THE JEWISH GUIDE TO

C000165595

The
JEWISH
GUIDE
to
ADULTERY

*How to Turn
Your Marriage into
an Illicit Affair*

RABBI SHMUEL BOTEACH

PAN BOOKS

First published 1995 by Pan

an imprint of Macmillan General Books
Cavaye Place London SW10 9PG
and Basingstoke

Associated companies throughout the world

ISBN 0 330 34135 9

Copyright © Rabbi Shmuel Boteach 1995

The right of Rabbi Shmuel Boteach to be identified as the
author of this work has been asserted by him in accordance
with the Copyright, Designs and Patents Act 1988.

1 3 5 7 9 8 6 4 2

A CIP catalogue record for this book is available from
the British Library

Typeset by CentraCet Limited, Cambridge
Printed and bound in Great Britain by
Cox & Wyman Ltd, Reading, Berkshire

For Debbie

ACKNOWLEDGEMENTS

I EXTEND MY heartfelt thanks to my dedicated assistant, Kathy Brewis, who edited this book and served as a sounding-board for the various ideas expressed herein. A young woman with a strong personality, she helped to balance and shift some of the book's ideas away from a strictly masculine orientation.

The same is true of my other very dedicated assistant, Julie Markoff, who offered scathing criticism and every once in a while a compliment ('I really like the particular typeface that this chapter is in'). Being Jewish Julie felt the need to argue on every last point and to abuse the book incessantly (she's jealous of the fame and fortune). She tried desperately to erase every last copy of the book from our computer hard disks, but I managed to salvage some of the work none the less. (The original manuscript was 1900 pages. I was able to reduce it significantly by deleting every second use of the word *sex*.)

I also thank my editors at Macmillan: William Armstrong, the Publisher, Susan Hill, and especially Ingrid Connell. It was Ingrid who had the most unpleasant task of having to edit down the massive original manuscript against my steadfast resistance. I insisted on retaining every last letter and every dot of every 'i'. The one concession I was prepared to make was to delete my middle initial from the book jacket. Thus, whole sections of this book and much unparalleled wisdom which could have cured the world and established relationships on a solid footing for ever have been lost to posterity due to Ingrid. If you reach a section which appears as though its guts have been ripped out, we have only Ingrid to blame.

Acknowledgements

I wish to extend my appreciation as well to Chrissy Iley whose original article on this book, which appeared in the *Sunday Times*, and subsequent advice with regard to publishers led to this marriage between myself and Macmillan. It can be said of Chrissy that her weekly column raises just a few more eyebrows than even this book.

The book itself is culled almost entirely from the hundreds of hours spent counselling and serving as an ear to the complaints and thoughts that people have about their marriages and relationships. As such, I must thank the many people who flattered me by taking me into their confidence. We all inhabit this planet together and we humans find ample occasion to lean on one another. Far from this being taken as a sign of a weakness, the need for human friendship, warmth or advice is the key to fraternity and brotherhood. But in order for this to be effective, there must first be trust. And I thank all those who trusted me with their personal lives and intimate details of their relationships. In appreciation, I have included small photographs of them adjacent to their respective stories and their home telephone numbers.

If I were to be asked what my great blessing is, without any hesitation I would say that it is my wife Debbie. But it is one thing to know that something is true. It is quite another to act in accordance with that knowledge always. Suffice it to say that my wife is devoted and loving to me in a manner which I find almost impossible to reciprocate. Still, any beautiful insight I have learned into the mystery of human relationships I have discovered with her at my side. Her sixth sense which penetrates far deeper than my own more superficial view of love has made so many things more understandable, and in this sense this book is as much hers as it is mine (although I am not sure she wants to be associated with it, much less credited for its authorship). Together, we are blessed, thank God, with four beautiful children but not much money (although your purchase of this book has already gone some way toward redressing that imbalance).

Finally, I thank the benevolent Creator for His infinite kindness in all areas, and especially in providing me with a wife who makes me feel necessary and wanted and seeks my happiness always. This book is dedicated to ensuring that we all reciprocate.

Shmuley Boteach
November, 1994
Oxford, England

CONTENTS

Contents

Contents

MAKING YOUR SPOUSE INTO YOUR LOVER

'Personally I know nothing about sex because I've always been married.'
Zsa Zsa Gabor, 'Sayings of the Week', *Observer*, 16 August, 1987

THE MAIN REASON for my undertaking this study has to do specifically with the fact that I am a Rabbi. If there is one thing that I have always sought both as a religious thinker and a religious individual it is the synthesis of heaven and earth. What I mean by this is to lead the kind of life in which religious teaching on the one hand, and the experiences and truisms of everyday life on the other, are not only compatible, but identical. I have always believed that if the teachings of heaven cannot be corroborated, or even discovered, through everyday living, then not only may we question their actual validity and authenticity, but worse, they are totally irrelevant to man. If God has nothing to say to man that actually works, and that he can actually verify with his own heart and mind, then His teaching might just as soon remain only in the heavens where it can benefit the angels and disembodied creatures, rather than descending to earth and confounding man. You may well ask, 'What is a rabbi doing writing a book on adultery?' This book is a serious attempt at helping to make marriages work by addressing the biggest marital problem of all: the loss of passion in monogamous relationships.

And this is where, ironically, the subject of adultery comes up. Adultery serves as one of the bridges between the religious and secular worlds, and one of the areas in which they seem to be in near agreement, referring to its commission as a *sin*. Whether or not the prohibition and societal loathing of adultery began as a religious teaching is debatable. Where there cannot be any disagreement, however, is that adultery is the only sexual offence whose subject transcends both religious and secular thinking. Even the most rabid secularists agree that adultery is wrong and that the pain that it causes is among the most severe to be found in any area of life. While the attitude towards so many other forms of human behaviour is still being debated between religionists and secularists, on the subject of adultery they are (nearly) all in agreement, betraying the belief that marriage is a religious institution and people have a greater respect, reverence and awe for marriage than if they regarded it as a mere social institution.

When I was eight years old, my parents separated. Try as they might, and they certainly made a go of it, they simply could not live together. A combination of radically different upbringing, social and financial backgrounds, and plain stubbornness made their life together less than peaceful and pleasurable (to use the British understatement). They ended up parting, and it was quite difficult for everyone involved, especially my brothers and sisters, since we were all very young at the time. And yet, even amidst my exposure to the acrimony of their marriage, I never gave up on the idea of marriage. In fact, I committed myself to try not to repeat the same mistakes which they had made, and which were so readily apparent. I basically said to myself, 'Marriage is a good thing. My parents, however, didn't go about it in the right way. There is therefore nothing wrong with marriage, per se. In this instance, there was simply a problem with the way *these two individuals* went about their married life together. The problem was with the *people* and not with the *institution*.'

After my parents divorced we moved from Los Angeles to Miami Beach and I was transported into a far more affluent Jewish neighbourhood and day school. I found myself perfectly at home because there were very many other kids in my class whose parents had divorced. Still smarting from the effects of my parents' divorce, I felt an immediate camaraderie and kinship with these children, befriended them easily, and went to their homes. It was when I began frequenting their houses that I noticed that we had nothing in common at all. Sure, their parents were divorced too. But they were the best of friends. Their fathers came to their homes and sat and joked with their mothers. Most of these kids did not see the unpleasantness that I had witnessed at all. They saw something completely different, and the divorce affected them differently as well. Their parents got along fine. They had simply lost interest in each other. They had fallen out of love. They were no longer attracted or excited by one another. And the consequence was this: whereas I always spoke with my friends in an endearing way about marriage, and often pontificated about whom I would marry, they did not. They had no time for it all, and when asked would almost swear that they would never marry. The reason was simple. They saw a flaw in the *institution* of marriage. The whole thing was a sham. After all, here were their parents, who got along and laughed together, but had still got divorced, because marriage did not work. Monogamy did not work. People simply could not stay married and interested in each other for long stretches of time. They were bound to lose interest in each other after a time.

When people say to me that the way that my parents divorced ('inharmonious' being an extreme understatement) and the acrimony that still exists between them to this very day is wrong, I disagree with them vehemently. I say I don't want my parents, who are themselves divorced, pretending they once were not married. I don't want them speaking as if they are mere friends. I don't want them acting as though what they shared

3

with one another was just casual. They were married, it was intense. Either it remains as intense as marriage or it doesn't exist at all. But to transmute it to the point where those who were once married can now be just like ordinary friends is a harmful farce. To pretend that your wife can become your best friend or pretend in any marriage that if you are best friends that is good for the marriage, is rubbish. It destroys whatever chance we have in life for sustaining something intense. When marriages can be peaceful in divorce it means that the people involved felt nothing for each other even while married. And while I agree with those who argue that parents can at least be civil to each other for the sake of the children, civil and cordial do not mean a continued association of friendship. I tell husband and wives who divorce: 'Face it, you never were friends. You were married. You once were lovers. Do not delude yourself.'

Anything that can become so casual was never really intense. Therefore when marriages end in divorce, they should break completely. They should find it difficult to converse. They should harbour negative feelings toward one another, because this is infinitely better than harbouring no feeling at all. Let them react and believe that this thing they were once in was still intense, so that they can have hope for success in their next marriage. They can still feel excitement. They can feel the energy that can pull them together like magnets and keep them attached to another human being for the duration of their lives.

At my own wedding my parents could not even bring themselves to congratulate each other. I am often asked by friends whether that bothered me. 'Not at all,' I say. On the contrary, if they sat and spoke together at the reception amicably, that would bother me. Because then I would forever ask the question, 'If you can get along so well right now the way you are, they why did you get divorced in the first place?' But since they cannot get along, I have my answer. They fought, therefore they divorced. It wasn't that their feelings for one another dissipated

4

and disappeared until they just drifted apart. Thus, I still have hope in marriage. It can remain intense. Just look. Even after so many years, my parents still feel all the hurt, pain, anger, and frustration. Because marriage is indeed intense, and those feelings never change.

Ever since my parents divorced, I have had a passion in life: to make marriages work again. I believe with all my heart and soul that the greatest human calling is to heal the world and make this earth a better place. Man has a mission, and I believe that man's first religious calling is not just to pray and recite hymns, but to help his fellow man lead a better, more joyous life. Some people accomplish this by becoming great doctors and curing disease, others become economists, teaching people how they can increase their material assets and raise the quality of their lives, and still others become full time parents, bestowing all of their love on their children. I have no greater wish than to have my contribution to humanity come in the form of making husbands and wives fall in love with each other all over again, and remain fully focused sexually on one another, rather than sharing intimacy with others outside the marriage.

Over the past few decades many self-help books have appeared with the express intention of restoring passion in marriage and enhancing the quality of married life. Where this book differs from its predecessors is this: whereas many of them deal with symptoms of problems, this book goes straight to the essence of those problems. Whereas what these other books offer is primarily *techniques*, this book offers a new state of mind.

Take for example the celebrated book, *The Joy of Sex* by Dr Alex Comfort. It offers the opportunity for a reinvigorated married life through improved sexual technique. Dr Ruth and Masters and Johnson offer more of the same. Other books offer techniques for improved understanding and communication between the sexes, such as Dr John Gray's recent and popular, *Men Are From Mars, Women Are From Venus*. I don't deny that these books are helpful, but by dealing with specific problems and offering techniques to solve these problems, they ignore the central malady in today's marriage: husbands and wives are drifting apart. They appear to be bored with each other, and the monotony of their lives leads them to argue and bicker about the most trivial items, or avoid conversation altogether by digesting copious amounts of television. To rectify this situation, what is needed over and above individual techniques addressing individual problems in marriage is a new state of mind, a new way in which we look at and perceive our spouse; something which in our eyes will always make them seductive and exciting. I completely concur with the sentiments expressed by Erica Jong in *Fear of Flying*, 'All the best-selling sex manuals are such gyps. They teach people how to [make love] with their pelvises, not with their *heads*.' What we need is not only techniques that will improve our sex lives, but a conscious focus on how attractive and exciting our spouse truly is, and a subsequent desire to share their bed always.

If we can renew our sexual interest in our spouse, then many of the overt problems, like continuous arguments and bickering, will fall by the wayside. A great Jewish sage once said, 'When you have nothing to do, you end up doing what you ought not to do.' Similarly in marriage, when we are bored with our spouse, when we feel we don't want to be married to them, we pick a quarrel on the silliest pretext. In this book you will see marriage, adultery, and sexual attraction in a completely new light, and learn proven methods by which to rediscover passion in your marriage.

Why Learn from Adultery?

This book begins with two very simple observations. First, there is a very dramatic rise in extramarital affairs in the world today.

Adultery is exciting and getting more exciting all the time. Second, whereas husbands and wives, even if they love each other, can feel bored with having sex together, the same is not true of lovers involved in adulterous affairs. The sex life of the average husband and his mistress, or of a wife and her lover never seems to dissipate in the way it might if they were married. Since your primary, and sometimes only, interest in the man or the woman in an adulterous affair is having sex, you therefore never seem to forget the fact that they are just that, a man or a woman, rather than a husband or a wife. The term 'man and woman' suggests exciting sexual beings. The term 'husband and wife' has a sense of familiarity, and perhaps even weariness.

This book identifies what it is about adultery that makes it so exciting, so attractive and irresistible to so many people; what it is about a new sexual partner that causes such passion, and explains how to transpose those same feelings into marriage. In other words, it is designed to help you look upon the woman you married not just as your wife, but as your *mistress*, or to make the man to whom you were wed and whose bed you share become not just your husband, but your *lover*; to boldly restore the place of sex in our married life to the central position it would occupy if we were indeed having an affair with someone outside the marriage. Looking forward to sharing intimacy with your husband or your wife, and having a satisfying sex life, is the essence of marriage. Nothing is more important. In the final analysis, getting married is and should be first and foremost about having a sexual partner with whom we look forward at all times to sharing the same bed and the same life. Our eyes should never turn to other men and women, not because we are repressing our sexual desires, but because our marriage is so exciting that we will never want to stray.

7

The Catch 22 of Marriage

There exists a dilemma which every marriage must overcome if it is to be successful. Every marriage, every long-term relationship between a man and woman, involves an inherent Catch 22. It is what I call 'the terrible cycle of marriage'. Simply stated, it goes something like this: the closer a husband and wife draw together in marriage, the more they fall in love with each other, the more familiar they become as well. The more they become 'best friends' (which is what some people portray as the ideal in marriage) the more they become tired or bored with one another. They may indeed have a greater love and feel a far closer affinity as time drones on, but almost inevitably their sex life will commensurably suffer.

This is because all those things in life which we consider to be exciting are new and fresh. We love buying and putting on new clothes. We love shopping for new things. We love driving a new car. We love moving into a new house and rearranging the furniture. We consider those things with which we are too familiar, which we have grown to know too well, dull and monotonous.

The fact that excitement and passion is gradually lost in marriage is a contention that I have never heard anyone disagree with. During the course of writing this book, I was invited to lecture on the subject in many countries, including South Africa, the United States, Germany, Australia, Norway, Sweden, Canada, and of course throughout the length and breadth of Britain. The lectures always contained something in the title about restoring passion to the natural dullness that is bound to ensue in marriage. Never once, in all my travels, did a member of the large audiences who came to hear the lectures ever stand up and say, 'What the hell are you talking about? What monotony in marriage? That certainly hasn't happened to me.'

It seems that every person I have ever met understands exactly what I am saying when I speak of the *almost inevitable* loss of passion in marriage and monogamous relationships.

How do you overcome the lack of novelty in marriage, when you have the same sexual partner every time, and wake every morning to the same face? It's a major problem. How does a wife feel when she undresses at night, and her husband continues to read the newspaper? The very success of the marriage works against you if you become closely-knit. If you do everything together, if you travel together and tell each other every secret, if you share everything and enjoy each other's company, you also run the risk of losing the fire in your marriage. It is as if God has placed inherent imperfections in life. The more dedicated and devoted a spouse you are, the more it seems that your partner will fantasize about someone else's heretofore unexplored body. It is only if you embark on long periods of separation and don't see each other very often, that you might long to be reunited physically.

The familiarity which marriage and monogamy create can mean that there is nothing left about you to conquer or discover. Your spouse can't embark on a journey of adventure with you because you are such a well-known quantity. You could even be supplanted by someone far less devoted simply because they *are* undevoted and *unknown*. Your spouse adopts the 'been there, done that' attitude towards you and the erotic pleasure they enjoy with you as partner. But they can look upon a business colleague or new acquaintance who is known to them only in a superficial way and think, 'My, how inviting. Now wouldn't that be interesting!' They represent the prospect of a new discovery.

This is the Catch 22 that every marriage is presented with and must overcome if it is not only to survive, but to flourish and prosper.

The good news is that a marriage *can* transcend the apparent mutual exclusivity of familiarity and passion. I believe and shall demonstrate in this book that marriage actually presents the greatest possibility for synthesizing familiarity with passion, thus affording the opportunity of reaching the highest summits of sexual excitement and passion.

Chasing as many sexual partners as possible, having someone new in your bed every night, is not the answer. Admittedly, when one beds a different partner every week or every month, the novelty and constant change will probably not breed monotony or boredom. And yes, it probably will be passionate and exciting. But it will lack the other essential ingredient which makes sex such a pleasurable and wonderful experience. It will lack *familiarity and informality*. When a couple barely know each other and have sex, they are as focused on impressing the other person and demonstrating their sexual prowess as they are on enjoying themselves and making sure the other has a good time. They are also conscious of the fact that they, their bodies, and their performance, are being judged. In other words, because they do not know each other so well, and are hell-bent on making sure that they themselves score well they simply cannot relax and be themselves. And so while the experience may be very passionate, it still may not give total fulfilment. It will not be as exciting as sharing the same experience with someone you love, who you know is not judging you, and with whom therefore you can simply focus and let go, be natural and have the most enjoyable sex possible: namely, the kind of sex that is totally spontaneous, uncontrived, instinctive and electric, the kind of sex that leaves you with a far closer attachment to your partner when the experience is over, so that it is not a one-off event but one which has a lasting effect. This is the kind of sex which can only be found through familiarity, closeness, long-term commitment and marriage.

Sociologists point to the leading causes of divorce in the past as being primarily financial or parental in orientation. After the

Second World War, the world embarked upon a period of unparalleled prosperity which did much to unsettle human relationships. Husbands and wives sometimes found themselves more pulled apart by their professional aspirations than united by their marriages. Likewise the cataclysms and social upheavals of the sixties led to a rejection of parental authority and society's more traditional and restrictive institutions like marriage. Free love seemed an appetizing alternative to a dead-beat marriage and divorce served to sever the chain that bound the spirit. The seventies did see a move to greater stability in marriage but this has been undermined by the greatest marital challenge of all – sexual boredom, which became the number one cause for divorce in the 1980s and 1990s. You're not divided over issues of substance but by trivialities that are accorded significance through the lack of satisfaction in the marriage. You grow tired of one another or you 'fall out of love'. This has led to the fascinating phenomenon of the *peaceful divorce*. These couples admit that they were more or less getting along fine, but they start to feel that their marriage is utterly boring and simply grow apart until they no longer feel married. When they come to people like myself for counselling, they speak of feeling 'as if we are not even married'. They are correct in expecting marriages to be intense, and what they now feel for each other is very casual and relaxed.

The Soul of Adultery can Invigorate the Body of Marriage

The only way to overcome this deadening of the emotions and sensations in a relationship, and the only way to remain at all times passionately in love, is by ensuring that marriages become as sexually exciting as they possibly can be. In explaining how this can be achieved, we will draw many lessons from sex both before but especially outside of marriage, identifying why it seems so much more exciting. We'll take an in-depth look at adultery, and bring its soul into marriage.

Don't worry for the moment about all the other problems that may exist in marriage – the constant bickering, the lack of respect for one another, the arguments and the needling. I believe firmly that if our sex lives become as inviting, exciting, and pleasurable as they once were, then all these other things will fall by the wayside. They may still exist, but they will not be as important. Husbands and wives who find themselves arguing over the laundry, the scratch on the car, the time spent away from home, will find these things melting into insignificance because of the satisfaction that they feel with one another in the most important area of all: their intimate lives together.

Why else is it that these things can be blown so completely out of proportion in marriage, if not because those things which were once much more pleasurable are no longer so? How else can we explain why coming home to dinner on time or remembering to buy flowers can become more important than going to the bedroom and enjoying each other's touch? I have a close friend who, as one of the leading divorce lawyers in Britain, has represented many celebrities in their divorce battles in court. She claims that over half her divorces are between men and women who complain that the other partner is too untidy for them and thus they find that they cannot live with them. Can you imagine husbands and wives leaving each other because they find one another too untidy! Do you believe that any of them are really more interested in always having a tidy home, a clean kitchen, no toothpaste smeared on the bathroom basin, than in having the most wonderful sex life together?

When a single man or woman is invited home by a member of the opposite sex for a nightcap, they don't first look around to check whether or not the room is tidy, or whether or not the air is fresh. They are interested in one thing, and one thing only, and that one thing is so inviting and so desirable that everything else – the colour of the room, its preparedness and decoration – falls into oblivion.

I recognize that a one-night stand is, of course, radically different to marriage which is more about having to get on with someone in an everyday context in which totally different life-styles can become important. It may seem naive to say that if you have a great sex life nothing else matters. Nevertheless, I believe that one of the strongest modern-day fallacies is that successful marriage is more about *compatibility of interests* than anything else. If this is true, then homosexuality makes much more sense than heterosexuality, and men should marry men instead of women. After all, they grow up with fellow men, and the average man and woman shares more in common with members of the same sex than with the opposite. And still, we look forward primarily to sharing a life with the opposite sex, which teaches us that marriage is primarily about *attraction*, rather than compatibility. And it is uniquely the power of a satisfying sex life that can transform the tedium of waking up to the same face and going to bed with the same body into a welcome experience.

This is the power of passion, and why it is so necessary. Because real, true passion forces us to focus on the most beautiful gift of all: not a beautiful home, not a super fast car, not a wonderful career, but rather the affection, closeness and warmth of another human being. And those who marry do so because they feel that this is what they desire most: to share the same bed, not just the same house, with the person they love. What often occurs, unfortunately, is that later in the marriage shopping and cooking and earning a living often become more important than intimacy as the bedroom yields slowly to the kitchen, dining room and office as the focus of the family's activity, the nerve centre of the married couple.

The cycle of adultery, even that of the wife, usually *begins* with the husband, and goes something like this: men innately desire (some would say require) many sexual partners and associate passion with newness. They may love their wives, but they still seek out new bodies. After a few years, or even months, of marriage, they become restless with their wives, or more properly, with the limitations of monogamy. It is not that there is anything really wrong with their wives, but rather that they are too familiar with them to retain their husband's excitement.

The monotony which they begin to feel in marriage causes them to begin to ignore their wives. In the worst cases, they forget their marital vows and actually pursue new excitement outside of marriage. But in either scenario, the wife feels neglected, undesirable and 'old'. She knows that her husband's mind is not on her, and therefore she feels rejected. Whether or not her husband actually commits adultery is immaterial. As the preeminent sex researcher Shere Hite put it, 'The basic cause of women's search for love and enjoyment outside of marriage has to do with women's emotionally alienated state within marriage. The condescension and lack of emotional closeness women are experiencing in their marriages is having a disastrous effect on women's ability to survive emotionally while staying completely within a marriage . . . women are not looking for affairs basically for "more sex" or "sexual variety" . . . women often feel more powerful emotionally in outside relationships (they are), because they cannot be taken for granted, they must at least be listened to, so that they won't leave.'

A wife therefore begins to yearn for the love and affection that once existed at the outset of her marriage. If she is lucky, and both she and her husband work hard enough, she will once again get it from her husband. But if she gives up the hope of her husband being affectionate, especially if she knows his attentions to be on other women, she will either close up and become an unhappy and embittered spouse, or she herself will look to men outside the marriage to make her feel desirable and beautiful, once again.

The objective therefore is to nip this cycle in the bud, stop it before it spreads. Therefore, amidst the many useful items that will be found to enrich marriage and prevent adultery in this book, none are so important as the techniques by which to achieve passion and newness in marriage. A husband who can be taught always to see his wife in a passionate light will be able to cater to his natural disposition and attraction to new lovers without repressing his essential sexual nature. The result will be that his wife will feel like the most desirable woman in the world. Both will abstain from adultery, not only for religious or social reasons alone, but because they feel themselves to be immensely happy and sexually satisfied. And they will revel in their life together.

It is to restoring the intimacy and eroticism of our marriages by examining the phenomenon of adultery that this book is dedicated. I seek to use adultery, or rather, *the possibility of adultery*, to give us the most exciting marriages. The possibility that even the most committed husbands and wives might stray is something good and beneficial in marriage. What follows is a journey of discovery into the requirements of a successful marriage; how we can make our married lives truly special and passionate, so that we may focus all our sexual energy on our spouse, always longing to be with them, and truly feeling and becoming indivisible. We are seeking to curb adultery not through religious diatribe and condemnation, but by making monogamy and marriage even more inviting and pleasurable.

CHAPTER ONE

MONOGAMY AND THE SIN OF ADULTERY

Is Monogamy Viable?

WHEN I HAD just turned twenty-one, I returned to the United States from Australia where I had been a student for two years. I was sitting with a close married friend talking over old times in a hotel lounge in Manhattan, when a young couple walked in together, immediately catching everyone's attention because of the amount of noise they were making. The man, who had a handsome dark complexion and was dressed in the finest Italian suit, looked very suave and charismatic, and was quite obviously the quintessential 'ladies' man'. His wife, although attractive, looked dishevelled and distraught. They sat down at a table not far from us, and even if I had had no intention of eavesdropping on their conversation (and I was tempted), I could not have avoided it because of the way she shouted. 'You promised me never to speak to her again. How could you? After everything that we have been through because of her, how could you smile at her and be so nice to her?' She was pounding on his chest. 'How could you? You promised. I thought she was out of our life forever. And here you go and pull her right back in. How could you?'

Her husband, clasping both her hands in his, was trying desperately to calm and quiet her down. But it was not working. She was clearly very, very hurt and upset, devastated even. He spoke to her softly and calmly, caressing her cheek as he spoke, but even he did not seem to care whether or not people were listening. He was only concerned with consoling her. 'Honey, you know I love you. You know that she meant nothing to me. I promise. She's history.' He petted her softly as he spoke, kissed her on the lips, and it appeared as though she would forgive him. She allowed herself to drop softly into his arms, apparently to relieve her fatigue. But then immediately, she recoiled, and with a vengeance. She stood up, pounded her fists against his chest, and shouted even louder, 'No! I won't let you do this to me again. No, I won't forgive you. You *don't* love me. If you loved me you wouldn't do this to me.' And she pounded harder. They argued a bit more in this way, with her shrieking and crying and pounding his chest, amidst his futile attempts to calm and console her, and his promises of future fidelity.

What I remember most from the cinematic drama unfolding before our eyes was the unconcealable look of pain and bereavement on his wife's face; the frazzled hair, the long black mascara streaks forming black lines down her cheeks. She was evidently hurt so badly that she was oblivious to the spectacle she was making of herself. She did not care about her appearance or about others' impression of her.

I also remember that her pain was something I could not understand. I was not yet married, nor had I ever had a serious girlfriend or even a casual relationship, for that matter. In the Rabbinical Seminaries (Yeshivot) which I had attended, we were strictly single and celibate, and had very limited exposure to females.

But there was another reason I could not understand her pain. Had someone died, I asked myself? How could this possibly be so serious? The story was obvious. Her husband had been unfaithful to her, or at the very least shown serious affection towards another woman. And his wife acted as though she, or her husband, was no longer living. She behaved as though she were bereaved of her husband who now had to be mourned. Hence my state of confusion that so completely absorbed me into the unfolding drama. 'Lady! Why are you so hurt?' I said to myself, wishing that this total stranger would confide her secret in me.

I looked over to my right and saw that my married friend was even more absorbed. After the episode was over, and we were both feeling guilty for eavesdropping and being so enamoured with someone else's conversation and life, indeed their pain, my friend sat staring silently and very thoughtfully into space. Our conversation had long since died, and I saw that suddenly he was not in the mood for talking. I interrupted his reverie to ask what he was thinking about. He turned to me slowly and spoke.

'What I have just witnessed has brought back terrible memories and made me think. Shmuley, you know that I've been married for three years now. I am fortunate in that I have a loving wife and we are very happy together. But in the first year of marriage, I was working very hard to build up my business and was keeping very late hours. After a few months, my commitment to my business became an outright abuse of the time I should have been spending with my wife. She begged me to give her more time. Every night she would ring and ask when I was coming home, and my response was always the same: just a few more minutes. Invariably she would give up on me at about ten or eleven and go to sleep on her own. I felt that my neglect of my personal life was justified by the fact that I was at the early stages of building up my business, which was for both of us, and inevitably, because it was new, it was going to be difficult and very time-consuming. I was confident that after this stage was over, I would be free to spend all of my spare time with my wife. Therefore, I asked her to be patient. It wouldn't always be like this. At times I even accused her of selfishness and of having the luxury of taking it easy at night while I had to work hard for our mutual benefit.

'Well, after a while, I began to notice that she didn't wait for me to come home the way she once did. Her mind was not on me the way it once was either. She worked as a part-time librarian and I suspected that she was developing a liking for a co-worker, a very soft and friendly young man. She spoke about him constantly, and acted very unnatural around him when the three of us were together. One day, I confronted her and asked her what was going on. I never suspected anything improper; my wife was just not the type. After much denial, she confirmed that she had very warm feelings towards him, and she suspected that he felt the same towards her. She told me that nothing whatso-ever had happened between them, but they usually ate lunch together in the cafeteria and had wonderful conversations together. Still, they had never discussed their mutual affections. But she did say that she was very attracted to him, often fantasized about him, and had even dreamt about them kissing each other on several occasions.

'I was devastated. I would gladly trade the hurt and anguish I experienced on that evening for any form of physical pain, even though I knew that nothing sexual had taken place. I was lucky in that I was able to reverse the damage caused by my neglect by showing my wife extravagant love, attention, and affection. But I still believe that she harbours a special place in her heart for that man. Whenever I question her on the subject, she refuses to speak about it. And she still looks starry-eyed whenever he is mentioned. And if we occasionally bump into him, she cannot be herself but becomes very self-conscious. I just wish she'd forget him.'

This episode served as my first real-life exposure to adultery, its general theme and consequences. It was particularly memor-able because, having had very limited experience of women and dating, I had a very romanticized vision of marriage. I looked forward to the day I would marry with glee and excitement and often wondered who my wife would be. The loneliness which I felt in Rabbinical seminary led me to believe that marriage incorporated everything that was good and loving, and could cure a person's desolation for ever. But here I was, before even having had my first date with a girl, and I had already become a cynic. Perhaps one of the greatest tragedies of the breakdown of love and relationships in general, and of adultery in particular, is that it affects all of humanity. There can be no human being with a feeling heart who could witness this woman's grief, her husband's pleading, or hear the words spoken by my friend without being adversely affected, the glitter of marriage becoming somewhat diminished. This episode, coming as it did at the very finale and culmination of my bachelorhood – thank God, I was engaged to my wife just three months later – served as the earliest inspiration for this book.

The Rise of Infidelity

Adultery has become commonplace in modern society, especially among husbands. Though the statistics provided by different surveys, studies, and reports are not uniform, they all point to an overwhelming number of spouses who are finding sex outside of marriage.

When the first report of sexual behaviour, *The Kinsey Report*, was produced in 1953, American readers were shocked to discover titillating new sexual facts: 'Seven out of ten farm boys did what?!' Kinsey also shocked America by reporting that 83 per cent of his male respondents said that they had had sexual intercourse before marriage; half of the men had had extramarital sexual relationships, and more than a third had had at least one homosexual experience after puberty, generally during their adolescent years. Kinsey's findings also demonstrated the extent of female sexuality. Half of the women questioned had had premarital sexual experience, and a quarter of married females who responded had had extramarital relationships.[1]

Since then, the numbers have gone up dramatically. According to the latest survey carried out by the *Janus Report on Human Sexuality*, published in 1993, one in four middle-income men reported an *extraordinarily high* rate of regular and ongoing extramarital sex. A corresponding rate of only 8 per cent of women reported 'often and ongoing' extramarital sexual liaisons. Among women, a survey conducted by *Cosmopolitan* magazine in the mideighties came up with the startling fact that 51 per cent of its readers had committed adultery. Similarly, in 1989, *New York Woman* magazine polled its readers and reported that almost one out of every two wives surveyed had cheated on their husbands. Similar findings have been reported in most recent surveys on the subject.

Despite the criticism by some that there are 'lies, damned lies and statistics', the empirical evidence is overwhelming and leaves no doubt that adultery comes more commonly to men than to women, just as commitment comes more easily to women than men. Those who deny this are arguing with fact. To quote from the *Janus*'s significant findings about marriage and divorce: 'More than one-third of men and more than one-quarter of women admit having had at least one extramarital sexual experience, but extramarital affairs account for fewer than one-quarter of all divorces . . . Among the divorced, men cite sexual problems as the primary reason, three times more frequently than women. Women cite extramarital affairs twice as frequently as men.'[2] But perhaps the greatest indication of the phenomenal rise in adultery, and an even more shocking finding in the area of human sexual relations is the admission, in the more recent studies of human sexual behaviour, on the part of the very religious of gross infidelity in marriage. We have now discovered that the very religious of various denominations are not necessarily practising what they preach. The *Janus Report* maintains that a third of all 'very religious' respondents, and 26 per cent of all 'religious' respondents reported having had extramarital affairs 'at least once', with 14 per cent of 'the very religious' admitting to 'often and ongoing' extramarital affairs. As the authors remark, 'Another finding may be even more disturbing, given the faith many Americans have in religion as the strongest curtailer of illicit passion: the very religious were *most likely* to report often and ongoing adultery.'[3] Whether or not this finding results from the fact that as some would argue in some denominations religious life dictates a strict adherence to a sexual code and can thereby result in severe repression remains to be seen. Still, there can be no doubt that these statistics are alarming. And yet, I am convinced and have been for a long time that it is specifically within a religious framework that not just marriage, but passion in marriage can best be maintained and developed. Those who attack and disparage religion as being repressive are not correct. Judaism, for example, has never advocated sexual repression, but rather calls upon humans to harness and focus all their sexual energy on their chosen partner, the rewards of which are considerable, as we shall see. While suppressing innate human nature can lead to harmful neuroses, focusing and channelling human nature is absolutely essential to a productive and meaningful life.

Is Monogamy Viable?

A far more serious question that arises from all the above is at the heart of civilized Western living and the Judeo-Christian ethic: Is monogamy viable? Was it ever viable? In the face of such extreme marital infidelity and the rampant spread of adulterous behaviour among the population, must we not really begin to question whether monogamy is not just some wishful fantasy imposed upon humans by religious mores, with no firm basis in reality?

From all indications it would appear that marriage is on the decline, while divorce and adultery are on the rise. This societal trend points not only to an erosion of the very institutions which maintain the stability of society, but worse, to the complete failure of sexual monogamy as a way of life. In addition to the figures on adultery already quoted, in the United States and many other parts of the Western world one of two marriages ends up in divorce. Of those who remain married, only one in four remain faithful to one another. Thus, only one quarter of 50 per cent, or an eighth of the population, seems to be happy in monogamy, or at the very least subsisting within a monogamous relationship. That is not very many at all and is certainly not very encouraging to young people contemplating marriage.

What these statistics seem to indicate is not just that marriage is in desperate trouble in today's society, but also that monogamy as a way of life is either disappearing, failing, or both. Monogamy simply is not viable according to these statistics.

Is Adultery Positive?

Today, following the sexual revolution of the 1960s, there are even those who argue – and there are a surprisingly high number of them – that extramarital affairs are a good thing, healthy for marriage, and should not be decried at all. Noted psychologist and author, Dr Albert Ellis, maintains, in *Thy Neighbour's Wife* by Gay Talese, that marriages can sometimes be helped by what he calls 'healthy adultery'. Many other researchers and authors who concur argue that at times having a lover on the side can help to keep husbands and wives together. In study after study, report after report, many married men and women assert that, while they still desire to remain married, the only thing that allows them to do so is the fact that they are having extramarital affairs. In many instances, a good marriage will be missing one component or ingredient, which can sometimes only be provided by someone outside the marriage. Sometimes the missing element is sexual passion. At other times it is the desire to experiment and 'see what one is missing' in a monogamous relationship. If this leads directly to the long-term viability of the marriage, a satisfaction of curiosity for example or a means by which a husband can release his anxiety instead of constantly arguing with his wife, then what makes it so wrong?

In her *Report on Female Sexuality* Shere Hite, the expert sex therapist who has written respected (if controversial) report after report on the state of today's male/female relationships, quotes an unfaithful wife who argues: 'I required love and sex – both together when possible. I could not have survived had I not fulfilled these needs, so [the affair] enriched my life and helped me to seek a good platonic relationship in my marriage, which actually saved the marriage. My husband did not know.' Whilst it is dubious in what sense the marriage could be said to have been 'saved', and whether 'a good platonic relationship' is what should be sought, this case is by no means unusual in that a married person feels the need to look outside of the marriage for something he/she feels is lacking within it. Hite concludes: 'The condescension and lack of emotional closeness women are experiencing in their marriages is having a disastrous effect on woman's ability to survive emotionally while staying completely within a marriage. Thus, for many women, having an outside relationship is one of the few ways to stay in the marriage. Having an affair can put new love and humanity into one's world, enabling one to go on living.'[4]

Of course, these arguments for the good which an adulterous affair can cause are countermanded by the simple fact that every single adulterous affair must hurt and cause terrible pain for all parties concerned. Nonsense is made of Hite's and others' arguments for the benefits of adultery by such observations as this made by another of Hite's female respondents: 'Overall though, I think the effects have been emotionally harmful, because there is no way to carry the relationship through to a happy ending. It must always end sadly. There is always hurt.' Indeed, adultery is a road that leads to nowhere but despair and oblivion, and serves not to alleviate the problems in a marriage, but to escape from them. Surely, it is better for a couple to rediscover love and passion in their relationship rather than find it with someone else, when it cannot last. Marriages are not saved when more complications are thrown in their way.

Yet, observing the meteoric rise in adultery statistics, it seems amazing to me that one thing still has not changed: the almost universal condemnation which adultery receives. In this modern age where old scruples and religious teachings have largely been consigned to the dust heap of history, attitudes towards adultery have not. To be sure, I have just mentioned that there are those who would argue that adultery may even have positive consequences. Such opinions are not, however, aired within mainstream society and they specifically call attention to themselves because of their rarity. Apart from a few authors who have written titillating books on the subject, there seem to be few people who would argue in favour of adultery at all.

As I write these lines, the most comprehensive survey of British sexual attitudes and practices has just been published by the *Independent on Sunday*. Simultaneous with this report being released, there has been a very big scandal in Britain in which two leading Conservative ministers have been discovered to have practised ongoing and flagrant marital infidelity. Both ministers were forced to resign, one after the horrific suicide of his wife, upon discovering that her husband had had a fifteen-year affair. Even before the survey was published, its findings were reported in all the main British dailies. To quote from the *Independent on Sunday*'s front page: 'Whatever the failings of their political leaders, the British people are overwhelmingly in favour of monogamy. Nearly 80 per cent consider extramarital sex to be always or mostly wrong, thus echoing Dr George Carey, the Archbishop of Canterbury, who denounced adultery as a sin yesterday. But the large majority of people see nothing wrong in premarital sex.'[5]

The extent to which the world as we know it has changed, and to which the sexual mores which once prevailed upon society, in public at least, have been overturned, is staggering. To quote the Kinsey Institute in *Sex and Morality in the US*:

> Never before in our society have public representation and discussion of sexual matters been so extensive. Magazines with pictures with full frontal nudity are available at corner drug stores; movie theatres with films that depict every kind of sexual behaviour; best-selling books often include down-to-earth advice on sexual performance and relationships; and even television, which enters most homes, is gradually expanding the erotic content of both its documentary and entertainment offerings. People's behaviour seems different as well. Premarital cohabitation among the young is no longer extraordinary; jokes about sex have come out of the locker room; the revealing bathing suit has lost its shock value; 'single bars' are to be found in any city of size.[6]

In most places up till the 1950s, such sexual openness was simply non-existent, except among a small avant-garde. So much seems to have happened since then that some commentators see the sexual revolution as successfully completed. As one journalist noted in 1975:

> For a revolution to be worthy of its name it must struggle against the accepted values and customs of a society. By that

27

standard, the sexual revolution became tame and toothless some time ago. Male prostitutes are now convivial guests on the daytime talk shows. Paperback copies of *The Joy of Sex* are tossed into the grocery shopping bag with the asparagus. Wife swapping and group sex are . . . old topics of suburban patio conversation. It's kind of difficult for a revolution to keep up a head of steam in a culture that has long ceased to put up even a token show of resistance.[7]

So why is it that, when virtually every form of human sexual behaviour is now condoned or even encouraged, adultery alone is still thoroughly and universally condemned?

Premarital sex is not only no longer condemned, but those who abstain are seen as old-fashioned and outdated, indeed as a bit barmy. According to the *Janus Report*, over 80 per cent of men obtain extensive sexual experience before marriage, and I suspect, having served as Rabbi to university students for six years, that the numbers are far higher. Before the turn of the century this would have been unthinkable. Victorian society could never countenance such rampant premarital experience, not openly anyway. Neither would puritan, Protestant America. But all that has changed now, and premarital sex has definitely become the norm.

The same can be said of many other so-called 'sexual vices'. Just a few decades ago homosexuality was not only condemned, but actually prohibited by American civil law in over twenty-four states. Yet today mainstream society would label as a demagogue and fascist anyone who condemned homosexuals in public. Serious public debate surrounds the subject of whether homosexual couples should be allowed to adopt children, and their case seems to have overwhelming support. Homosexuality has come a long way from being labelled 'a crime against Nature' as recently as a century ago, and a 'human medical pathology' up to only thirty years ago, to being accepted as a viable 'alternative lifestyle' in the modern age.

This also applies to group sex. While it may not be as widespread as premarital sex, the *Janus Report* claims that 17 per cent of men found group sex 'very normal' or 'all right'. A far greater number actually admitted to having been involved in group sex at one time or another. In fact, there are very few sexual deviances left which society refuses to tolerate or which have not been labelled 'normal' and routine. In *Janus*'s words, 'much of what [Freud] considered deviant has become part of the everyday sex lives of many Americans.' Similarly, 'Many sexual practices that were once deemed wrong or sick or forbidden appear to be commonplace today.'[8]

I can see only two exceptions to this rule. The first is child sex and abuse, which is still seen as evil and hideous by society at large; the other is adultery. The *Janus Report* maintains monstrously that only 2 per cent of men report personal experiences of adult sex with children. Society still views those who molest children as being sick and in need of serious psychological help, not to mention deserving of severe retribution and punishment. The gross violation on the part of an adult, usually male, sexual offender of the innocence which we attribute to a child is an offence society will never forgive or tolerate.

But what can we make of the lingering distaste, indeed revulsion, toward adulterers? When it comes to child abusers, the reason is straightforward and simple. These are disturbed adults who prey on the helplessness and natural openness, naiveté, and innocence of a child. In short, child abuse goes against the grain of everything which we hold dear in this world. But the same rules do not apply to an adulterous husband or wife, whom we seem to detest or at least denounce almost equally. There must be a reason for our loathing and deep disrespect for those who cheat on their spouses.

Western audiences warm to the messages of films like *Fatal Attraction* and *Indecent Proposal*, both of which portray the terrible and irrevocable damage which adultery brings in its wake. In them, we witness the all too real and physical pain being brought about through an insensitive and irresponsible act of infidelity. The point is that the disastrous consequences of adultery are felt in the here and now and the damaging results are all too clear.

Commenting after the aforementioned Governmental controversy, the Archbishop of Canterbury added: 'Adultery and the breakdown of faithfulness and trust that it represents is more than a mere indiscretion. It's a sin. It is a failure to live up to the kind of standards we expect from all people in authority . . . It cannot be said that reliable evidence of hypocrisy, untrustworthiness, irresponsibility or selfishness in one aspect of life is irrelevant to a person's general credibility. People do not switch morality on and off like a light bulb.'

I disagree. The nature of human sexuality is such that it is impulsive and instinctive and therefore can indeed be switched on and off like a light bulb. We all know that there are moments when we feel intensely sexual, and other moments when the entire sexual enterprise seems uninteresting and even rather odd. On the whole, however, men and woman gravitate toward each other naturally. It is precisely for this reason that Judaism, taking a realistic and forward-looking approach to human sexuality, forbade unmarried men and women from finding themselves in secluded settings which may lead to compromising situations. Judaism recognizes that men and women are first and foremost *sexual* beings, and this recognition is a compliment to both. The fact that some people may fall prey to human nature does not automatically disqualify them from public office, or even seriously compromise their integrity. I totally reject the notion that betraying one's spouse is akin to being a dishonest used car salesman. Committing adultery, however heinous we believe the act to be, is not a total statement of what a man or woman is and does not immediately make them totally immoral people.

To be sure, marital infidelity is far more serious than stealing money. But it is not always as conscious and the culprit is not necessarily as culpable. In this respect, the Archbishop has erred in his comparison. To state that someone who commits adultery will definitely be untrustworthy in his public life, is to assume that both are indiscriminate acts of dishonesty, and they are not. Harbouring such notions may even betray a superficial knowledge of human nature and behaviour. When we discover that a man or a woman has committed adultery, the question that should really be asked is not why they have done so, but rather, *Why didn't it take place sooner?* Why did they agree to monogamy in the first place? As we shall see, it is marriage and monogamy that are totally unnatural, while adultery and polygamy are in complete consonance with the natural state of man. Stated in other words, one does not *choose* to commit adultery. Rather, one is naturally pulled in that direction, and must choose *not* to commit adultery. Adultery is prevented when a man or a woman puts on the brakes, in the name of their marriage, religion, ethics, or what have you. Theft or murder, by contrast, involve conscious efforts to commit the crime, rather than a conscious effort to prevent oneself from the transgression.

There is perhaps no clearer case in point, or refutation to the Archbishop's words, than the example of the great humanitarian hero Oscar Schindler. He was a wretched husband, who cheated on his wife on numerous occasions and finally even left her. And yet he risked all to save 1000 helpless Jews. And ever since Steven Spielberg's epic *Schindler's List* appeared on the screen, countless writers have asked how could so awful a husband have been so great a humanitarian? But what is the meaning of the question? There is simply no significant relation between the two. Because you cheat in your marriage does not reflect an overall character defect. It does mean that you are not making a

31

strong enough effort to channel all your sexual passion into your marriage, and the result of your lack of exertion is a terrible sin and boundless pain caused to your spouse which must of course be corrected.

Adultery Within a Marriage

Yet with all the empirical evidence of the disastrous effects of adultery the role of extramarital sexual activity in divorce is paradoxical. Whereas about one in five divorced women and one in five divorced men cite extramarital affairs as the primary cause of their divorce, some extramarital sexual activity can apparently occur within an otherwise stable marriage without causing a breakdown. The *Janus Report* found that 28 per cent of married men and women had had more than one extramarital sexual contact without their marriages dissolving.

Nevertheless, it is patently obvious that extramarital affairs are poor ingredients for a trusting marriage. In the time that I have counselled and observed married couples I have found there are understandably numerous examples of marriages dissolving, often violently, after one single case of infidelity. Surveys and statistics seem to support this as well, with the incidence of extramarital affairs serving as an important primary reason, especially among women, for break-up.

But I have also been involved in many cases where the wife or husband is highly forgiving of the other's infidelity, and believes that their love for each other is far more important than a momentary breach of their marital bond. More often than not this happens in cases where the spouse is honest enough to inform their partner of their unfaithfulness. Since the very first casualty of adultery in any marriage is the trust upon which the marriage is built, this is somewhat reinstated by the spouse's unprompted and unsolicited confession. The instances where the marriage survives an adulterous affair or one-off sexual encounter depend upon the belief on the part of both partners that their love for each other by far outweighs the adulterous act, and is strong enough to overcome any breach of faith. But if the marriage is healthy enough to sustain the impact of an extramarital breach on either side, why did it not prevent it from happening in the first place?

This question is not easy to answer, and if dealt with superficially can lead to grossly inaccurate and wrongful conclusions being drawn. I believe wholeheartedly that adulterous acts and adulterous behaviour do not necessarily betray any serious problems within a marriage. In fact, adultery is far more of a statement about human nature than it is about the state of matrimony. There is one important proviso to this statement, however: it applies only to acts of adultery committed by the husband. While acts of adultery on the part of husband or wife are equally sinful and equally serious, still when it is the wife who strays it is indeed indicative of a serious problem within the marriage. Stated in other words, when a husband is unfaithful, often the cause is not his marriage at all, but a natural sexual predisposition towards variety. When a wife commits adultery it is not because of her nature but rather because of her *marriage*. Statement after statement on the part of husbands show that, in their minds, even if they stray they still love their wives and they are doing nothing to really hurt the marriage. 'We both chose not to tell our spouses. I knew it would only hurt my wife, she wouldn't be able to see that I did not love her less . . .' 'I have had extramarital experiences unknown to my wife. They pulled me out of a mental slump that seemed to be destroying me. *They didn't affect my marriage in any way.*'[9] The point is that many husbands actually believe, however mistakenly, that their acts of infidelity do not seriously disrupt their married lives. Later in the book I will demonstrate the fallacy of their thinking.

Now I understand that these statements are highly contentious, and I could easily be accused of applying a double standard, implying that the infidelity of the wife is far more serious than that of the husband. Nevertheless, I ask the reader to please hold off judgement until I am able to better clarify this point later in this book, as well as bringing ample proof to support my case. While I shall have much to say about this, specifically in Chapter 3 detailing the differences between male and female sexuality, I shall say at the outset that there is a chronicled and proven difference between the reasons why men and women commit adultery. The large number of men who admit that they commit adultery although they are very much in love with their wives, seems to tell us that men do not look for strong emotional attachments with their girlfriends and mistresses and are far more prone to the sexual element and one-night flings. *In the minds of many adulterous men, love is something they get from their wives; excitement is something they get from their mistresses.* In this respect, the statement of Britt Ekland that 'I say I don't sleep with married men, but what I mean is that I don't sleep with happily married men,' is a farce because statistically speaking, nearly all the husbands who commit adultery are 'happily married' albeit feeling innately unfulfilled by monogamy. So they often talk themselves into the belief that they are unhappily married and their wives don't understand them, when really all they are feeling is a palpable sense of boredom brought about by a natural inclination away from monogamy. Emotional fulfilment has little or nothing to do with it.

There can be no question that men are not naturally monogamous and seem naturally unsatisfied with one sexual partner. Thus, their acts of infidelity are more a statement of their innate sexuality than the results of the state of their marriage.

In this I differ with many authors who time and time again emphasize that adultery is a statement of a fundamental illness within a marriage, or of a highly unsuccessful and dissatisfying sex life between a couple. I feel it is very important to say this because I not only believe that in most cases a marriage should not break up as a result of a sexual indiscretion on the part of a spouse, but moreover, I truly believe and shall argue throughout this book that it is specifically the *possibility* of adultery that can resolve the greatest of all challenges to marriage: the loss of sexual passion in long-term relationships.

Adultery is a Sin of Omission

What is the true sin of adultery? It is a sin of omission. People seem to think adultery is a sin of *commission*: you do wrong, therefore it is a transgression. But it is not. It is a void. It is wrong not because you have done something wrong, but because *you haven't done something right*. All of the affection, emotion, and attention you lavish on the person you seek to seduce should be shown to your spouse. You are taking what your spouse deserves and rightfully belongs to them and giving it away to someone else, a stranger. Instead of putting it into your marriage you're focusing outside your marriage. A marriage is a hungry animal, an electric, alive institution. It needs to be constantly fed with attention, devotion and love. Adultery then, far more than being a sin, is an act of *diversion*. Your affair may end, but the consequences of your marriage having been depleted of attention and energy for a sustained period of time can be catastrophic. It may even end the marriage. A man and a woman do not live together naturally. They must make a constant effort to show each other their devotion if a marriage is to succeed. Thus, the principal crime of adultery lies in its depleting a marriage of its necessary life-force and life-giving sustenance.

In my first year at Oxford a woman who was twenty-five years old wanted to be divorced after only two years of marriage. Why? Because her husband had been unfaithful to her. She caught him red-handed in the matrimonial bed with another woman. She was hysterical. 'Out,' she cried to the woman who was scrambling to find her clothes. After she had left, she shouted and cried to her husband at the top of her lungs, 'You're a beast, you're an animal. You brought that whore into my house and into our bed. How could you?' And she cried and cried for three weeks, inconsolable, until she just decided that she was leaving him. I was on very good terms with both of them, and struggled to try and keep their marriage together. I said to her, 'Look, Judaism is a forgiving religion and people deserve a second chance, so if he feels regret then why won't you forgive him?'

'Shmuley,' she said to me, 'I don't want the divorce only because he committed this abomination. Had he been a husband the rest of the time – had he been considerate, compassionate, caring, loving; had he called me when he was away, been concerned when I was unwell, or complimented me on the efforts I made to enrich and beautify myself for him – then I might be able to overlook it. But he has never acted like a husband. He never helped with the housework, and never even took the time to talk to me and tell me what was happening in his life. If he is not a husband at all then why should I overlook his mistake? I can forgive my *husband* for doing something wrong, but this man is a stranger. Love can assuage hurt. But here there is no love.' I use this story to illustrate a very important principal: adultery is not about hurting your wife. Rather, it is about taking the affection and desire which is hers by marital right and giving it away to a stranger. In other words, *by committing adultery you do not become an adulterer. Rather, you cease being a spouse.*

From time immemorial it has been debated whether or not a man or a woman can love two people at once. Can a husband indeed love his wife and his mistress equally? Can a woman remain focused on her husband and her paramour simultaneously? I do not know how to resolve this dilemma, and nor do I care. The question is completely immaterial because one thing is certainly clear. Even if a man could *love* his wife and mistress simultaneously, he still cannot show them both enough attention and affection to properly sustain his relationship with them both. And the same applies especially to women, who seem to get more emotionally involved in their extramarital affairs. And marriages do not thrive and subsist on what we *feel*. Rather, they live through *what we do* about our feelings. That is what is most important in every marriage. No wonder then, that the number one way in which husbands and wives discover about each other's affairs is not directly, but *indirectly*. It is not through walking in on one's husband while he is with his girlfriend, or hearing about it from a friend. Rather, the process is far slower and more subtle, and usually begins with noticing that one's spouse is distracted. No longer are they as loving, attentive, or concerned. Their thoughts are far away and their sexual desire for their spouse is usually very much diminished as well.

In her book *Tempted Women*, psychologist Carol Botwin cites this distraction as the main give-away in uncovering 'the whole secret affair'. She writes: 'The majority of unfaithful wives become mentally consumed by their extramarital relationships and may appear to their husbands to be lost in thought or preoccupied, less thoughtful or attentive in general . . . [They] are less interested in making love to [their] husbands than they used to be.'[10]

But perhaps the greatest proof that adultery represents an omission in a marriage is the final 'clue' to discovering an adulterous affair which Botwin describes: 'You stop trying to change things that were bothering you before. If you felt that you weren't getting enough sex, you stop attempting to entice your husband. If you were complaining that he didn't communicate enough, you stop trying to open him up. If he drank too much or had other bad habits, you stop railing at him about them. After finding some satisfaction and fulfilment with the other man, you give up on your husband and stop bothering him about things that you were carrying on about before.' Thus, adultery serves as a double wrong, first because it betrays a marriage and causes terrible pain to one's spouse, and second because it robs a marriage of the input it needs to survive and prosper. On a more individual level adultery erodes, if not utterly destroys, the faith and trust that one partner has in the other. It causes never-ending pain to the partner who has been betrayed, and a terrible sense of humiliation. Worse, it causes an almost incurable feeling of inadequacy that the partner who has been cheated against cannot shake. 'What do I lack that he found with someone else?' the wife asks herself. 'Have I not been loving or caring enough?' the husband asks himself. What is particularly unjust about this introspection is that it is the *victim* who feels responsible. So in addition to the pain which the infidelity causes, the soul-searching on the part of the partner who did nothing wrong just compounds and makes matters far worse.

> 'It's all my fault. If I'd been nicer, smarter, funnier, prettier, thinner (like she is), none of this would have happened. Why did I get so furious when he wanted his mom to move in with us, or when he wouldn't clear out the garage? If I'd only been a better wife, if only I hadn't gone back to work, we'd still be together.'[11]

This feeling of inadequacy is particularly acute with aspects the betrayed spouse feels just cannot be changed and leads to the worst feelings of inadequacy. It is one thing for a wife to feel that perhaps because she focused too intensely on her career, she showed too little affection to her husband and must now reorient her life in the hope that the warmth he gets from her will cause him not to search for it elsewhere. But what if the wife discovers that her husband's lover is unusually beautiful and sexy? How can she avoid the feeling of being an inferior lover, and being unable to compete with the stronger feminine qualities of the competition? The same is true if a husband discovers that his wife's lover is far more successful than he or is of unusual athletic build and strong masculinity. Is he therefore an inferior being, he asks himself.

Causes of Adultery

I much enjoyed Naura Hayden's book *How to Satisfy a Woman Every Time*. Although it has quite a risqué title, the book is actually about bringing passion into *marriage*, and I commend her for her beautiful statements about marriage within the book. 'Now we come to my favourite subject, marriage . . . I truly believe in the commitment of marriage. I think it's the greatest relationship that two people can ever have. A partnership with someone who loves you. What could be better. I hate it when a married man makes a play for me. Even if he's the handsomest, most darling man-about-town, it truly distresses me. I don't want him to embarrass his wife by flirting outrageously with me or any other woman.' But even she falls prey to the belief that adultery is always a statement about the problems within a marriage: 'So why do so many people fool around outside of marriage? . . . I believe most of it stems from incomplete sex lives. The men fooling around are doing it because they sense their wives are not deeply in love with them. Most women are deeply dissatisfied sexually with their husbands and their marriages, and are looking around for "Mr Right" to fulfil them in this very important way.'[12]

Nonsense! Many men who fool around are fully aware that their wives are completely and totally in love with them. In fact, this can often serve as the very reason for adultery. When a wife loves her husband too much and shows too great a degree of devotion, and never any sexual attraction to another man, and conversely no men show an interest in her, the husband searches elsewhere for excitement for his wife presents no challenge to him, and no flattery since, on the surface, no one else seems interested in her. Men want a woman who is desirable to others as well. It is one of the most natural human emotions. The greatest cause of adultery among men is certainly not a search for 'deep emotional love', but rather *failing to see one's wife as a desirable woman*. It can hardly be erotic and sexually seductive to see one's spouse first and foremost not as a woman but as 'my wife'. And yet, as soon as a man discovers that his wife is sexually interested in another man, and conversely, others are interested in her, he goes crazy and wants her back. The reason: he now recognizes that indeed she is not merely *his wife*, but a sexual creature, and that itself makes her irresistibly attractive and desirable.

What I am prepared to concede is that adultery points to a serious ailment in the marriage in that all the passion, time, energy, and creativity that unfaithful couples are putting into their relationships with others could be put into their marriages. And since a marriage needs constant feeding of emotion and sexual energy, it will suffer enormously from this depletion.

So, whilst a bad sex life may not be the *cause* of adultery, it almost certainly will be the *result*. In this respect, I believe that Hayden's statements ought to be reversed. Since men are not naturally monogamous, if they do not make an effort to transcend their natures and focus all their sexual energy on their wives, the result will be that wives will feel deeply dissatisfied with their intimate lives, because their husbands are simply not wholeheartedly participating in it and committed to them. They may then embark on a quest for 'Mr Right', and even if they do not, they will be deeply discontented with their husbands. This in turn will cause husbands to feel that they are not fully loved, which, at least in the short-term, is true. Love, as King Solomon so beautifully reflected in 'Song of Songs', is largely reciprocal – 'like the waters of the sea that reflect the human face, so too the heart reciprocates the emotions shown to it'. Therefore, no wife can feel completely in love with her husband when she witnesses his undying obsession for someone else. Of course, this wicked spiral just continues to corrode the relationship, unless a stop is put to it quickly.

Conversely, the very small number of women who are in love with their husbands and yet still commit adultery seems to suggest that women search for a paramour primarily if they feel ignored or neglected by their husbands. Thus, their infidelity does betray a serious marital breakdown, although certainly not irreversible. Hayden's statement about unfulfilled wives gives the false impression that any wife who is not married to a real-life Casanova, or who is not a sexual tiger, or who has not read every Masters and Johnson book and every sex manual and who has not experimented with every sexual position, will of necessity feel dissatisfied.

But this is erroneous. It is not *positions* that men and women want in sex, but *attention*. There is nothing so erotic as the knowledge that the partner you are with is totally interested in you, and only you. They delight in just looking at your body, and gauging your response to the activities they initiate. And the ultimate turn-off is to feel that your partner is not fully interested in you, or that their thoughts are elsewhere. Hence, even the sexiest prostitute, with all the sexual knowledge in the world, is not worth even a penny for her favours. There can never exist any deep erotic pleasure with her since *she is being paid*. Come to your senses! She is just not interested. She couldn't give a damn about you, and every erotic movement and sound which she makes is contrived.

I once heard a sex therapist speaking on CNN. Interestingly, this therapist was herself a former prostitute. She said that whenever she counsels couples about marriage, she walks over to the husband and asks him to point to his principal sexual organ. Inevitably, the man blushes, and instinctively looks down to the area of his crotch. She then says to them, 'Wrong! This is your most powerful sexual organ,' pointing to his head. 'It is the interest you have in a person that turns them on.' This is absolutely true. Sexual excitement and elation lie in the mind, not in the genitals.

It is for this reason that marriage, and marriage only, possesses the greatest erotic potential. Since marriage involves the greatest commitment, it also serves as the greatest statement of interest. It is a statement by two people that they are so interested in one another that they are even prepared to close off all other sexual possibilities and partners. I know that to some readers who are married, this will sound absurd. Marriage – the most exciting? The most erotic? If this is so, they will ask, why is it that in virtually every account of an extramarital affair, the partners will invariably describe the most exciting sexual moments of their lives, transcending by far anything that could be found in marriage? The answer is that the full potential of marriage has yet to be unlocked. If only we could identify exactly what it is that brings such excitement to adultery then, remembering that all sexual erotica is in the mind, this could easily be transferred into marriage and bring a couple to life. And in marriage the excitement will be far greater because there is no need for apprehension or shyness, or the concern that one's sexual performance is being 'rated' by a stranger in contrast to their other nightly partners. To make this commitment effective it is necessary to see the marital bond primarily as a sexual commitment. Instead of seeing marriage only as a statement of 'He loves me and therefore he wants to spend the rest of his life with me. Thus, he asks me to marry him,' we must equally view it in these terms: 'He sees me as so sexually desirable that he wishes to spend all his days talking with me, but also his nights with me in my bed. Thus he asks me to marry him.'

But conversely, this can also serve as the reason why *adultery* can be so exciting. A woman who has an affair with a married man might be prepared to put all morality and ethics, and the knowledge of the hurt that she is causing to another woman, on the back-burner, since she says to herself, 'Can you imagine how attracted this guy is to me? He is prepared to sacrifice everything for me. He is risking *everything* for me. He really loves me.' Thus, even women who are normally very sensitive and caring can suddenly find themselves becoming the lovers of married men, and in the process hurting another woman in the worst possible way. Why? Because regardless of how terrible the consequences of the adulterous act may be, the man still wants them, and cannot deny their attraction. And for many women, their passionate interest in them serves as an offer so inviting they just can't turn it down. What we all want, above all else, is to be adored and needed. That perhaps is the principal reason for the excitement that lies in adultery, and will account for the complete character transformation that overcomes so many women who are willing to sleep with married men. 'It is exciting to think that a man finds you desirable when he has a woman whom he obviously found desirable at some time waiting at home.'[13]

But this too is a farce. He is not prepared to sacrifice everything for you, even if he says he is. In fact, he sacrifices nothing. It is all an illusion. He uses you secretly and in the process loses nothing but his own innocence. He keeps his wife, and children, and has commitment-free sex with you. In his mind, there is no risk, since he is sure he will not be caught. And even if he is, he thinks his wife will forgive him, rather than risk divorce and the breakdown of the family, and life will go on. There are reasons which might compel a wife to be forgiving. In a widely quoted report by sociologist Lenore Weitzman of Harvard University, a woman's standard of living was said to drop 73 per cent after divorce. If this is not the case, and he truly does love you, then why does he not carry on his affair with you in public? Let him celebrate and proclaim his association with you to the whole world, including his wife.

The Marriage Commitment

Marriage does not come easy to anyone who undertakes its commitments. Nor should it. I have always believed that the greatest statement of love from one human being to another is when a constant, ongoing effort is made to remain loyal, faithful, loving and caring amidst the natural inclination to selfishness, apathy, and sexual experimentation. People just naturally love novelties. 'I started this just for excitement and to see what it would be like to be with someone else. But I fell in love and I can't lose him.'[14] Any husband and wife for whom marriage comes easy are deprived of making the most sublime statements of love to each other, i.e., I love you and care for you, so much so that I seek to transcend my nature by remaining loyal and loving and totally focused on you at all times.

The simple fact is that anything in life for whose attainment effort does not have to be expended is simply not worth having. Marriage is the greatest proof of this statement. There is nothing more special, more loving, more worthwhile, more sublime, and better able to cure humankind's hurts and woes than marriage, when it is done right. But conversely, there is nothing so miserable, hurtful, devastating or tormenting to the soul than marriage when it goes wrong, and when one's shared life with a partner is spent in constant bickering, one's purpose in life becomes only the causing of pain to one's spouse. Thus, we must make an effort, our greatest effort, to be at all times loving, caring, and faithful partners, even amidst a natural atttraction to men and women outside our marriage. Monogamy is not a concession which religion asks humans to make in the name of holiness and decency. On the contrary, it is the very vehicle through which the ultimate sexual passion can be experienced and sustained to make our marriages pleasurable, glorious, and above all holy.

SOURCES — CHAPTER ONE

1. *The Kinsey Report, Sex and Morality in the US*, 1989
2. *The Janus Report on Sexual Behaviour*, 1993
3. ibid.
4. *The Hite Report on Love, Passion, and Emotional Violence*, 1991
5. *Independent on Sunday*, 16 January 1994
6. *The Kinsey Report, Sex and Morality in the US*, 1989
7. ibid.
8. *The Janus Report on Sexual Behaviour*, 1993
9. *The Hite Report on Love, Passion, and Emotional Violence*, 1991
10. Carol Botwin, *Tempted Women*, 1994
11. Diane Baroni and Betty Kelly, *How to Get Him Back from the Other Woman*, 1982
12. Naura Hayden, *How to Satisfy a Woman Every Time*, 1982
13. *The Hite Report on Love, Passion, and Emotional Violence*, 1991
14. Carol Botwin, *Tempted Women*, 1994

CHAPTER TWO

THE UNNATURAL STATE
OF MARRIAGE

THE POTENTIAL and natural inclination towards adultery is especially highlighted by the extreme unnaturalness of marriage. Every human being is first and foremost adulterous and non-monogamous, and only after an effort is made and sexual focus attained do we become monogamous. A woman came from London to see me in Oxford. She was already hysterical when she walked in, and I wondered how I could calm her down. Susan, a young wife of thirty-three, had been referred to me by a colleague in London after discovering that her husband had had a six-week affair with a woman he had met on an aeroplane. Susan had discovered the affair, ironically, when another airline had called to inform her husband at home that his flight had been cancelled and therefore he and his travelling colleague would have to fly the following morning. His intended companion was his mistress, and instead of taking the next morning's flight he instead spent his time trying to dissuade his wife from leaving him. They had three children and he begged me to help keep the marriage together. But whatever arguments I used to persuade her to forgive him, she wouldn't listen. She just kept ranting and raving, 'How could he? I gave him the best years of his life. How could he?' Finally, I bent over my desk, looking her in the eyes, and said, 'How could he *not*?' She looked startled and hurt, and turned to leave my office. Before she did so, I explained myself.

So many people make the mistake of asking how a faithful spouse can stray. On the contrary, the real question is how could they remain faithful! Make no mistake about it, adultery is what is natural and intuitive. It is marriage and monogamy which run against the grain of human nature. So the real question in adultery is not, 'How can anyone commit adultery?' but rather, 'How can anyone commit themselves to marriage and monogamy in the first place, and what can we do to make people behave *unnaturally* and remain faithful?' I told Susan that what was surprising about her husband's behaviour was not why he committed adultery, but rather why he was ever faithful in the first place. I advised her that based on this understanding of the inherently promiscuous nature of all humans she should perhaps be more forgiving, so long as her husband firmly undertook never again to repeat this terrible mistake, and acted towards her with added affection and closeness.

Let's take a closer look at this. Is it natural to be married? Is marriage a natural aspiration of life? Is it an automatic human impulse? Is marriage an intuitive culmination of desire on the part of single beings to join together and thereby permanently assuage their loneliness? And most importantly, is monogamy natural?

The answer is an emphatic: NO! Forget it. Monogamy is as unnatural as the desire to remain hungry. I contend without any reservation whatsoever that marriage is not a congenital human state. I further contend that the knowledge that marriage is not natural is the single most important element of any successful marriage, and the quicker we realize it, the better, because we will then be on guard constantly to make our marriages work, and ensure that we are devoting and dedicating ourselves totally to its success. Judaism maintains that the fundamental challenge of human living is for man to rise above his nature. We dare not allow our natures to rule us. Rather, we must endeavour to exert our mastery over our own human inclination. Only then can we be guaranteed fulfilling and extraordinary lives which are not the product of mere impulse and whim.

I read a story once about a white Bengal tiger in the Miami Zoo who ate a zoo keeper. It was decided not to destroy the animal. Part of the reason was that the white Bengal tiger is virtually extinct already. But the more important consideration was that the zoo keeper himself had made the fatal mistake of leaving the cage open as he fed the animal. It was felt that the animal should not be punished merely because of its predatory and voracious nature in the face of human error and subsequent provocation. But such clemency would never be granted a human. He would be expected to rise above his nature. If you are sitting innocently in a bar, and a man comes up and repeatedly insults you and provokes you, you'll end up going to jail and possibly even the electric chair if you take out your gun and shoot him. Because you're human, and not just an animal guided by instinct, you are expected to control your emotions, and will thus be held accountable for your actions.

The same applies to humankind's natural gravitation to many sexual partners. The fact that your nature leads you to stray will never serve as an adequate excuse for hurting your spouse and destroying your marriage, which is why the woman above was so unforgiving. Therefore, when we speak of marriage as a holy institution, and when we speak of marriage as a Godly institution, ('holy matrimony'), we must attune our ears to the serious implications of these words: *it means that marriage is not a natural institution*, but a supernatural one. And that means that it does not come easy; we do not slide comfortably into marriage or monogamy. They must be worked upon, and we must never take them for granted.

But before I am accused of sounding negative, or in any way diminishing marriage, just hear me out!

It is certainly not natural to be married. In the next chapter, we shall speak extensively of man's natural propensity to search for a variety of sexual partners, and how monogamy is a constant challenge to our natural state.

Imagine if I made you the offer of a lifetime: a beautiful country mansion is yours, with every luxury and amenity provided, at 50 per cent below market price. I will sell it to you, but with one caveat: you must move into the house and never move out again. You cannot sell it or rent it out. It's wonderful, but you are absolutely stuck with it. There may be some slight provisions for moving out, but they will be accompanied by severe financial penalties, emotional drainage and pain. Are you still interested? Or do you see the catch?

What if I offer you a great bargain on a car, but along the same lines: would you purchase it? And if you do, are you sure that when a younger, more modern and better equipped model is released, you would not regret your earlier life-long commitment? While your car ages and loses much of its original gloss and shine, will you not look with envy at your neighbour's more modern purchase?

Or what about employment: all you lawyers out there, I will offer you a great job, with a considerable salary at a highly rated firm. And it comes with total job security, namely, you can't lose it: it's for life. If you accept the offer, there is no way out. You must work there for ever. Again, you may earn your independence if you subsequently prove unable to withstand the commitment. But beware. The price of your independence will be extraordinarily high. Now, are you prepared to sign on the dotted line? Are you sure that once a better offer comes along by some firm who witnesses your professionalism and wants to make you theirs, you won't regret your life-long contract? For those of you who aren't taken by the offers outlined above, and I suspect that this is not an insignificant number, you must ask yourself, *why then are you prepared to be married?* In fact, there is no other example in life where an individual is prepared to commit themselves, amidst any possible eventuality, to a life-long prospect. How could we? How would we know that things wouldn't go wrong? I am not so naive as to deny the power of love. But if you are indeed so infatuated with someone that you wish to marry them, go ahead and live with them! Hold them in your arms and make them yours. But for God's sake, don't be silly enough to say things like 'Till death do us part', or 'I will love you forever', when you have no guarantee that you will wish to preserve the relationship fifty years hence. Certainly, don't be silly enough to sign away your commitment, and your life in the process! Take things gradually, see how it goes. It's the reasonable, logical thing to do. You wouldn't commit yourself this way in any other circumstance. Why, then, for marriage?

Had God Never Thought Up Marriage, Human Beings Wouldn't Have Either

The answer is that marriage is not a human, but a *divine* institution. It is an irrational institution; it really doesn't make sense. I suggest sincerely and with no fear of refutation that if God had not commanded us to marry and thus instituted marriage as a most basic staple of life, mankind would never have come up with it. We simply would never have thought of it. To be sure, humans might have devised some vaguely committed style of living together, but it would be entirely predicated on the emotions of the moment, and with no provision for commitment into what is at best a questionable future. We are only all too aware of the unpredictability of emotions. The man you can't live without today, you can't live with tomorrow. The woman who seems so comely now, might seem repulsive just a bit later. Men and women might have made a life together and be waiting around to see how long it lasts; how long the sexual and emotional attachment retains its passion and magic. But why the commitment under the wedding canopy?

It might even be argued that the need to formalize a

commitment in such a serious way, as is done in Jewish marriage, betrays a serious flaw in the love which the couple have for one another, since if they really felt so deeply, there would be no need to contractualize their affections. Surely, if two brothers enter into business together, one will take offence at the other's insistence that their lawyers sit down to draft contracts and ensure the other's commitment, faithfulness, and honesty!

Powerful contemporary proof to the effect that marriage is an exclusively religious institution with no basis in logic is this: marriage and marital fidelity are being diminished commensurably with the evaporation of religion from mainstream society. And it is specifically religious communities that have the highest rate of marriage and at the youngest age. Elsewhere, the average couple are finding increasingly little reason to marry and are opting to live together instead, often with no view towards marriage whatsoever. What on earth for? They love each other and in their minds this is sufficient. It is undeniable that religion and marriage have gone hand in hand from the earliest times.

The Rationalists' View of Marriage

If marriage were a logical and/or moral imperative, if it were a human creation, it would be gaining strength in this supreme age of rationalism. But the historical fact remains that many great rationalists, indeed many great philosophers, have always been fiercely opposed to marriage. Most of the great libertarian thinkers viewed marriage, and especially monogamy, as the most oppressive of all institutions, and labelled it as such. The Oxford book of quotations lists sixty-two entries on the subject of marriage. Only four are positive, a few neutral, and the rest, over fifty, very negative. The consensus basically is that getting married is about as satisfying as root canal, and should be treated accordingly. As Jonathan Swift wrote: 'What they do in heaven we are ignorant of; what they do *not* we are told expressly, that they neither marry, nor are given in marriage.'

I especially like this quote of George Bernard Shaw which expresses the ultimate cynicism of marriage: 'Those who talk most about the blessings of marriage and the constancy of its vows are the very people who declare that if the chain were broken and the prisoners left free to choose, the whole social fabric would fly asunder. You cannot have the argument both ways. If the prisoner is happy, why lock him in? If he is not, why pretend that he is?'

The power of course of the quotation is the impression it makes on the reader. For how could Shaw just write as a *prima facie* assumption that those who are married are not happy, unless he feared no disagreement from the great majority of his readers? No, marriage is not natural, and the belief that marriage is natural has led to terrible misconceptions and inestimable damage in relationships. Happiness in marriage, unlike the passion of adultery, requires effort and the quicker we realize this, the more secure our marriages will be. And because it is a divine rather than human construct it requires the blessing of Heaven to endure. Every effort to bring greater depth into married life through spiritual and religious observances and closeness can only assist in a marital bond.

'The Person I Married is not the One I Fell in Love With'

There is a common contemporary complaint among married couples that things change once they get married. They claim in many cases that the person whom they married is different, sometimes radically, to the person they were dating. They feel that their husband, or wife, was somehow more sensitive, more caring, more responsive while they were going out together, as opposed to when they finally tied the knot. In the words of a female friend: 'The probability that my husband would open the car door for me now, as he did when we were dating, is the same probability that I will bring him breakfast in bed, as I did every Sunday in our first few months of marriage.'

When the couple first started going out, he was on his best behaviour, always careful to be a gentleman. Now, here they are married just four months and already he breaks wind in his wife's presence and digs out the wax in his ears, not even noticing how disgusted his wife is with this vulgarity.

How can this be? From whence spring these changes? Does marriage then have a magical, yet sinister capacity for changing a woman from Snow White into Attila the Hun just by standing under a canopy? Can the act of a man putting a ring on a woman's finger suddenly transform him from Doctor Jekyll into Mr Hyde? I somehow doubt it. And yet it is true that often marriage is not nearly as pleasant or exciting as dating, and countless couples complain of this treacherous transformation. It is this reality that has given rise to the oft-repeated aphorism, 'How to kill a great relationship? Get married.'

The real explanation for the sudden rude awakening is described above: couples mistakenly believe that it is natural to be married. Therefore, whereas when they date they exert every effort to impress their intended partner because they understand this is vital and necessary and that it is difficult for someone to *commit* to marriage, when they finally marry they suddenly exert no effort at all, thinking that bliss will just flow automatically from their union. They do not see marriage as a constant struggle, a constant challenge, in which a person must be on alert at all times. Rather, once you get married, you need hardly do anything at all. You simply stay married.

In her book, *The Erotic Silence of the American Wife*, sociologist Dalma Heyn describes the problem as follows. There's a theory that some men are what sociologists call 'situationally expressive' – loving and forthcoming during courtship, when they are eager to win a woman, but inclined to withdraw expressiveness once they win her. When she describes this condition to women during interviews she finds that many recognize its key elements. 'It all happened so soon, to me and my friends. I mean I think something slipped away incredibly fast.'

Every man and every woman knows that in order to build up and sustain attraction with a member of the opposite sex, one must work very hard. To be sure, there often is love at first sight, or an immediate attraction. You meet in a restaurant, and you just know that you would love to go out with the girl sitting at table number seven. But even this sort of attraction will dissipate almost immediately if nothing is done about it. If you do not ask her out, you will forget about her quite rapidly. If you do ask her out, you must do your utmost to impress her. Why else should she be interested?

When a man and a woman date, they are always on their best behaviour. They want to impress one another. He refrains from any manifestation of temper in her presence. She refrains from using foul language. He tells her of his very exciting job and the influential people he meets. She mentions the challenging academic work in which she is engaged, and how she hopes to finish her Ph.D. before summer. In short, they display the best side of their personalities in order to create a favourable impression.

I remember this well from my own experience. I was a student in New York with no means of transportation when I first took out the woman I wanted to marry and whom I was eager to impress. We went out to dinner to a beautiful kosher Chinese restaurant in Manhattan. A cab-driver offered us a ride back to Brooklyn, and on the way back I asked him if he knew of a car rental company who would rent a car in New York to someone under the age of twenty-five. He began to drive us to

Coney Island Avenue in Brooklyn, saying he had a friend he could speak to who required a $300 deposit since I was under twenty-five, in addition to the $200 fee for a week's rental. He told me to give him the money when we went in so he could negotiate with his friend, giving me his car keys as 'security', and the three of us walked out of the car towards an office that said 'Car Rental'. As we emerged from the car, like a bolt of lightning he ran back into the car, obviously possessed of a spare set of keys, and he was gone, into the wild blue yonder, together with my $500.

I was a poor student and the blow was devastating. I will say as an extreme understatement that I was angry. My first instinct was to erupt and verbally consign him and his offspring for a thousand generations to the nether reaches of hell, a place where I had consigned many such scoundrels before. But I looked to my right and there was this woman who was innocent enough to have been clearly puzzled and troubled by everything that had just transpired. 'Is he coming back?' she asked. 'No,' I said. 'I've been ripped off.' She wondered what my response would be.

I sighed, and then said in a quiet voice, 'Poor devil. Can you just imagine how impoverished he must be, how desperately he needs the money, to have had to resort to that act of connivance and theft? I wish him well with the money, and may God look after him. After all, we are all humans and have our faults. And just as I would not like others to judge me, so I too overlook the infraction of this poor lost soul.' There was not a shred of sincerity in those words and never in my life have I uttered something so disingenuously. In fact, I wanted to tar and feather the man, and then stuff him into the engine of a 747 jumbo jet. But, it worked. And Debbie, who was later to marry me (poor soul), gave me a deep and satisfying look and said, 'I can't believe it. The average guy would have been so angry, would have wished him dead. But you – you're so kind and loving.

55

You're amazing.' So much for knowing your partner before marriage . . .

There is a universal recognition of the need to manifest one's most caring side in the act of wooing the member of the opposite sex whom we want to convince to marry us. We recognize that it just doesn't happen *naturally*. People don't fall for each other if they don't do anything for one another. People recognize that impressing someone enough to win their approval for marriage is a highly laborious and time-consuming process which essentially runs against the grain of human nature. People will not commit themselves to a life-long endeavour impetuously.

But then, it finally works. He gets on a knee and pops the big question. She blushes and with elation says yes, and the deal is done. The big day comes, and now they are married. What now? He is no longer on his best behaviour, losing his temper frequently and with little cause. Nor is he as generous, complaining that they must save all their money in order to pay the mortgage. Nor is she as patient with him and as loving as she once was. They sit around with their heads in their hands wondering what went wrong.

And yet the answer is staring them in the face. They have made the mistake of assuming that once a couple get married, the process of impressing one another is over. Stated in other words, they think that marriage is something which one does once only, and then *is* married. But marriage is a constant act, and we must always engage ourselves in the act of *becoming* married. Marriage is not a natural state, and the natural resistance to its monogamous demands and huge commitment necessitates a constant and conscious effort to make it successful.

Marriage Needs Constant Nourishment

The knowledge that we never *become* married, but rather must always *engage in the act of becoming married*, can have enormous implications for passion in marriage. I will mention in the chapter entitled 'The Ten Commandments of Adultery' that the words 'lover' or 'mistress' carry with them an erotic mystique. So do the words *man* and *woman*. But the words husband and wife do not. To think of your wife not as a *woman* but as a *wife* is to consign her to the depths of familiarity and boredom. An alluring woman has the power to attract new men, whereas a belaboured wife often loses her husband's affections. A mysterious new man can often excite the passions in the way that an everyday husband cannot. The knowledge that none of us ever becomes a wife or a husband, but always remains just a man or a woman who try their best to remain faithful amidst a powerful, natural inclination to do otherwise, serves as a constant reminder that we are married to sexual creatures who are not naturally monogamous, are deeply attractive to others, and we must therefore work to preserve their loyalty always by showing them love, attention, and romance. Remember this all-important rule: on one ever *becomes* married, and no man or woman ever becomes a husband or wife. Rather, they, just like you, are alive and alert sexual beings who must ward off their attraction to strangers constantly and reaffirm their sexual fidelity to you specifically and realign their sexual energy accordingly. This knowledge is the first major step in reinvigorating a stale and boring marriage. Do not take your spouse's fidelity for granted.

That no man or woman ever becomes a husband or wife is reflected in the Bible. There is no word for 'wife', for example, in Biblical Hebrew. Rather the word is 'eishes', which translates as 'the woman of'. Thus, Sarah was 'the woman of Abraham', but not his wife. She, along with other women, constantly remains a woman whose fidelity, affection and sexual focus must be constantly re-engendered by their husbands. And the same applies to men whose love for their wives must be constantly elicited.

In this respect, the only success we will ever have in marriage is if we always focus on what we can put into marriage, and the same of course applies to every relationship. We must never focus solely on what we can take out of it. In my job as a Rabbi, I hear all too often of young couples complaining that they do not get anything from the relationship. Statements abound along these lines: 'I do this for him and that for him. And what do I get? Nothing!' Before marriage a man and woman are separate and distinct beings. If they are to join together as one, then they both must reach inward towards one another, constantly contributing to each other. But if the couple is to focus on what they can receive from one another, instead of what they can give, then each partner is reaching outward, effectively *away* from one another. How then can they be joined? This is especially so with regard to human sexuality. If indeed monogamy is unnatural then people can only be satisfied with the most exciting and passionate intimate lives and we must make every endeavour to satisfy our spouse.

This should not sound radical because I am not arguing that we do not deserve any benefits from marriage. Nor am I suggesting that there are no legitimate needs on the part of each spouse in a marriage. If both husband and wife focus on what they can *contribute* into a marriage, it follows that automatically they will both receive anyway. In this scenario they will not be receiving and enjoying the benefits of companionship and marriage as strangers, but as loving halves of an indivisible whole.

CHAPTER THREE

DO MEN AND WOMEN *NEED* MANY SEXUAL PARTNERS?

'Women are more naturally monogamous than men. It is a biological necessity. When promiscuity prevails, they will always be more often the victims than the culprits. Also domestic happiness is more necessary to them than to us, and the quality by which they most easily hold a man, their beauty, decreases every year after they come to maturity.'
(C. S. Lewis 'We have no right to happiness' *Saturday Evening Post*, 1963)

WHAT DO YOU make of the following wife's complaint: 'My husband has not been faithful to me. How do I feel? Mad with fury. I am angry and it hurts. It is like having some kind of illness that is slowly eating away at me. I cannot just turn off my feelings and simply stop loving him like I was turning off a light. I want my husband to be monogamous. I don't think I am expecting or asking for anything more than he is asking and expecting of me. The worse thing he has ever done is sleep in another woman's bed when he should have been at home with me in our bed. He may have someone else. I'm glad I don't know.'

Is the statement reasonable? Is the woman correct in assuming (a) that by expecting her husband to be faithful she is merely asking what he asks of her; and (b) that comparisons and

59

expectations that can be made of women can also be made of men?

I have argued earlier in this book, and believe with the firmest conviction, that monogamy is not a natural state for a man, and this statement is true whether we approach it, like myself as a Rabbi, from the religious perspective, or even a secular Western perspective. Beginning with the latter, the scientific theory of evolution maintains that man is a product of slow development from the animal to the intellectual: not only is there a kinship between man and animals, but man *is* an animal, although endowed with higher cognitive faculties, among which is the power for verbal communication. Monogamy among male animals is extremely rare. This is not only an empirical fact but an easily verifiable observation. It is one of the fundamental assumptions of evolution, through its essential mechanism of natural selection and the survival of the fittest, that survival will be guaranteed to any species that can best propagate its off-spring, both qualitatively, but especially quantitatively. The only definitive action that will ensure the 'selection' or survival of a species is if the males copulate and inseminate as many females as possible. Thus, monogamy is not only unnatural, but can prove deeply deleterious to a species. The fact is that according to evolutionary theory, which is not only widespread today but is accepted, virtually unscrutinized, as fact, the males in every species will search for as many sexual partners as possible. Socio-biologists have long argued that the male is inherently promiscuous, going from partner to partner to ensure the most widespread possible distribution of his gene pool. The conclusion of the socio-biological argument is supported indirectly by many sex researchers who cite numerous surveys showing that males are far more likely than females to have extramarital affairs.

Male Sexuality

According to the Bible, and the religious view of male sexuality, the same is true. Whereas modern society is largely of the opinion that men and women differ only with regard to their reproductive systems, the Bible maintains that men and women differ in many important respects (but which of course have no bearing on their equality), but none so much as the area of human sexuality. It is in accordance with these differences that Judaism, as a religion, enacts different religious obligations, corresponding to the unique masculine and feminine traits possessed by each gender. The exact obligations in question are beyond the scope of our current discussion, but what is of tremendous significance is that whereas the Bible does not countenance polyandry for women, and even considers it an abomination, it does allow polygamy in theory for men. Regardless of the discouragement for polygamy which was pronounced for many reasons, among which that it creates enmity between two women who will compete against one another for their husband's affection, and that the Jews were being scorned and beaten by the majority Christian population, which was monogamous, the fact that the Bible does allow this for men and not for women seems to be a *prima facie* recognition of the natural differences that separate the sexes. Abraham had two wives, Jacob had four, King David six, and Solomon topped them all with what we understand to be hundreds.

Men naturally seek many women, many sexual partners. Allowing polygamy was a concession made by the Bible to accommodate this natural male need for more than one sexual partner. The Bible does however make the case that monogamy is a far better, holier state within which to live, and to which man should aspire (and later the Jewish Rabbis forbade polygamy as a Jewish lifestyle outright). Nevertheless, it does acknowledge the make-up of the male drive, and allowed for polygamous marriage in order to accommodate it, even amidst its discouragement. The same was not granted to women and polyandry was outlawed by the Bible because they do not seek many sexual partners so much as a deep emotional involvement with a single loving and caring man.

But I do not seek to repeat clichés about male and female sexuality without any empirical proof, especially since the issue is contentious and highly debated in society today. The most impressive proof of what I am saying is, of course, empirical. It is *the women* themselves who are astounded at the natural male tendency to promiscuity, finding nothing within themselves, amidst a very strong sex drive, that would match that of the males' inability to be satiated with one sexual partner. The *Hite Report* quotes many women who are flabbergasted at how unfaithful some of their friends' husbands truly are: 'I honestly believe I could seduce my best friend's father if I wanted to – some fidelity these guys have.' 'My husband's best friend (who was married and assured me it was fine with his wife) told me I was the only woman he wanted to go to bed with. Then a married judge tried to get me in bed, a married accountant, a married jewellery salesman, etc. etc.'

Yet again: 'I do not get involved with or date, nor have I ever even been attracted sexually to, a friend's husband, boyfriend, or date. But I sure have had my friends' husbands, boyfriends, dates, and friends try and do it with me – in fact, most of them. Usually when the guy makes a pass, I think, "What more does he want?" It seems many men are seeking newness, which they equate with passion. Newness meaning lots of women.'[1]

Female Sexuality

Many would refute the above conclusions by pointing out that the latest studies, especially that of the *Hite Report*, maintain that women have nearly as many extramarital affairs as men, especially since the sexual revolution of the 1960s. In 1953, Alfred Kinsey found that 26 per cent of women were having sex outside of their marriages. In the *Hite Report*, published in 1987, 70 per cent of women married five years or more are having sex outside their marriage. Many other surveys have reached a similar conclusion that female infidelity, while not quite as high as men's, still reaches above 50 per cent. Even allowing for different statistical methods, this points to an enormous increase, which would mean that women's rate of extramarital sex has almost tripled in thirty-five years, and is almost equal to that of the men's rate of 75 per cent after five years of marriage.[2]

But these figures can be quite misleading. The first important point to bear in mind is that, whereas male extramarital sex tends to be of the 'one-night stand' nature, that is, rapid and often, the female type tends to be far more of the long-lasting, emotionally involved type. 'What the largest number of men are seeking is a sexual adventure for its own sake. They are after novelty, a fresh body, someone to excite their senses again.'[3] 'Most women's affairs are not with "casual" partners, but are long-lasting relationships.'[4] What women covet far more than a sexual liaison is a loving partner, and they are even prepared to find it outside marriage if need be. For women the sex is ancillary to the extramarital affair, whereas with the men it is *central*.

In fact, among women, extramarital affairs rarely lead to divorce (only 17 per cent), but tend to continue in intense relationships as a stable way of life for years. The average number of years for wives' affairs that are not one- or two-time meetings, is, surprisingly, four years; longer than many marriages last these days. It seems curious that most women opt to stay in a marriage even when the love in the affair is deeper – although financial necessity and the unavailability of the man in question (since most married women's lovers are married themselves) would help account for this. We must conclude that women who divorce their husbands usually do so because of what is lacking in their marriage, not because they are in love with someone else.

'The majority of women having affairs say they feel alienated, emotionally closed out, or harassed in their marriages; for 60 per cent, having an affair is a way of enjoying oneself, reasserting one's identity, having one person appreciate you in a way that another doesn't,' writes Shere Hite before introducing the personal revelations of some adulterous women. The point in all the quotations seems to be that they sought the affair not just to have sex, but to find love, attention, and comfort.

'I felt so unappreciated at home and was given "love" and appreciation in the relationship. The effect on me personally was to build me up, support me, and help me to cope with my marriage.'

'The reason for my affair for three years now has been hunger for affection. I told my husband several times I could not live without affection.'

'My husband chose to ignore me for years . . . and years . . . Eventually I started having affairs . . .'

'My husband and I argued . . . I was to blame for *everything* . . .' this woman too embarked upon an affair.

Hite writes of the female nature: 'Women are not looking for affairs basically for "more sex" or "sexual variety," as men at least often say they are – although some women do want more excitement and romance. Women often feel more powerful emotionally in outside relationships because they cannot be taken for granted, they must at least be listened to, so that they won't leave.'

Perhaps this accounts for the reason why a wife's partner

in an adulterous affair is always referred to as a lover, in contradistinction to the husband's adulterous partner who will usually be called a girlfriend, or a mistress, but rarely a lover. For the husband the affair might not be anything more than 'sex', for the wife it is usually a 'loving' relationship.

That women enter into extramarital affairs *primarily* for emotional, as opposed to sexual reasons, can be further substantiated from the *kind* of women who are most likely to have an affair, which according to the statistics is very surprising. One might have been led to believe that this huge increase in female infidelity would have taken place primarily among the new class of female business women and professionals, who, working outside of the home and as equals alongside their male counterparts, would fall in love with a peer. But this is not the case. It is specifically the women who do not work outside the home who are having more affairs, at least according to most studies. So, it is not the 'new women' or 'career women' who, having entered the previously male world, are now emulating male sexual activity, but the women who are economically dependent on their husbands and who may have fewer outlets to turn to in an emotionally unfulfilling marriage.

But perhaps the most significant proof that female infidelity is a response to an emotional vacuum, and not necessarily a straight desire to have more sex, can be ascertained from the relatively low number of affairs among women, only 6 per cent, who are in love with their husbands and find their marriages emotionally fulfilling. The simple fact is that the overwhelming number of women who claim to be loved by their husbands, and are shown that love, do not have extramarital sex. Even this 6 per cent is high compared to the 98 per cent of women who claim to be 'in love' with their husbands and are therefore totally monogamous, as opposed to the previous 6 per cent who express themselves as 'loving' their husbands, but not being 'in love' with their husbands.

In fact, it might even be argued that the cause of female infidelity is that women are no longer willing to stand for their husbands' affairs. Now that it is common for the women to be equal breadwinners for the family, they are not prepared to give a man love, obedience, and fidelity when he does not reciprocate. Women now put greater emphasis on what they are giving emotionally, so that they are more acutely aware of men who do not return their affections. With this increased economic power, achieved over the last twenty years, women according to Hite 'are less likely to believe or accept the ideas women expressed so often as recently as the 1950s: "That is just the way men are, you just have to accept it." Women want to have a real life with someone now – emotionally, psychologically, intellectually, and physically.'

One loyal wife who, after discovering that her husband was having an affair with another women, said: 'I am a social being – a human being with gifts to give and needs that have to be filled by other people. I'm beginning to think of looking outside our marriage for some of my affectionate needs.' And again: 'I think that if I do start seeing other people it will give me bargaining power, which I'm lacking. Many times I feel like he has all the power – makes most of the decisions and I just comply – which infuriates me.'

Similarly, another proclaims: 'I cheated on my husband after he shattered my world by cheating on me. I did it for revenge and also to be told I was pretty and wonderful, etc. – the romance. I felt terribly guilty afterwards and only truly loved my husband. I forgave him but he never truly forgave me. It had a damaging effect on our relationship, things were never the same.'[5]

These extracts illustrate the feelings of the highly increased number of women who are today practising extramarital sex, the percentage of which is nearly that of men. However, despite this, the traditional differences that are posited to exist between men and women are not compromised. To be sure, there are many who militantly maintain that men and women have the same sexual drives. They affirm that there are no sexual differences whatsoever between men and women, aside from physiology and plumbing. In *The Erotic Silence of the American Wife*, Dalma Heyn makes an impassioned argument for this position:

> How often have we heard: Women are by nature monogamous. Happily married women don't have affairs. Women do not desire a variety of sex partners. Women must love a man to have sex with him ... Women are not aroused by men's physical appearance ... Equally disturbing is the tendency on the part of some women to believe that while men really want sex, women want relationships. I question this: it is often a semantic distinction men and women are socially taught to make when in fact both may want both, and because it implies that sex is not an integral component of women's pleasure in relationships ...[6]

I agree with Heyn that there are indeed many women whose powerful sexual urge is just like any man's. Being a rabbi to students, I know of several women who openly declare that they go into a relationship for sex only, just as male students may. One American student even told me of a former girlfriend who broke off their relationship because of her desire 'to have sex with men in all fifty states. I think she only has Hawaii and Wyoming left to conquer.'

But here we are not debating individual cases of male or female sexuality, but *rather the right to generalize*. Although there will always be exceptions to the rule, I believe we can generalize about male and female sexuality. I have met far more women who are interested in the totality of the relationship than the sex, and who indeed would not go to bed with a man whom they did not love. I have also quoted all the statistics above which plainly show that in the overwhelming majority of cases, wives will not take a lover unless they feel unloved or ignored by their husbands. The same certainly cannot be said of men. For all her anger at the traditional stereotypes of female sexuality, Heyn brings no evidence, apart from a few interviews with very sexually active (married) women, to counter those stereotypes. Likewise, even amongst the myriad very vocal women who violently oppose these same stereotypes, I have yet to hear an adequate response to the statistics which show that male and female infidelity occur for entirely different reasons. The question of whether these differences are innate or socially conditioned, while highly interesting, is beyond the scope of this book.

A Wife Taking a Lover Betrays a Serious Flaw in a Marriage

However unpopular to modern commentators it may be, the evidence is that men are naturally prone to extramarital liaisons while women seek a deep and fulfilling emotional commitment with a man. It follows from this that female infidelity betrays a far more serious problem in a marriage than male infidelity. To be sure, male adultery is a serious and terrible violation of the marital vows, but a wife should not necessarily have to question whether or not she is desirable to her husband just because he feels attracted to other women. The fact is that this is natural, although it can and must be curbed and he must focus his attention on his wife.

But if a wife loses interest in her husband, and begins to find love and romance outside of the marriage, then the chances are that she is being ignored or marginalized by her husband, and this is serious indeed. Thus, while each act of infidelity must have a response and a cure in accordance with the specific causes of each occurrence, we can, in fact, generalize with regard to how to separately curb male and female infidelity. The latter requires that a husband begin to respond to his wife's needs, and put her before everything else; to make her feel that, in a world with roughly two and a half billion women, she is the most precious and the most special to him. If he doesn't, then she will explore the terrain and find someone who does feel that way. I don't claim that it is really all that simple, and neither do I deny that there are many women who are the exceptions to the rule and, like men, desire vast quantities of success with many different partners. But still, a husband who shows his wife extravagant love and affection has taken a huge step in the right direction.

It is the response to male infidelity that becomes more complicated and problematic. How does one reverse their nature? Marriage begins to work against a couple. The more deeply they fall in love with one another, and the closer they become and feel, the more familiar and comfortable they feel with one another as well. And the more familiar they become, the more the husband might naturally seek a novel sexual partner affording plenty of mystery, adventure and newness. One of the oddest things about adultery is how many husbands there are who will go to bed with women far less attractive and sophisticated than their wives. Why do they wander if they have a far more exquisite creature in their own beds? It is for the same reason that a woman will put on a brand new dress she bought to go to a party, even though it is far cheaper or inferior to a dress that has been sitting in the wardrobe for some time. It is the 'newness' of the object itself that makes it attractive. Likewise the wife represents the old, and the lover the new. We don't get excited about the nicest outfit we own, but the newest. That's all there is to it.

What then is the cure for male infidelity? How can we assure a man's complete and undivided focus of his sexual attention and energy upon his wife? And how can we make a wife, and a husband, for that matter, always appear novel and exciting to their spouse?

SOURCES — CHAPTER THREE

1. Shere Hite, *The Hite Report*, 1987
2. ibid.
3. Carol Botwin, *Tempted Women*, 1994
4. Shere Hite, *The Hite Report*
5. ibid.
6. Dalma Heyn, *The Erotic Silence of the American Wife*, 1993

CHAPTER FOUR

CAN WE RETAIN PASSION IN MARRIAGE?

ONCE ON A visit to Miami with my family, a few old classmates were kind enough to take me to a basketball game of Miami's new and very exciting team, the Heat. The game was entertaining and stimulating, and yet to be honest I was not focusing on the players or the ball. I could not take my eyes off a middle-aged couple sitting in the row right in front of me. I can almost swear that during the entire evening this man did not take his arm off the shoulder of the woman he was accompanying. Even after he returned from buying some peanuts, he immediately sat down and his very first gesture was to put his arm back around her shoulder. When one of my friends who held season tickets for the games in that row, saw me looking in them in wonderment, he bent over to me and said, 'For three years I have been coming to these games and for three years I have also watched in disbelief how this husband holds on to his wife throughout the game, every single moment. I promise you he does this every game and has never stopped. There is definitely something wrong.'

On the drive home from the game we debated between ourselves how this could be possible. How could this husband be showing such extravagant warmth to his wife. Not surprisingly, the conversation immediately turned to one of understanding what could possibly be wrong with the man. One friend insisted that he must be having an affair with another woman, and overly compensating for it by showing his wife such sustained and

71

extravagant affection. Another friend suggested that they themselves were not husband and wife at all but two lovers having an affair, albeit an indiscreet one, attending basketball games together for three years. This proposition was quickly rebutted by my friend with the season tickets who knew the couple and verified that they were married. Another explanation proffered by a friend was that she was probably dying, had very little time to live, and hence her husband was being so kind and loving. What the exact explanation was I never found out, nor is it really essential for the point of this story. What is important is that everyone in the car unanimously agreed that there must be something wrong with the man because it is impossible to remain so loving in marriage after that long a period of time. And while I personally did not necessarily agree with some of the more ludicrous explanations being bandied around, I, too, was confused as to what this couple's secret was.

Looking back it seems incredible! Not only have many of us lost the capacity to be at all times romantic and loving, and not only are we convinced that it is humanly impossible to sustain such love, we are even prepared to assassinate the character of those few odd couples who are totally romantically involved with each other and posit the most sinister motives for their extraordinary behaviour. But what was this couple's secret, and can we put it in a way that is easily acessible to us, and that we can easily insert into our own lives?

Sexual Desire and Desirability Are All in the Mind

As a religious individual, I have always rejected the prevailing religious thinking that all things physical are necessarily ungodly. This premise, promoted virtually across the board by most world religions, is not present within Judaism. The very first verse in the Bible reads, 'In the beginning the Lord created the heavens and earth', implying that both were equally created by God, and thus both are holy and special; 'and God saw all that he had made, and it was good'. This understanding is crucial. If physical existence is not special, and if it indeed represents the antithesis of things spiritual, then we as a collective race must fight the flesh and blood desires of our human nature. It is evil and must be either repressed or reversed. But if human beings are holy, then human nature is commensurably holy. Rather than fighting human nature, we must harness it. Rather than reversing it, we must focus it. Rather than being ashamed of it, we must understand it and use it to our advantage.

Monogamy is not a natural state for humans, although it is the best option since it offers the finest possibilities for a real combination of love and passion, when practised properly as we shall continue to explore. Still, the inclination for married people to look, even just glance, at other people outside the marriage for sexual possibilities, cannot be denied. Rather it must be respected and understood. Once we have analysed what is so downright exciting about the possibility of a new sexual partner, we must then attempt to transpose that excitement into our marriages.

Let me relate the true story of a forty-two-year-old man who had a thirty-eight-year-old wife. They got along fantastically well and felt themselves to be true companions. They trusted each other with every secret and comforted each other in their sadder moments. Only one major component was missing from their life together: passion. The husband accepted that this was primarily his fault. He loved his wife, but he no longer found her exciting. To be sure, he readily agreed that she was very attractive, and was told so on numerous occasions. But still, after sixteen years of marriage, the novelty had worn off. It had been years since they had had a truly exciting intimate encounter. His lack of sexual interest was, of course, felt by his wife, which led to a further deterioration of his marriage. The more she saw him looking at younger women, the more she began to crave attention from other men. And when he flirted openly with women at parties, she was positively enraged. The situation deteriorated to such an extent that they no longer felt themselves capable of discussing the matter. They reconciled themselves to the fact that their marriage provided stability, albeit at the expense of passion.

This deterioration led the husband to begin contemplating the possibility of having an affair. He thought that he might regain his youth and the lost excitement of early love in a mistress. He found himself eyeing many of his female co-workers, as if he were picking out a potential candidate. There were times when he was startled to find just how easy it would be to have an affair, and how many willing partners there were. Thoughts that had not been more than a passing fancy in his mind throughout all his years of marriage were now being entertained in great detail in his head. Commensurate with his entertaining the possibilities of marital infidelity was an even more troubling development. Whenever he was in bed with his wife, he thought about other women. He simply felt the need to ponder and contemplate other women in order to find his sexual experiences with his wife exciting and satisfying.

But the husband noticed something. Whenever his *wife* stared at other men, or whenever he felt that she had a real interest in another man, he suddenly felt passionate about her once again, albeit to a limited extent. What were these deep dark emotions rising up within him? He knew that a sociologist would dismiss them as mere territorialism, and a feminist would cite this as yet another example of the patriarchal society. But deep within him he felt that this was more than just trying to reclaim what was rightfully his. Rather, he felt that he was once again viewing his wife as a *woman*, as a sexual object. Every time she displayed an interest in another man, and even more so when another man displayed a liking towards her or stared deeply at her, he was being reminded that his wife was indeed a sexy woman and an object of sexual desire.

But what was he to do about developing this? Should he encourage his wife to have an affair and then tell him about it? He would not countenance such a thought. Besides, he knew that the kind of jealousy which would arise from such an experience, and the kind of hurt he would feel, would destroy him. He resolved to close that possibility. And yet, he felt that the excitement of seeing his wife with another man might be the saving of his marriage.

He suggested to his wife that they go away on holiday together to the US Virgin Islands in an effort to spice up their withering love-life. There, they spent the first two nights together, but still felt unsatisfied with their marital relationship. The husband then suggested to his wife that they had to take radical steps in order to resurrect their marriage. He presented her with a choice. Either she would agree to a woman, presumably a prostitute, joining them in a threesome, or they could instead invite a man into their hotel room. He knew his wife would absolutely object to both of these possibilities, so he told her that all he wanted was for her to agree to be massaged by a man in his presence. Her husband also made it clear that while the masseur would not actually have sex with her, he might go a long way down that path. After much haggling and cajoling on his part, she reluctantly agreed.

The husband made a few calls in his wife's presence, and found a male 'masseur' who supposedly also had other specialities. It was arranged for the masseur, whose name was James, to come that night. The husband was surprised to find that his wife was actually showering, applying her make-up with care, and putting on her best lingerie in order to ready herself for the experience. Just before the appointed hour arrived, the husband came up with a strange stipulation. He told his wife that she would have to wear a blindfold. 'I don't mind you being with this man; in fact, I know that you are doing it for me. But I don't want you to see his face. You simply can't see him, because then the experience would be too intimate.' His wife agreed that this was a good idea, saying that she would be far too shy if she had to look at him anyway.

But here came the twist. *There was no James.* The husband himself was to be James. He had already paid a hotel bellboy to first call the room at ten p.m. and, after having his wife answer the phone, announce that he was James and that he would be coming up. Next, the bellboy was to come up to the room, knock on the door, and announce himself as James the masseur. Earlier, the husband had bought new cologne which his wife would not recognize and an expensive wig that gave him shoulder-length hair. He devised a completely new sex routine that he had never practised on his wife.

When the appointed time came, he told his wife that he would sit in a corner while 'James' gave the massage and asked if she was ready. She lay down, all the while with the mask on her face, and nodded. She was thoroughly fooled. He approached her and began to massage her back, slowly, patiently, and better than he had ever done before. He moved over every part of her body, paying more attention to detail than at any previous time in their married life together. He caressed and kissed her so that she felt as though he appreciated every part of her, and slowly she turned on like a light to a man whom she thought was a complete stranger. Her husband continued to mix and match, trying and experimenting every way, in order to throw his wife off the track. He was thoroughly successful. His wife didn't have a clue. How could she? The man that she was married to had never treated her in this way before. 'James' was romantic and wonderful and found her vastly desirable. He lavished more attention on her in his intimate routine than her husband had ever done before.

After a full hour of touching, the husband became more ambitious. He knew his wife to be naturally shy, and was sure that she would resist his undressing her. But she did not. He took off every inch of clothing, and she did nothing to protest. Next, he began to go far beyond his mandate, and still she permitted him to go further. He held her hand softly, and she clasped his back. He kissed her passionately, and she kissed him back. In the space of three hours they shared full intimacy. His wife came alive like never before, and he began to wonder if she was indeed the same woman that he had been married to all these years.

When the event was over, 'James', without saying a word, kissed the woman gently on the cheek and left. Her husband opened the door to allow him to depart, and then returned to his wife and removed the blindfold. His wife looked radiant and joyous. She thanked her husband for having organized the night, and told him how much she had enjoyed it. She also insisted on knowing whether or not he was upset, since things had far surpassed the original intention. He insisted that he was not, but deep down he felt a curious but immensely potent blend of passion and excitement mixed with shock and immeasurable hurt. His wife had in theory allowed herself to have sex with another man. Even though it had not really occurred, it had in her mind. He could never look at her in the same way again. The loving, caring, loyal and devoted wife whom he thought he knew had turned out to be none of those things. But on the other hand, his disappointment and anxiety were also the direct cause of his excitement and passion. Here he was married to such a passionate woman, such a sexual creature, that she would risk anything in the pursuit of physical fire and pleasure. He now saw his wife in a totally new light. She was not just his wife. Indeed, she could not be fully possessed. She was a *woman*. And a sexy woman at that. A woman who had responded to the love and affection shown her by another man. Perhaps she would respond to her husband as well if he just tried a little harder.

For the next two days these antithetical emotions ran through his mind, driving him crazy. What did he want? A loyal wife or an exciting, adulterous wife? The passion he now felt for her, knowing what she had done, had never been so strong. Indeed, it exceeded anything he had ever experienced before. He felt reborn, and his sexual life with his wife was unsurpassed. He now found her truly the most attractive woman in the entire world. So powerful was his attraction that he was not even tempted to look at the bikini-clad women on the beach, but instead gazed lovingly upon his wife the entire time.

But he was also scared. As far as his wife was concerned, she had had a much better time with another man than she had ever had with her own husband. Would she therefore search for other men? Would she ever be satisfied with her own husband? When she closed her eyes at night during intimacy, who would she be thinking of: the dark mysterious man who had excited her but whom she had never seen, or the dull husband who was so uninteresting by comparison? In the end, he decided that he must tell her the truth, and he did. For her part, she could not, would not, believe it. At least not until he offered her all the evidence: the wig and the cologne.

Now, what had happened here? Why all the contrasts and contradictions? And how could they both have been so transformed by a single experience? Up until the moment when 'James' had started his massage the husband had seen his wife as all wife and no woman. He had become accustomed to her, so that the novelty wore off. He had not forgotten that she had passionate sexual needs but he had refused to accommodate those needs, and in turn decided to focus his energy on other women. Even though he was not actually unfaithful, he had forced her to assume a compliant and dull role. *She had no fire because he had snuffed it out.*

But the moment that she agreed to the bargain, he began to see her as a sexual creature, a sexual animal. No longer was she a wife, but a fiery woman. A temptress. A woman who would do anything for sexual excitement and pleasure. She was alive and vigorous; not predictable and boring. Playing the role of a possible suitor who would live or die by his sheer appeal, he had to impress her. He had to win her over. He had given up trying to impress his own wife long ago. Their intimate life had assumed an unimpressive, yet acceptable routine. But here was a woman who was taking great risks to allow a paramour into her life. Moreover, he was supposed to be a professional. He had better be good if he was to be acceptable and desirable. He would also, of necessity, have to try to do completely new things. Any element of their normal routine would expose him immediately.

For her part, she had been totally fooled, not really by the cologne and wig, but by the interest this man took in her, and the way he totally focused on impressing her. She was accustomed to a husband whose attitude in bed betrayed the been there, seen it, done that attitude which is so patronizing and offensive. In short, she had been made to feel that she bored her husband. He was interested in younger and newer women. But 'James' was different. James genuinely liked and desired her. In fact, he desired her so much that he was willing to take risks for her, even to exceed his mandate and do something forbidden. Her husband wouldn't even do those things which were allowed! So, he made an attempt to impress her. And she came to life as a woman like never before.

I discovered this strange tale when the wife, who was fairly religious and observant, came to me to ask whether or not she would have to repent. She wanted to know whether she had done anything wrong, since she didn't actually commit adultery, although she *thought* she had. After hearing the story, I went to her husband, who was a close friend, and questioned him about his motives, and the consequences of his actions. The results of this story, according to him, are quite mixed. On the one hand, the husband swears till today that he never thinks of any other woman when he is in bed with his wife. Nor does he need to. He insists that the mere memory of that night is enough to excite him for the rest of his days. He also insists that now he is far more passionate about his wife, and cannot forget what a sexy woman she is.

On the other hand, he has become far more insecure about his own standing. When he goes on business trips, for instance, he doesn't ever contemplate having a fling with a new acquaintance, because his mind is far too occupied with what his wife might be up to. He finds himself thinking about her most anxiously, and telephoning her constantly to check up on her. He now knows that she is indeed capable of having an affair with another man. But is this really a bad thing? If the possibility of her being adulterous causes him to be totally absorbed in his wife and to think of her constantly, is it really negative?

Adultery is Destructive; *the Possibility* of Adultery is Beneficial

Up until now I have said, and I shall maintain throughout this book, that the effects of adultery are entirely negative and destructive. They eat away at a marriage, and destroy the basis upon which it is built: trust and love. Still, what about the *possibility* of adultery? Can we not use to our advantage the recognition that the possibility exists at any moment, that the spouse to whom we are married is so driven sexually, and is so desirable to the opposite sex, that they can betray all their marital vows and indeed jeopardize their very lives? If we live with this recognition, will it not lead us to a constant attraction to our partner, inspiring a real commitment to impressing them so as to retain their affections and concentration upon us, and keep us refraining from marital infidelity ourselves, since we are always focused on ensuring, and taking the necessary steps to make certain, that our spouses themselves remain loyal and focused.

Stated in other words, *adultery can only come about in a state of complacency and boredom.* Only when a husband feels that he is dissatisfied, and while he is running around his wife is safely at home minding the children, does he go about having an affair. Only when a wife feels that she is neglected while her husband spends all his time at the office does she look for someone new. In fact, this is one of the most common refrains heard from husbands and wives who are having affairs. Asked whether they think that their husband or wife is also having an affair, they almost always respond that this is impossible. They insist that they are simply not the type. 'My husband? Forget it. He's just not the type. He's just not interested enough in sex to do something like this.' 'My wife has, I believe, never been "unfaithful" to me. Knowing her lack of interest in sex, I would be astonished to find out she had ever indulged herself elsewhere.'[1] Of course, they often come in for a very rude awakening when they discover just the opposite. And when they do they feel flabbergasted and upset. But why? If they themselves are having an affair, why shouldn't their spouses?

The answer is that if the average wife knew that her husband was the type to have an affair, then she never would have searched for a lover in the first place. Why should she? The loving passionate sexual firebrand that she was looking for was right here in her own bedroom. The problem is that he has never demonstrated that previously. He simply never showed that side of himself.

Sexual attraction is basically all in the mind, and the recognition that this is so provides the greatest hope for restoring passion back into monogamous relationships. Because what you really need, if romance or passion is missing in your marriage, is not a new partner. *You need a new attitude.* And being made aware that your spouse is capable of having an affair causes you to see them in a completely new light.

Strong proof to support the assertions that it is specifically seeing our spouses as sexual beings that makes us passionate about them, and that it is all in the mind, which would also mean the passion in marriage is never beyond salvation, may be found in the overwhelming first response of a husband upon discovering his wife's infidelity. In her book *Tempted Women*, Carol Botwin writes in the chapter 'Facing the Music' that as soon as a husband discovers that a wife has had an affair, 'Your husband may want to have sex with you right after learning about your affair. It is a strange enough phenomenon, but it happens frequently enough. Some men may get excited thinking about you as a sex object again. Others get a perverse thrill from imagining you with another man.'

What has happened here all of a sudden? Why would a husband, amidst discovering perhaps the most hurtful and painful news of his life, react first by having sex with his adulterous wife? Nearly every writer with whom I discussed this book, and asked this question, told me that the explanation was simply that the husband wished to reassert his authority over his wife, to veritably reclaim that which is his. His immediate sexual response towards his wife was nothing more than pure territorialism. Botwin herself advances this explanation: 'Others use the sex to express their hostility or even ownership of your body. Do not expect tender sex at this time – it is likely to be more as if he is taking you than making love.' Similarly, when I asked the celebrated sex researcher, Shere Hite, in an interview, what she made of this phenomenon, her response was that this was the ultimate display of the patriarchal society, a husband showing his wife that her body belonged to him.

But I disagree with this interpretation. If the husband wished at this point only to show his territorial authority over his wife, then why not beat her to a pulp, or strangle her? Not only would this be far more effective in showing his dominion over her, but it would be killing two birds with one stone: he could get out his aggression and anger, *and* display his control.

Even the territorialism is a sign of sexual passion. Why should he want to 'take you', or express 'his ownership of your body' unless he thinks you to be sexy and worth possessing. If he wanted to express his ownership of you in a servant or slave capacity, then he would hardly have sex with you to make his point. He would, in his rage, order you into the kitchen, or make you scrub the floors in order to humiliate you for your infidelity. But here, even if this is a show of territorial rule, he is expressing his ownership of your *body*, your sexual dimension. The boring wife he thought he had secured and therefore ignored, possibly even leading directly to the affair in the first place, is now a sexual firebrand. And the most exciting kind imaginable: an adulterous wife, the kind of woman who just can't get enough. These are the women who excite men, and to discover that you've had one all along in your bedroom but never paid attention is enough to drive a man through the roof, both with rage as well as passion.

The problem of course is that *actually having* an affair, apart from the moral or religious abomination which it constitutes, is terribly destructive to a marriage and must be avoided at all costs. But the possibility of adultery is something which can be harnessed and used to our advantage. If a husband and wife can somehow always understand that the person that they are married to is an attractive sexual being, with real sexual needs, and so great is their sexual desire that if it is denied them they are prepared to find it outside the matrimonial bed, then they will live in a constant state of sexual passion with their spouse. The problem is achieving this awareness, and remembering it constantly. These are the methods that we are about to explore.

SOURCES — CHAPTER FOUR

1.   Carol Botwin, *Tempted Women*, 1994

CHAPTER FIVE

THE TEN COMMANDMENTS OF ADULTERY:

Making them Work Within Marriage

'There can be no doubt that the lives of a very large proportion of married men and women are being enriched and made more meaningful by secret sexual relationships.'
Tony Lake and Ann Hills, *Affairs*, 1979

M R LAKE AND MS HILLS may be right, but there probably exists a far greater number of people whose lives have been deeply scarred by extramarital relationships, families that have been destroyed, betrayed spouses who have utterly lost their self-confidence, and men and women who only wish that they could turn the clock back and reverse their adulterous liaisons.

Why did they do it? For a variety of reasons, but mostly excitement and rejuvenation; an end to the monotony of marriage. So what's the solution? If marriage and monogamy are doomed to lose their spark and become boring, but an affair betrays everything you believe in and can ruin your life, what are we to do? Give up on life? Bow our heads and submit to the inevitable loss of excitement that afflicts all long-term relationships? Choose stability and permanence over passion, youth and vigour?

The answer is to have a secret, passionate sexual relationship with your spouse. Turn your husband or wife into your lover. Make your marriage into a clandestine adulterous affair. Give your marriage all the ingredients that adultery has. Tap into its secret, and then bring all of those secret ingredients into your marriage. I will now analyse those essential ingredients, and demonstrate how they can work for you in your marriage. What does it take to have an exciting, illicit affair?

Essential Ingredients for an Adulterous Affair

I. ADULTERY IS FIRST AND FOREMOST ABOUT SEX. IT MAKES EACH PARTICIPANT INTO A DESIRABLE SEXUAL OBJECT

Yes, there are adulterous affairs which become deeply emotional and loving. But by and large adultery is about great sex and is entered into by both men and women who seek some spice in life, an end to their everyday routine, and a partner who really appreciates their bodies, treating them as if they are the most desirable person on earth. Adulterous affairs are not bogged down by problems of housework, cleaning, children and worries over finance. As the responsibility of marriage increases, as bills pile up, as children are born, and as jobs become more demanding, often a couple's sex life is put on the back-burner. Everything else takes precedence and as a result their lovemaking suffers dramatically. An affair, however, is different. It is the essential sexuality of the men and women who enter into an extramarital affair which is accentuated – everything else is less important, or totally unimportant.

Chapter 6 will show you the essential secret of how to bring your sexual life with your spouse back from its hiding place to the foreground. You will learn of the centrality of lovemaking in every marriage, and how a good sex life has the power to remove those incessant petty squabbles which bog so many marriages down in the mire. You will also learn to establish a mindset whereby you are always aware of the sensual attractiveness of your spouse, that they are a desirable sex object, which will make you want to restart your affair with them.

2. ADULTERY THRIVES ON SEPARATION AND EXPECTATION

A large part of the excitement behind an adulterous affair is the constant waiting and yearning to be with your illicit partner. Since the relationship is unlawful, and you don't want your spouse to catch you, you are living apart from your lover, always in a state of *expectation*. To an extent, you want what you can't have, and this is largely responsible for the erotic excitement of adultery. Statistics show that adulterous partners who leave their spouses and move in together usually end up separating soon after. Once you get what you have been chasing, you're suddenly not so hungry any more.

In an adulterous affair, since you don't live with your lover and have no sense of security, you think about your lover all the time, waiting and yearning to be with them. Unlike your spouse, since you can't have sex with your lover any time you wish, your mind becomes obsessed with them and the sex you have with them. You are constantly erotically engaged in thinking about sex with them. You yearn for what at the present moment is just outside your reach. To an extent you compensate for the void by playing out the affair in your mind. You even tell yourself how you will make up the lost time by having the most wonderful sexual encounter upon your next reunion.

In Chapter 7 you will see how temporary periods of sexual abstention and separation can do wonders to reinvigorate your marriage. You will discover how a husband and wife enjoy a fiery, as opposed to a 'watery' love, and you will see how brief periods of sexual separation nurture that fire. You will also learn how the all-important 'possibility of adultery' which exists in every marriage can be used to your advantage to live in a perpetual state of expectation with your spouse, even though you share the same house and the same bed each night.

3. ADULTERY THRIVES ON A STATE OF IRRECONCILABLE TENSION

There can be no doubt that the thrill of the chase, the fear of getting caught and not knowing when you'll next be able to see your lover adds to the excitement of adultery. Strange as it may seem, it is this which keeps the adulterous affair alive and exciting. You never have time to settle into a routine and stagnate. You are constantly on the move, setting up secret meeting places, tapping into your most creative and resourceful self to outsmart all those curious eyes around you, and keep your affair going. Your highest and most creative faculties are fully engaged in the relationship, a relationship which ultimately has no real solution and thus generates constant tension.

In Chapter 8 you will read how the natural attraction which even married people feel for other men and women outside the marriage, far from betraying the commitment of marriage, can ensure that we are constantly occupied with *choosing* our spouses anew. The anxiety that is caused by our natural gravitation to other men and women, amidst our steadfast commitment to our spouse, guarantees that our marriages will never become stagnant or monotonous.

You will also learn how to utilize to your advantage the natural tension that exists between wishing our spouses to be seductive and hypnotic all round (which makes them attractive to others as well), yet wanting to possess them entirely, and the intense feelings of jealousy brought about by the glances that others might give them, and which they return.

4. ADULTERY THRIVES ON SECRECY, MODESTY, AND MYSTIQUE

I know it sounds strange, but yes, modesty. The foundation of an adulterous affair is that only the two of you know about it. This itself is part of its excitement. In life, those things which are hidden and concealed always retain their lure and excitement. Conversely, things which have become too public are quickly forgotten. I know a man with a vast art collection, included within which he has real Picassos and Van Goghs. At any given time, only one or two are on display in either his office or his home. The reason: he wants them to be precious in his eyes and his viewers' eyes. Therefore, they are revealed on only rare occasions. Likewise, a couple who are having an illicit affair thrive on the knowledge that they have this wonderful secret. In fact, once the affair becomes known to the world the excitement begins to dissipate.

In addition, those who are involved in adulterous affairs, however much we might condemn or despise them, carry with them an air of seductive mystique. Think of the great literary adulteress heroines: Tolstoy's Anna Karenina, Flaubert's Madame Bovary, Lawrence's Lady Chatterley, and Hawthorne's Hester Prynne. Being wanted by someone else in a sinful relationship bestows a certain erotic quality of mystery on the object of another's desire. Hence their sensuous attraction.

In Chapter 9 you'll learn about the importance of modesty in marriage, and the harmful effects that sexual overexplicitness have wrought. You'll also learn what you can do to make your marriage secretive again, and how modesty will lead your spouse to cherish your body once more, and create an environment of mystery and intimacy. You'll discover techniques to alter your perception of your spouse, leading to an aura of seductive mystique.

5. ADULTERY INVOLVES INTENSE FOCUS

The points about separation, expectation, anxiety, secrecy, mystique and viewing your spouse as a total sexual partner together contribute to the real power of an adulterous affair: the complete sexual focus which one has on one's lover. Lovers who yearn for each other are not distracted by anything; they think only about each other. When they are in bed together, they do not feel the need to call up past images of other sexual partners to excite them. On the contrary, their passion is such that they are totally involved with one another and what they are doing at that moment. Not even thoughts about their marriage, security, or their children get in the way of their affair together. *Too much about marriage is casual, whereas everything about adultery is intense.*

In addition, the risks lovers have taken to be with one another serve as a catalyst to reveal their total sexual sides, and involve them in the relationship in a way unknown in marriage. It is as if the danger pressing against them reveals their complete personalities. They become total sexual partners. They disclose their secret sexual fantasies to each other and let go of all inhibitions. In short, lovers in an illicit affair become magnets to one another, engaging each other's complete interest. This accounts for why adultery, with all its pains, still seems so fulfilling.

In Chapter 10 you will learn the secret of becoming a total sexual partner within marriage. You will discover the importance of sexual focus, the technique of making your spouse your only sexual outlet, and the immense passion and satisfaction which this generates.

6. ADULTERY IS ABOUT INTENSE JEALOUSY

The great majority of married women who enter into adulterous affairs do so not with single, but with married men. Thus, every time the couple separate after a rendezvous and return to their normal lives, the woman knows that her lover is going back to his wife, and she lives in a constant state of jealousy. She knows that in the final analysis she is the second woman in her lover's life, always a subordinate. When he goes on holiday, he does so with his wife and children, and indeed he spends the majority of his time in her company and most of his nights in her bed.

In addition, since every act of adultery involves a betrayal of one's marital vows, you are always aware that the person you are involved with is duplicitous. They are always telling their spouse that they love them and that they are faithful, and then they leave their house to embark upon this double life. This knowledge that your lover is not faithful to his/her spouse, leads you always to suspect that perhaps they are not faithful to you either. At the very least you know that they have the potential for betraying you, just as they have betrayed their spouse. This knowledge is painful. It is also instrumental in inducing a state of jealousy. You know that you have no security – there is no home, children or even commitment to bind you – and thus you always fear being discarded in favour of someone else. Your lover may even choose to return to their spouse.

This jealousy induces you to want to possess your lover even more, so you exert every effort to sustain their attention. You always dress your best, speak lovingly – in short, you are on your best behaviour always.

In Chapter 11 you will learn about healthy jealousy and how indispensable it is to every marriage. Too many people complain that their spouses dressed better, spoke more kindly and treated them much better before they were married. You will discover how, if your spouse felt far more jealous about you, their desire to possess you and their behaviour towards you would increase incredibly. You will learn that, in truth, no one has any real security in marriage and thus you must expend great energy on earning the attentions of your spouse.

7. ADULTERY IS ABOUT TRUST

Sounds odd, doesn't it? But even after everything I have said about jealousy, ironically and paradoxically, adultery involves a large amount of trust. The adulterous party puts immense faith in their lover. They trust them not to tell anyone about the affair, unless they both agree on disclosure. They trust each other not to make their sexual encounter a one-night stand only. Let's face it, adultery involves terrible risks and can leave utter destruction in its wake. Many a person has even chosen to end their life in the wake of an adulterous affair. No man or woman is prepared to undertake these risks unless they feel they trust their partner to make the affair somewhat lasting, and not just 'to love them and leave them'. So great is the trust that a woman puts in her married male lover that although a startling 87 per cent of husbands who promise to leave their wives for their lovers do not in the end do so, still 82 per cent of the women who are promised this still believe it, and stay in the affair after an ultimatum has been issued to 'either leave your wife and move in with me, or I go packing'. It is this immense trust which adulterous parties put in one another that serves to bind them and feel comfortably sexual with one another amidst their very precarious situation.[1]

In Chapter 12 you will rediscover the centrality of loving trust in marriage, and the huge pay-off in closeness it brings. You will discover the benefits of *abstaining* from extramarital affairs, and how to re-instil truth, faith, and real companionship in your marriage, even after a spouse has been unfaithful. You will also learn how the faithfulness you show your partner by channelling your sexual energy in their direction actually serves as the single most powerful aphrodisiac, creating immense sexual – and erotic – passion.

8. ADULTERY IS ABOUT ATTRACTION

Marriages today seem to be predicated primarily on compatibility and common interests. We are sexually attracted to and excited by the person we wish to marry, but we are perfectly prepared to abstain from marrying them if we feel that we don't have enough in common, if our communication is bad, backgrounds are not similar, and if financial considerations are not favourable. Even if we feel an immense attraction to a member of the opposite sex, we might overlook them as a potential marriage partner because we fear that attraction is simply not enough. Of course, commonality of interests is important, but it is never as important as raw sexual attraction. It is this that keeps marriages together. People simply have to be interested in each other as individuals and not just in each other's *individual interests*. The mistake of believing that *primarily* we must share things in common leads to the problem that, as time goes on, often the common interests begin to outweigh and supersede attraction, so that even couples who love going to the cinema together, enjoy the same kind of music, and read the same books, can begin to drift apart.

Not so in a adulterous affair, which is run entirely on the basis of attraction. Lack of common interests is subordinated almost entirely to the physical lure posed by that seductive member of the opposite sex. Many affairs begin with complete ignorance about the person in question. Thus, you go to bed with them not because they too love the opera, but because they make your skin tingle. In marriage we need to feel the same level of magnetism.

One of the most important things you will discover in Chapter 13 is the absolute centrality of physical and emotional attraction in marriage, and how real compatibility comes from the fact that you are one sex, and your spouse another, and not because you both love the opera. As such, you will learn always to see the *man* in your husband, and the *woman* in your wife, so that you constantly feel pulled towards one another in a far more powerful way than common interests would afford. You will also learn how the power of physical attraction can be employed to your benefit in removing and resolving marital strife.

9. ADULTERY BOOSTS THE EGO; AS SUCH, IT IS AN ACT OF RE-CREATION

As one woman quoted in the *Hite Report* said, 'The affair was wonderful for me emotionally. He was so powerfully attracted to me, thought I was beautiful.' Many people justify what they know to be a wrong move because of the need to feel rehabilitated after being ignored in their marriages, or after sharing their lives with an uncaring, insensitive spouse. The fact that someone else shows such an immense interest in you, coupled with their willingness to risk so much to enter into an affair with you, makes you feel once again as if you are the most desirable person on earth.

If no one takes any notice, you feel as though you don't exist. Most people, especially women, enter into adulterous affairs after being neglected by their spouse. What adultery affords is the chance to feel wanted again. We human beings are actually creators. Whenever we are attentive to our fellow human beings, whenever we care for them and listen to their woes, far more than simply treating them kindly, we call forth their existence from nothingness. When people are ignored or neglected, they feel as though they don't exist. Worse still, they often wish that they were dead. Thus an adulterous affair, for many people, makes them feel alive again, as if they were re-created.

Californian marriage and family counsellor Daphne Rose

Kingman says that 'next to the death of a loved one the ending of a relationship is the single most emotionally painful experience that any of us ever goes through.' Instead of causing this pain I will show in Chapter 14 how the elaborate and extravagant love you focus on your spouse will yield an immense emotional and sexual attraction. You can re-create your spouse anew and bring novelty and freshness into your marriage.

10. ADULTERY IS ABOUT PASSION, EXCITEMENT, AND NEWNESS

I saved the most important factor until last. Overwhelmingly, men enter into adulterous affairs simply because of the attraction posed by a new sexual conquest and a new body. Everything in life about which we are passionate is new, and almost everything which is new is exciting. Think about buying a new car, or a new dress. Think about the thrill of starting a new job, or visiting a new country. And think about the excitement felt the first time you ever had a romantic encounter. The very *familiarity* of marriage can work against it, while the novelty of adultery has ensured that it has remained the most indulgent and erotic vice since the beginning of time. Simply stated, adultery affords the opportunity for something new and different, while marriage offers more of the same.

But newness doesn't have to mean acquiring a new object. It can come in the form of rearranging the furniture of the house, re-upholstering that old sofa, re-spraying the car. It can also be achieved when you lose an object, or thought you had lost an object, and find it again. What this affords is a new opportunity to rediscover what you already possess; to bring excitement and newness to those things which you take for granted because, *to you*, they have become monotonous and boring, even though, in reality, this is a fallacy.

Passion, excitement, and newness are not empirical concepts, but mental ones. They are all in the mind, and can therefore be easily induced with the proper techniques. The most important thing which you will learn in this book is a proven method by which to constantly rediscover your spouse, thus guaranteeing more passion in your married life than you could ever experience with adultery.

What's this? Marriage, not *just as*, but even *more exciting than adultery*? Yes, far more. Read on and you'll see.

SOURCES — CHAPTER FIVE

1. Tony Lake and Ann Hills, *Affairs*, 1979

CHAPTER SIX

BECOMING A TOTAL SEXUAL PARTNER

I. ADULTERY IS FIRST AND FOREMOST ABOUT SEX. IT MAKES EACH PARTICIPANT INTO A DESIRABLE SEXUAL OBJECT

M Y FRIEND JAMES was severely embarrassed when his wife
Linda began scrutinizing the Visa bills which kept on
coming up with charges for 'Apparel' from an obscure place in
Leeds. Her curiosity led her to telephone the bank and get the
number of this strange establishment that had already cost them
over £200. To her surprise a very seductive female voice picked
up the phone on the other end. The stranger's first words were
not the usual, 'Hello,' but rather, 'What is *your* fantasy?' The
number she had dialled was none other than a sex-talk line.
Linda was flabbergasted that her husband would spend their
precious funds on such nonsense, and she was personally insulted
that he needed this. She felt humiliated and inadequate. Was
talking about sex with another woman even more exciting than
actually *having* it with his wife, she asked herself. He was too
embarrassed to answer any of these questions. What did he talk
about, she asked him. What was wrong with her that he felt he
needed to have sex over a telephone? Gradually she began
venting her rage at her husband for his silence until they came to
me for advice.

James refused to discuss the issue until his wife left the office.
Quietly, I persuaded her to do so. He then opened up. With an

agonizing look on his face he told me how Linda was a beautiful woman, but very squeamish, even shy, about sex. Yes, they could do it whenever they wanted. But they could never *talk* about it. He desired sexy talk with his wife, but she would always silence him. He wanted to know her fantasies, and wanted her to know his. Finally, in frustration, he began wasting their money on fantasy lines.

This story and countless others like it raise the subject of the extent to which today's husbands and wives are sexually involved with one another, and the need to become a total sexual partner within marriage. Adulterous parties have far more complete, and hence satisfying sexual lives than the average married couple. The risks that they are taking, and the very strangeness of their situation together, leads them to come out of their shell for more than a husband and wife. In essence, by committing adultery they have established the sexual supremacy of their character over and above all other facets, something which is not always true in marriage. Husbands and their mistresses, wives and their lovers, not only *have* more sex with each other, but think about it more, talk about it more, and expose their deepest darkest fantasies to each other. In her new autobiography, *Fear of Fifty*, Erica Jong relates how her current and third marriage seems to be succeeding where the others failed, and identifies one of the essential ingredients in preserving the sexual passion in the marriage as being her new habit of writing down and reading her sexual fantasies to her husband. The operative word in adultery is 'obsession', and adulterous partners are obsessed about each other constantly. While this overindulgence with one's lover strains a marriage terribly since one finds it difficult to concentrate on one's everyday life and one's spouse adequately, it does transform one into a total sexual partner with one's lover. Now we'll see how to bring this into marriage.

Repression is Always Destructive but Sexual Focus is Always *Productive*

Judaism does not believe in repression. Rather, it believes in channelling one's energy, vitality and all one's character dispositions into beneficial areas as dictated and determined by holy doctrine and religious and ethical teaching. Of course, Judaism as a religion is filled with restrictions regarding human behaviour. But, whereas other religions restrict certain forms of human behaviour in their entirety, Judaism forbids certain acts in one area, but opens an arena for the performance of the very same acts in another. The key to apprehending the Jewish world view is this: Judaism does not accept that there is anything in existence which is intrinsically evil. Rather, everything is neutral, that is, it has no innate good or evil quality. It is the objective of man to try to bring all these neutral objects into the camp of holiness. The Talmud proclaims that everything which God forbade in one area, He made permissible in another. Judaism does not seek repression of human nature, but rather a focusing and channelling of human nature so that it always expresses itself in a positive and productive way. There is no better example of this than sex and marriage.

Judaism does insist on many sexual restrictions, most notably prohibitions against adultery, homosexuality and incest because these are seen as unGodly activities. But sex itself is not unGodly. On the contrary, used correctly it serves as the ultimate statement of human love and closeness emulating the celestial union of the masculine and feminine aspects that exist within the Godhead itself, as explained at length in Jewish mysticism. Whether or not sex is moral and holy does not depend on the sex act itself, but rather on how humans go about doing it. For instance, even in marriage sex can be unholy, such as when a spouse thinks about someone else while in bed, or when a husband has sex with his wife against her consent, an activity strictly prohibited by Jewish law.

If a person walks through the woods and finds a stick, he is given the choice either to use the stick to build a fire and give himself and perhaps others warmth, or he can use the stick to bang someone on the head and rob him of his possessions. The object is itself neutral. The use to which it is put is not. The same is true of God. In His kindness He gave us the most passionate and exciting way in which to bond with another human being in pleasure and holiness, thereby expressing our love for them. How we use or abuse this special opportunity is our choice. If we choose to squander our sexuality the only ones to suffer will be ourselves.

One of the most forward-looking things about the Bible was its unique ability to accommodate the psychological elements of humanity, including human sexual affairs. In one of the most liberal and significant statements of any ancient religious text, the Talmud states, in summing up the sexual practices which are allowed between a husband and wife, 'In the final analysis, a husband and wife can do whatever pleases them most,' meaning they should pursue sexual practices which excite them. The great many verses in the Bible dedicated to sexual prohibitions, with the exception of having sex during menstruation, virtually all apply to extramarital sex, not to sex between a husband and wife. There can be no greater illustration of the advanced Jewish outlook on sex, nor a better expression of how Judaism believes, not in repression, but in focus and sublimation. The same activities which are absolutely prohibited with another man or woman become not just permitted, but holy, when done with one's husband or wife.

What Humans Desire is not just Sex, but to *Be* Sexual

It is vital that we recognize the total statement of what human sexuality is. Far from being merely the act of coitus, human sexuality is humankind's most instinctive, congenital, and natural impulse. Indeed, it can be described as the very life-force and subsistence of humankind since it is this life-instinct which guarantees that humanity will never depopulate itself. But it is also very important to remember that humans do not merely have a need or desire to have sex. Rather, they experience a desire to *be sexual*. They need to think sexy thoughts, speak about and indulge in erotica, look at sexy things and undertake sexual acts. The best kind of sex is that which consumes us entirely. This is why premarital sex, where you are conscious of being judged and rated according to your performance, could never have the fulfilment of marriage where you feel completely relaxed and natural with your spouse. Sexuality is not an ancillary dimension or aspect of human existence. Rather it is a total and intrinsic statement of what people are and what they do. A recognition of this fact is essential if a husband and wife are to be happy together and completely satisfied with one another sexually. It is not impossible that the very first door is opened to the possibility of straying when a husband or wife does not serve as a *total sexual outlet* for their spouse. Don't ever give your spouse the excuse of having to find erotic outlets outside the marriage or home.

I know of a husband who was very kind and loving to his wife, yet still ended up committing adultery on a number of occasions, which resulted in his wife leaving him. In conversations aimed at salvaging the marriage, his wife told me that she was astounded that her husband found the need to have a sexual affair, since they had a very satisfying sex life together.

Her husband corroborated this in a subsequent conversation. So why did you do it, I asked him. Like my friend James quoted above, he said: 'Well, it started when I began calling phone-sex lines. I would often ask my wife very personal questions about how she felt about sex in an effort to have an erotic conversation. But she was extremely shy on the subject. I would ask her if she used to masturbate before we married, and she would turn red and change the subject. Well, one thing led to another, until I no longer felt she was a complete sexual partner. She's a great woman, but very reserved and thus cannot supply me with all my sexual needs. There were things which I just need to find outside the marriage.'

This of course is in no way a proper justification for adultery, and this husband is a fool for betraying his devoted and loving wife. Nevertheless, the story does provide an important lesson. Sex and marriage are at their best when a husband and wife are sexual together in every possible way. This is the essence of adultery and the secret of successful illicit lovers: they always put sex first. A husband and wife should endeavour to the best of their ability to destroy or transcend any sexual inhibitions that separate them and to become a total and complete sexual outlet for their spouse. This, of course, necessitates a concerted effort on the part of both. We are not so much concerned with the commission of adultery as the channelling of all one's sexual energy into marriage. Thus, even if a couple refrain from an adulterous affair yet do not involve their complete sexual selves in marriage, they have still lost. They have lost the opportunity to use sex to its utmost in binding them together.

To be sure, nobody has the right to immediately demand that their partner submit to their every sexual need, especially when the other is uncomfortable with certain activities. Rather, they must try to show their partner how important this might be to them, how it would benefit their marriage, and how it would assist in making them even more of an exclusive sexual partnership, strengthening their love. In this way, the couple can grow together as total sexual partners, rather than merely as two people who have sex together.

Stated in other words, in order for a married couple to enjoy and sustain a healthy, vibrant and satisfying intimate life, they must make their sex life together *central* to their marriage, and not just another aspect of it. One's spouse should not be seen as one's business partner, housemate, best friend, psychiatrist, and in addition to all these things, *also* one's partner for sex. Rather, a spouse must first and foremost serve as one's lover. Everything else is subordinate. If this is not so, then a marriage will undoubtedly flounder. Make your marriage into an illicit affair. Put as much time into creative sexual planning and techniques within the marriage that two lovers would do in an affair.

The simple fact is that having sex is extremely important to a great many people, and is perhaps the most important thing in marriage to the vast majority of people. In a study conducted by Dr Shiner, it was reported that the average man under forty thinks of sex six times per hour. But the problem is that the average married couple has sex 1.5 times per week.[1] If both members of a marriage do not see each other first and foremost as sexual partners and bedfellows, and subordinate all other considerations to this, then a marriage runs the risk of decline and infidelity. Remember the first rule: if our husbands and wives are totally absorbed with us sexually, if they can talk about sex with us, fantasize about sex with us, look forward to sex with us, plan the most exciting sexual encounters with us, and actually go ahead and have it all with us, then there is no reason in the world that they should have to look for sex outside marriage. It is principally in homes where a husband and wife make everything in their marriage and lives together more important than sex that one of them begins to stray.

What form does this straying take? Why, in finding a lover for the purpose almost exclusively of sex. In other words, the primary attraction of taking a mistress or a paramour is that one focuses together with them on sex almost exclusively, something that was not happening at home. So although people might have children together, buy each other beautiful clothes and jewellery, this still does not serve as a replacement for the primary purpose of marriage, nor will it therefore safeguard against the possibility of adultery. People marry for reasons of love and sex. They want to share the same bed with someone whom they cherish and adore, and they want to have a passionate sex life with the love of their lives. Once other considerations become more important in the marriage, one can safely assume that a couple will experience severe difficulties. You marry to have a permanent lover, not a best friend. It irks me when spouses refer to each other as best friends, thus degrading what they mean to each other.

In the final analysis, how sexy a husband or wife is depends largely on their spouse. Every human being has the capacity to bring out the sexual side of their partner, which everyone possesses, but which lies dormant within many, instead of being revealed openly. Every marriage involves a bit of give and take. A husband or wife must create a loving and accepting sexual environment within marriage, which adapts to the needs of both partners, thus accommodating their shyness for example, or whatever other impediment is present. But amidst this accommodation, the most important long-term goal of every marriage must be to create and maintain a healthy atmosphere that is conducive to and sustains a passionate sexual life. A husband and wife must seek to rid themselves of all sexual inhibitions, and try anything and everything together, within the confines of holiness and goodness, the parameters of which are determined for me within Jewish law, and have been touched upon earlier in this chapter. They must be able to speak to each other about all sexual things, and feel absolutely comfortable and excited with one another. I don't believe that there is such a thing as a 'shy' spouse. A person's sexuality must be brought out, and that is entirely dependent on how sexy and desirable one's spouse makes one feel.

To achieve this, we must take charge of our lives, especially the intimate dimension thereof. A husband should never feel the need to look at *Playboy* in order to see a woman in a certain item of lingerie or a certain position. A wife should never have to turn on a film to hear a man tell a woman poetically how beautiful or special she is. The moment a man sees a sexy piece of lingerie on a mannequin in a store, if it excites him, he should buy it on the spot, and fit his wife into it. Similarly, if a woman finds a particularly romantic novel inspiring, about a couple's trip to Venice, for example, she must persuade her husband to hop on a plane at their first available opportunity so they may enjoy the experience together. Go ahead and fantasize. But fantasize about your wife. Better yet, translate the fantasy into the actual by living out your dreams – together.

For those who would argue that this advice is impractical, and that there are children to tend to, jobs to work at, responsibilities to bear, so that packing up and going somewhere together is just not that simple or easy, I ask you this: If you were at work and heard that the plumbing at your house went haywire and was flooding all the rooms, would you not run home immediately? Well, why don't we do the same thing in marriage? When our home is in danger of physical destruction, we move heaven and earth to protect it. But when our marriages are in danger of dying a horrible death of monotony and boredom, we are all too often *too busy to save them*. No matter how much training it takes to convince us of this truth, our marriages are the most important things in our life, and we should, if we have to, accept ridicule, financial loss and even sacrifice our careers to boost and salvage them. We must put our marriages first, for only in this way can we become total sexual partners.

If a married man and married woman were having a sexual affair together, they would be forced to find the time in the middle of the work day to run to hotel rooms, and the like, in order to secretly spend some time together. But why should marriage be any less spontaneous? If we can find the time to run around behind our spouse's back, why can we not find time to run around *with* our spouse? Go ahead. Make arrangements for someone to look after the kids and run away to Paris for the weekend. Treat your spouse in no less a way than you would treat your lover.

Discuss Sexual Fantasies with your Spouse

Although marriage should be your only arena for erotic and sexual pleasure, what you choose to do with your partner is entirely up to you. The most satisfying type of marriage, and that in which the couple can grow closest together, is where there is an absolute trust between the marriage partners, without inhibitions, and where they serve as each other's total and complete sexual partners. In this situation, there is absolutely no need for a husband or wife to search for intimacy elsewhere, because everything is provided for within the marriage. One of the ways to do this is to practise revealing all your sexual fantasies to your spouse. It may not be easy at first, but will become second nature after a few times.

By telling your spouse of your fantasies, they become a total sexual partner to you. And by hearing them from you, they begin to see you as a sexual being who is creative and imaginative and they will grow excited with you again. You should be able to relate your fantasies to one another, and dress up in accordance with your partner's express wishes. In this way the possibility for adultery is largely nipped in the bud, and the passion in marriage greatly increased.

SOURCES — CHAPTER SIX

1.   Dr Shiner, *Why Men Are the Way They Are*, 1990

CHAPTER SEVEN

SEXUAL SEPARATION IN MARRIAGE

2. ADULTERY THRIVES ON SEPARATION AND EXPECTATION

'The time away [from his wife] had a salubrious effect on their marriage and each visit home was a renewed honeymoon . . . after seeing the children, they made love with a fervor reminiscent of their courtship.'
(Gay Talese, *Thy Neighbour's Wife*)

Ready and Willing for Sex

I DISCOVERED THE expression 'ready and willing for sex', from the husband of a Jewish woman who, together with her spouse, was studying more about Judaism and desired to become more observant. She and her husband had been married already for five years, and from their conversation it was clear that much of the spark of their marriage had gone out (he started frequenting a health club and his wife said jokingly that she didn't mind him getting running lessons from the big-chested woman in the tight leotard because 'it would be a miracle if he got excited about anything these days'). I suggested to them that they could kill two birds with one stone.

One of the central tenets of Jewish family living is what are known as the Jewish laws of family purity. The Bible stipulates

that once a month, for the five days of normal menstruation, and
for seven nights thereafter, a husband and wife should not engage
in intimate relations. This not only precludes having sex, but
even hugging or sleeping in the same bed (because one thing
leads to another). Thus, for twelve days a month, a husband and
wife live in physical separation. At the conclusion of this inter-
lude, the wife goes to a *mikveh*, or Jewish ritual bath, the water of
which is drawn from and always connected to a living spring, for
immersion, after which she reunites sexually with her husband.
The exact reasons for the laws are not entirely known, but one
explanation that has been offered is that Judaism sees life as
holiness, and death as the absence of holiness so in Judaism,
therefore, life and death are always kept separate and distinct. A
priest who works in the holy temple cannot enter a cemetery; an
Israelite who touches or comes into contact with a dead body
must immerse himself in 'a spring of living water'; a Jew cannot
mix meat (death) with milk (the liquid which nourishes life). So
too, the procreative act of sex cannot be undertaken while a
woman is experiencing a lost opportunity for life, her menstrual
flow, until such time as she too immerses herself in a pool of
water emanating from a living spring.

Irrespective of the fact that the exact reasons remain inac-
cessible to us, undertaking this period of separation constitutes
the quickest and most sound means by which to re-instil passion
in marriage. As every husband and wife who have been separated
from one another for two weeks should already know, the sexual
reunion which follows is explosive. As your wife comes home
from *mikveh* and enters the bedroom, you literally rip each other's
clothes off. As I have insisted throughout the book, the principal
and overwhelming cause of loss of passion in marriage is simply
the loss of novelty and newness. What separation does is repack-
age our old lovers as new. And although I do not believe that
this is an ultimate or complete solution to the problem of loss of
passion in marriage, preferring instead to create our partners as

'new' by means of a mentally-guided perception of their innate desirability and sexuality, it simply cannot be denied that observing the laws of Jewish family purity is extraordinarily effective in restoring passion in marriage. I would go so far as saying that there is no more proven or effective method to induce a state of erotic desire in marriage than this amazing institution of sexual abstention in accordance with the law of family purity. Many a Jewish author, in fact, has described the monthly, passionate night of reunion as 'a second honeymoon every month', and this it really is. If the abstention is total and complete, then the night of reunion can easily be as good or better than the wedding night. Thus, I instructed this couple that if they were looking to become more observant, as well as to instantly restore passion into their marriage, they should obey the laws of family purity and impose a monthly period of sexual abstention.

The reason that separation is only an incomplete and temporary solution to restoring passion in marriage is self-evident. It avoids dealing with the root of the problem. It says that in truth husband and wife can never sustain a passionate relationship, and must therefore go without being together for a while, in order that they should look forward to their reunification. The loss of sexual interest in one's spouse is a mental block, a problem in mental perception, that has no real basis in reality. Therefore, it must first and foremost be addressed in the eye of the mind. Having said this, however, separation does prove immensely useful and should be practised by everyone.

After this woman went to the *mikveh* for the first time, I asked her how she viewed the experience. 'It really was amazing,' she told me, 'and it made me feel the sexiest I've ever felt. For two weeks I didn't, and knew that I couldn't, have sex. Then, I went to *mikveh*, and afterwards, before going home, I put on my prettiest dress and most beautiful make-up, and underneath it all I wore my sexiest lingerie – all for my husband's benefit. I had to stop on the way home to fill the car with petrol. When I did so, I could tell that all the men at the petrol station couldn't take their eyes off me. I felt that I was very desirable. But I could also tell that the reason wasn't only the way I was dressed. Rather, it was the way I felt about myself, and how I carried myself. After having been off limits for nearly two weeks I was ready and willing for sex. I was a woman who felt very sexy, and everybody noticed. I wasn't at all flirtatious and wasn't dressed immodestly. And I didn't have to be. The men noticed me nonetheless. When I got home to my husband, we had the most memorable night of our marriage. I told him how all the men on the way home had looked at me, and my husband saw the same thing. I felt like he really wanted me.'

In the remainder of this chapter I will argue that human nature innately needs separation in order to thrive and flourish, and the love between husband and wife, being fiery as opposed to watery, operates on heightened moments of passion, with intermediate moments of lessened passion. In this way we become aware that even if our marriage is not always passionate, that's all right and there's no real reason to panic. Marriage needs hills and valleys, and not everything can appear new all the time. There are more exciting and less exciting moments. Thus, there is nothing to worry about if half the time you find your marital relations more calm, as long as for the other half they are passionate. In the final analysis, although I maintain that one of the most essential ingredients for a thriving marriage is attraction and sexual intimacy, we can't of course discount the centrality of all the other necessary essentials like good communication and just enjoying being together in a non-sexual context. The two abstemious weeks of a month actually strike a very good balance in contrast to the two more fiery, sexual weeks. They serve as periods when a couple can develop the non-sexual dimension of their relationship, especially their communication. But if you go more than two weeks a month without at least a strong breeze if not an outright earthquake, you must do something urgently and refer to the other suggestions in this book. It is very difficult to abstain from sex with your spouse, let alone not share the same bed. But the benefits really are rewarding and it should be pursued.

I have made mention several times in this book that whereas the principal cause of female infidelity is an emotional void, usually brought about through neglect on the part of the husband, the principal cause of male infidelity is not in any way the fault of the wife, other than the fact that she is a wife. Husbands seek and equate passion with newness. Psychologist Carol Botwin puts it succinctly, 'Women prefer familiarity and bonding over what men find so thrilling – the excitement of a new body. Not that there aren't some women who are more like men. But, at this moment in history, they are still a small minority.'[1] To further emphasize just how important it is for a wife to appear new to her husband as an immediate cure to the monotony of marriage, we'll take a quick look at some fascinating studies that have been conducted into the subject.

In 1986, researchers in the Department of Psychology at the State University of New York at Albany tested the ways in which males and females responded to repeated exposure to the same sexually titillating film, and then to new films of this genre. Sexual arousal that occurred during initial viewing declined after repeated exposure to the same film for men and women alike. However, when new erotic material was introduced in the form of two fresh films, one showing the same actors from the first movie performing different sexual acts, the other featuring different actors, a marked gender disparity showed up. Men responded with greater excitement to the new partners, while women's excitement escalated when they saw the same, by now familiar actors in the films.[2]

I will not now enter into the age-old argument as to whether these discernible differences are 'natural or nurtured'. Suffice it to say they exist. And if we desire passion in marriage, we must cater to them. One of the quickest ways to achieve this newness, which is instrumental in enhancing every marriage and maintain it, is through a monthly period of separation. The constant state of longing induced by separation makes marriage into an adulterous affair.

Separation Inspires Longing

If a couple maintains a period of separation, however difficult, they are guaranteed that they are going to be living in a constant state of longing for one another, and not in a constant state of longing for someone outside the marriage. People find an attraction in those things they can't have. The underlying reason for this is that the novelty it poses makes it exciting and its forbidden state makes it inviting. Another man's wife, in addition to the obvious attraction she poses as a woman, is also something that your wife could never be: totally off limits and forbidden. What lurks behind those constructed borders, he wonders, what delights does she have to offer? How does her personality alter in a sexual situation? How does she feel when she abandons herself to a man's touch? Adultery thrives on this forbidden state and separation, inducing a constant state of expectation and longing which we too can have in marriage through a period of sexual abstention.

Expectation Means Excitement

We have to make the separations in our marriages reflect the kind of separation that inspires adultery itself. Sexual expectation leads both parties to lean in towards one another, and is thus a powerful catalyst to their constant state of union. Much of the excitement behind an adulterous affair is the constant waiting and yearning to be reunited with your lover. Your sexual affairs are carried out in stealth. But far from this separation hindering the affair, it just adds to its excitement. You live in a perpetual state of expectation. You long for what is in essence not yours and this longing accounts for how the excitement of adultery, unlike marriage, can be sustained over long periods of time. Many affairs last for years. The people are not married. They stay together because they're enjoying it too much to call it quits. If the adulterous parties were to live together daily in a sexual situation over long periods of time, you can bet that before long they would grow tired of each other. Statistics show that an unusually high number of adulterous partners who leave their spouses and move in together end up separating soon after.

Abstention Leads to the Building Up of Sexual Energy

Temporary periods of sexual abstention and sexual separation can do wonders to reinvigorate your marriage. It is possible to induce a perpetual state of expectation with your spouse, even though you share the same house and the same bed nightly. If you are Jewish, I strongly recommend that you begin to observe these laws in their entirety and not only separate, but go to *mikveh* after the twelve-day separation period is over. The actual laws that govern this period are easy to follow, and many short guides about them have been produced (the best are *Waters of Eden* by Rabbi Aryeh Kaplan and *A Hedge of Roses* by Rabbi Norman Lamm). If you are not Jewish, I suggest that you institute a period of sexual abstention and separation in your marriage for at least the five days (upon average) of menstruation and for as many days thereafter as possible, up to a week. Try to keep it up for as many days as you can, up to seven. Many women in any event express a feeling of discomfort, even humiliation, about having sex while they are having their periods, and this also guarantees that wives feel comfortable about the moments when they choose to have sex. I'm aware that most couples will not go as far as moving out of each other's bed (as the laws of family purity demand). But still, in this period of sexual abstention you must really abstain. What we mean is a real period of abstention from any form of sexual release, not just coitus. Allow your sexual 'steam' to build up. Don't engage in any form of oral sex, or self-release. Let yourself become an obsessed sexual machine that thinks about your spouse constantly, and wishes to finally release all that pent-up sexual desire with your spouse.

The effects of implementing a short period of sexual separation are immediate. But, I reiterate, this will only work if you close off to yourself other forms of sexual outlet. Don't masturbate, and don't look at pornographic magazines or films with very explicit sexual imagery. A short period of sexual abstention will lead you to glorify your spouse and increase your dependence on them.

You will also find that you treat your spouse far more nicely and argue less during this period of pent-up sexual excitement. Closing off all other sexual outlets, allowing your sexuality to build up, and knowing that the only person with whom you can release this powerful build-up is your spouse will lead to a real feeling of dependency. You need your spouse. You think about them always. You long for that fantastic night of reunion which is just a few days time away. This state of expectation leads you to become reliant on them, and see them as an enchanted lover. Their attraction in your eyes is suddenly immeasurably enhanced through the power of your pent-up sexual desire.

In films we hear constant jokes about how men who have been in prison, or who have been prisoners-of-war for many years, react upon seeing their first woman. To them, she is an enchanted princess, irrespective of how she compares with other women. They have not had a sexual partner for many years, and they lust in a powerful way after this one woman who is now before them as if she were a goddess. I have a close Mormon friend who, true to the traditions of the Church, never had sex until his wedding night, which wasn't easy since he married at thirty-three. The wedding was to take place in California, and his student friends at Oxford all joked that the Californian authorities would prohibit him from conducting the wedding there for fear that he and his bride, who was also a virgin, might ignite the St Andreas fault and have the whole State fall into the Pacific. Well, you can make your wife into that same enchanted princess by following these easy steps. Remember:

1. Abstain from all forms of sexual contact for a period of between 5 to 12 days per month.
2. During this period refrain from any other form of sexual outlet or gratification, including and especially masturbation.
3. Plan your night of reunion in a special hotel, or send the kids to friends, or go away for the weekend. Every month you will be guaranteed not just another wedding night, but a good few days of the most exciting and passionate sex.

Love Like Water; Love Like Fire

I also want to mention that a period of abstention, far from being an admission of defeat that marriage cannot sustain long periods of passion, but needs separation, is really a reflection of human nature and the kind of love that keeps a husband and wife fastened together. By separating for a brief period every month, our life together with our spouse becomes a true reflection of the emotional bond that links us.

In Jewish thought it is explained that in the emotional

attractions found among humanity we observe two kinds of powerful love. One love is analogous to water and the other to fire. The love similar to water is that which exists, for instance, between a brother and sister; as they are relatives by birth, they feel comfortable with each other and experience an innate closeness from early infancy. Their love is therefore strong, steady, predictable and calm. There is no vast gulf that separates them or that has ever separated them, which would necessitate a fiery, passionate type of love in order to keep them together. Their love does not thrive on interruptions, and an extended period divorced of one another's company will not serve to enhance the relationship, but to hamper it. Their love flourishes on a consistent and calm interaction, which defines the very nature of the love from its inception. Thus, their love is analogous to a still, watery calmness.

But a man and woman in a romantic situation, the ideal of which is as husband and wife, enjoy the very opposite: theirs is a fiery love. It is fiery because of the extreme distance between them before they were married, when they were, in fact, complete strangers. In some ways, this distance continues throughout their lives together, because of the innate disparities between male and female. There is no commonality between them provided by the same family background, as there is for a brother and sister, and so they cannot enjoy a casual and calm love. Rather, their love must serve as an agent through which they overcome their differences and become one. The love must be aggressive enough to continually overleap divisive bounds. For them there is a deep dark gulf which separates them, and which will always separate them. As the flames of a candle stretch forth despite their being bound to the wick, likewise a husband and wife, irrespective of the fact that each is constrained by his or her fully-formed character, must stretch out over this vast distance to fuse together. Thus in the relationship between husband and wife there is a constant flux: separation and distance are followed by affinity and closeness, and these constantly alternating fluctuations are essential to the marriage.

A husband and wife live in a perpetual state of becoming distanced and then experiencing reunification. If a brother and sister were to have this kind of fiery love, it would consume them. It is not the appropriate emotional interaction as it does not suit or support their relationship. Brother and sister cannot be romantically involved. Similarly, the reverse is also true: if husband and wife were to experience a calm, casual love, their relationship would suffer. There would be no force significant enough to either contain the originally separate individuals or nurture their married unity.

By recognizing the dual eclectic nature and necessities of the husband-wife relationship, one may begin to appreciate the practical importance of the Jewish laws of family purity and going to *mikveh* that we discussed earlier. Up until now we have said that the abstention involved in family purity produces discipline in the marriage, keeps it fresh and vibrant, and allows a couple to communicate on something other than a purely physical plane. But the period of separation is also much deeper than that. Married life regulated by the *mikveh*, or sexual separation, far from being an artificial imposition, is a natural reflection of the type of love which exists between husband and wife. The love is one which constantly explodes like a glowing fireball, then recedes and subsides, only to burst forth once again with added zest and enthusiasm. To nurture this love, the lifestyle of husband and wife must in turn correspond to that emotion which they are attempting to cultivate and enhance. Their physical behaviour must reflect that emotional state in order to support it, so that even when physically separate, husband and wife are able to be reunited.

The fiery dimension of the love which exists only between husband and wife is alluded to in the Hebrew terms for 'man' and 'woman', '*Ish*' and '*Isha*'. When written in Hebrew, '*Ish*' is spelled 'aleph', 'yud', 'shin', while '*isha*' is spelled 'aleph', 'shin', 'hay'. The common letters are 'aleph' and 'shin', which together compose the word '*aish*' or 'fire'. When we combine the two letters that are unique to each one, 'yud' from 'Ish' and 'hay' from '*Isha*', we form one of God's names. In this way a remarkable insight can be gained. The love between husband and wife is meant to be of a fiery nature. On its own, however, fire is totally unpredictable. At times, it is positive and useful, but if it is left uncontained for long it can suddenly become very destructive. So, too, human passion when not directed will attract husbands and wives to strangers and thus damage their marriage. It is, therefore, imperative for us to realize and respect the sanctity of this fiery relationship. By heeding the practices of the laws of family purity, or a brief period of sexual abstention, as well as modesty and restraint in our marriages, and creating gaps in our passionate relationships, we make God, the Creator who is responsible for all regeneration and renewal, an active partner and both '*Ish*' ('man') and '*Isha*' ('woman') realize their full potential to regenerate by sexual reproduction, forge a powerful bond and unite.

SOURCES — CHAPTER SEVEN

1. Carol Botwin, *Tempted Women*, 1994
2. ibid.

CHAPTER EIGHT

ATTRACTION TO STRANGERS KEEPS MARRIAGE VIBRANT

ADULTERY THRIVES ON A STATE OF TENSION

*'Nobody bothered to tell you what marriage was really about . . .
You expected not to desire any other men after marriage. And you
expected your husband not to desire any other women. Then the
desires came and you were thrown into a panic of self-hatred.
What an evil woman you were! How could you keep being
infatuated with strange men? How could you do that to your
husband? Did anyone ever tell you that maybe it had nothing to
do with your husband?'*
(Isadora speaking to herself in Erica Jong's *Fear of Flying*)

A MAZINGLY, one of the greatest hopes for reinvigorating
marriage with newness and freshness comes from the very
side of human nature which is directly responsible for adultery:
the undeniable fact that even after marriage we are still attracted
to strange men and women. In the final analysis, adultery is only
possible because every man and woman, even after marriage,
retains an attraction to the various other men and women whom
they encounter in daily life. Is it wrong then for a husband or
wife to be attracted to other men and women? To an extent, the
question is a *non sequitur*. The simple fact is that even while being
totally in love with one man or woman, we are still never

oblivious to the attraction we harbour for others outside the relationship.

One of the seemingly sad, yet obvious facts of being completely in love is that it is not, in fact, ever complete. Even while we are fully and utterly in love and devoted to our spouse, this does still not preclude us from noticing other men and women, and at times harbouring a strong attraction to them.

Loyalty of the Mind

A student to whom I am quite close once came to my office to make a complaint. At the time, he was discovering Judaism for the first time and was endeavouring to lead a more religious life. He said, only half jokingly, that he found it difficult to be 'religious and pure' around our student society because of the distraction of all the pretty women who frequent our student centre. He made specific reference to one very attractive woman who had just made her first visit.

His comment in itself was not surprising, but what made it unusual was that he had a long-standing girlfriend whom he had been with for five years, and to whom he was about to get engaged. It had always appeared as though he loved her dearly. Indeed, his girlfriend seemed very happy with him and not at all neglected. So why the sudden mention of his deep attraction to another woman? Is it acceptable to be in love with one person and remain very attracted to everyone else around?

This is a vital question in every relationship. Does it betray a lack of love for one's spouse if one remains strongly attracted to other people, without ever acting upon such interest? I am not asking whether it is reasonable for one to notice the fact that other people are attractive, which is absolutely normal and to be expected. Rather, is it acceptable not just to notice the attraction, but to allow oneself *to be attracted* to other men or women besides one's spouse? Is it excusable if one's flesh heats up as a result of pondering the sexuality of someone outside the marriage? Stated in other words, is it acceptable to want to commit adultery, so long as the person in question never actually does it, always remaining loyal and faithful in practice? Following from my earlier arguments about how the possibility of adultery is not in itself evil but can be used to great effect in restoring passion to every marriage, in this chapter we will discover how the inescapable, natural attraction to other men and women, even when we are totally and utterly in love with our spouse, is positive, and forms a vital part of keeping marriage alive and fresh.

One of the most frequent complaints that wives voice against their husbands when they take them out is that often they cannot focus their attention on their wives, but instead notice and pay heed to every pair of legs that pass them by. In the words of the noted Jewish social commentator Dennis Prager, 'Many men's heads resemble radar towers, they are constantly moving around noticing every woman that passes. I call this the radar-tower syndrome.' Naturally, the wife is extremely insulted that his interests are focused on these other women and not on her. In virtually every class that I have given on the subject of relationships and mentioned 'the radar syndrome', the women in the audience nod their heads in agreement, understanding immediately what I am referring to. In Oxford many of the single female students cite personal examples of men who have taken them out, only to be distracted by other attractive women. Thus, you have this phenomenon wherein although a man may take a woman out and enjoy a wonderful relationship with her, this does not mean that he is not attracted to other women, sometimes strongly so, even while he is in the company of the woman he loves.

This behaviour is of course unacceptable and is justifiably considered to be insulting and insensitive. And yet, it remains a matter of fact that for every person there does exist a natural attraction not only for their spouse but also for strangers of the opposite sex. I strongly maintain that men must do their best to transcend their natural attraction for women and women for men and focus their sexual interest on their spouse. Yet, the story cannot end there. This is an undeniable and hurtful phenomenon that warrants closer scrutiny. It seems almost unfair, that although we can be so totally in love and devoted to a spouse, we still are very aware of the sexual appeal of many acquaintances. Why is this, and how can it be used to our advantage in marriage?

The Tension between Good and Evil

To answer this question, we must digress briefly and explore the nature of good and evil in Jewish thought. Those people who endeavour to lead good, righteous lives will notice that even if they have overcome the struggle to perpetrate an evil or dishonest act, it becomes no easier to choose good the next time round. It is just as difficult, and the same effort is required on each and every occasion. It will always be the same conflict to give ten per cent of one's hard-earned money to charity; it doesn't get any easier with practice. It is and will always remain difficult to wake up early in the morning to go to synagogue before our personal pursuits of business or study. It is possible that choosing the right thing may become marginally easier with the passage of time, and indeed the great medieval Jewish thinker Maimonides maintained that man has two natures, the first being innate, and the second acquired through repetitive action. The more often you do something good, even amidst fierce inner resistance, the easier it becomes to repeat the act, until it actually becomes second nature. And yet, there can be no doubt that the struggle will always remain. Life is not easy, and doing the right thing always is certainly not easy.

The question must then be asked why it is so difficult just to be a good person and to choose goodness on every occasion? Why can't we make one choice at the age of twelve or thirteen, when of mature and culpable age, to lead a good life, and remain that way for the rest of our lives? Why must these choices be made continually? Why did God make it all so difficult? Shouldn't it just be enough to want goodness badly enough that sheer willpower alone should propel us above all the negative possibilities and tendencies?

The Zohar, the most fundamental work of Jewish mysticism, provides the answer: whenever good is chosen over evil, the glory of God is raised infinitely higher. This means that Judaism as a religion does not believe in man making one choice of good over evil which lasts forever. Man cannot climb the mountain summit of goodness, become an exemplary human being, and then discard evil from his soul forever. Make no mistake about it. What God desires is not *righteousness*, so much as the *struggle* to do the right thing. He does not wish for man to love and choose goodness just once in his life, and pursue a righteous path thereafter unchallenged. On the contrary, what Judaism believes in is a daily struggle to choose good over evil, God over wickedness, charity over selfishness, compassion over judgmentalism, love over hate, and fidelity over adultery. The reason is that God is glorified far more if good is chosen constantly rather than just once; it is a far greater statement of a love for goodness if it is chosen constantly and consistently, on a regular basis. Choosing to do the right thing always makes goodness important in our daily lives.

To make the point on a more human level, we have discussed how the qualities of novelty and newness have the capacity to attract us to an object as never before. We so very much appreciate and look forward to something new happening in our lives, or buying a new item. The Creator desired that we never become bored of goodness, never allow it to go stale in our lives.

Thus, it remains a somewhat elusive goal, always beckoning from right in front of us, bidding us to strive yet further to attain it. Man is not meant to be weary, but enthusiastic about Godliness. Just as in a relationship the chase is always part of the excitement, the same applies to a Godly life. There is no time or room for complacency. *Choosing goodness must be a daily activity*, not something confined to our past. If we had the capacity to choose to follow a righteous path once and for all early in our life, then God would not be playing an active role in our lives. He would be associated with an ancient decision we made in our youth, and which we have not thought of since. Since it is not possible to commit ourselves to goodness once and for all, and it therefore must be chosen daily, we are afforded an opportunity to bring God and goodness into our lives and make His presence meaningful and felt in a very tangible way.

Some religions maintain that it is wrong for man to entertain evil thoughts or to have any attraction or compulsion towards depravity and that he must choose to rid himself completely of his amoral tendencies. To them, it is not the struggle which is important, but complete and utter righteousness. They are not so much into *choosing goodness*, as they are into *vanquishing evil*. Judaism believes that man is not out to slay this impulse but to conquer it daily. By choosing decency and integrity regularly rather than as an historical occurrence, we manifest our love for God on a daily basis. The choice of good over evil can never be a one-off event.

Judaism is not really concerned with evil, so much as with goodness, and maintains that the utter eradication of evil is an elusive and misguided objective. The purpose of evil is to provide choices. There are two essential ingredients in human behaviour which make an object attractive and desirable. The first is when it is new and fresh. The second is when we choose to make it our own of our own free volition. We are bored with things which are old, and we despise things which are forced upon us. Therefore, the existence of good and evil and man's initial neutrality afford us the opportunity of choosing good things daily, thus making them (a) fresh and novel, and (b) our own personal choice.

Marrying Every Day of Our Lives

In a similar vein, we may say that the reason that God created us in a manner in which we harbour an attraction to other men and women, notwithstanding our love and loyalty to our spouse, is so that we have the opportunity to express the greatest and most sublime level of love: that which comes about through choice. Since an attraction to others still exists despite the strong commitment of marriage, we are in a position to choose our spouse *constantly*. We cannot rely on a one-off event and statement made under the wedding canopy for our fidelity. Rather, our commitment is dynamic, constantly being reinforced and strengthened. Far greater than a past statement of love and choice is a statement which says, 'I love you and choose you ceaselessly. Not just once, long ago, but every single day.' Amidst the many billions of people in this world, amidst all the good-looking, funny, attractive, good-natured people to whom we harbour a congenital attraction, it is this one person to whom we have pledged our love and whom despite the struggle we continue to choose to adore. There is no more beautiful statement of love that can be made between two people. This kind of love is dynamic and fresh, rather than stale and old.

The Only Person in the World

That this is true can be borne out from a very simple example. A wife might consider it a compliment if her husband said to her, 'You should know that I am not at all attracted to other women;

I don't even notice them, only you. It is not even that you are the most beautiful woman to me, it is simply that you are the *only* woman as far as I am concerned. I am completely oblivious to everyone else. I am deadened to all other women, and they are to me like wood.' Naturally, a wife who heard this from her husband might indeed feel complimented and secure. But far more flattering would be the proclamation, 'There are many very beautiful, attractive women that I have encountered. And to be honest, I find them appealing and desirable. And yet I have chosen to be with you, because to me you are the most special, and nobody can compare to you. In a world of beautiful and attractive people, you are the *most* beautiful. Although there are many to choose from, for me there can be no other, only you.' In this scenario a woman is made to feel incredibly special, as if she wins a beauty pageant every day. Instead of making her feel that you love her because she is akin to being the only woman on a desert island, and essentially you have no choice but to love her, she feels rather that she has won a contest and is the most desirable woman, amidst some very stiff competition.

Because women also gravitate towards other men, and yet remain steadfastly loyal and in love with their husbands, firstly, the husband can really feel special. He is not *alone*, but rather he is *unique*, in a class of his own. The second advantage is that he understands that his life with his wife is not something stale or in the past. She loves and chooses him *constantly*. Thus, he can be assured of the excitement and passion in his married life increasing rather than dissipating with the passage of time. Choosing one's spouse constantly expresses the depth and intensity of the relationship. The most sublime way of telling someone 'I love you' is 'I have *chosen* you to make you mine, and I go on choosing you daily. I am never complacent about my love for you and my need to *do* something about it.'

Viewed in this way, there can be said to be a very positive dimension in the ongoing struggle for faithfulness and fidelity, not just in religious practice and observance, but in relationships. When a businessman struggles to remain honest in his financial dealings, even though he could get away with fraud, he shows that God is a living Being that occupies his thoughts and plays a central role in human affairs and determining morality. God is not consigned to the dustbin of history, because He informs and influences our actions regularly. He plays an active role in our lives.

The same is true of a spouse. If a husband or wife could be separated by a business trip, and find no necessity to struggle to remain faithful in heart, mind and deed to one another, what would this say about their marriage? Of course, it would mean that their marriage is very secure, but not passionate and alive. They got married long ago and now find no need to invoke the memory of each other while away in order to remain loyal and faithful, since they are not at all tempted by anyone else. But the husband or wife who naturally feels an attraction to a business associate or colleague to whom they are not married, in order to remain faithful must have recourse to the loving memories of their loyal spouse waiting for them at home, and thus they take the spouse, and their marriage with them everywhere. Although this involves strenuous effort, it is an exertion which is not only necessary but rewarding. The result is a marriage of the highest quality within which one's spouse is continually affirmed as being chosen, rather than merely being established once and for all as 'the wife' or 'the husband' and taken for granted from that point onwards. This is a beautiful insight into relationships which one may cull from Jewish religious thought.

The Tension in the Daily Need to Choose

It is often claimed that the greatest love in the world is that between a parent and child, but this is somewhat inaccurate: the greatest love in the world is that between husband and wife. This is because, even though a parent may love his child with an unbreakable bond, this love has in a sense been forced upon him; it is natural to love one's children. Not only is it natural, but in reality it is compulsory and we might even say that a parent has no choice but to love their child. In fact, when we hear of parents who do not show affection to their children we are mortified, and we speak of them as being 'sick' due to their unnatural behaviour. But when a husband chooses a wife or vice versa, from millions of other potential spouses who are equally qualified and equally deserving of love, it is for no other reason than the fact that one desires this person and makes them unique and special by declaring them as one's own. In this respect, what truly makes something unique and special more than anything else is that fact that it is *ours*. No wonder, then, that even upon returning from an exotic Caribbean holiday, we feel relieved to be home. The home is ours, the hotel room on the island is not. Human beings connect with things that they have chosen and achieved of their own accord far more than anything which has been given to them, or that has been forced upon them. No one forced you to choose to love this woman or man, unlike your children. The affection you show them is completely voluntary, and in this respect comes from the deepest, innermost recesses of your soul.

In the same way, by choosing one's wife or husband over all the other women and men who may be equally attractive, and by continuing to choose them at every minute and at every hour over any others who may be encountered, one demonstrates the highest form of love: the ability to be so absorbed and so engrossed in our loved one that we think of them always and choose them constantly. Adultery involves a constant state of reappraisal and reconfirmation of one's commitment to one's lover. Marriage needs the same. The anxiety forced by our natural attraction to strangers, on the one hand, and our wish to remain faithful to our spouse on the other, creates a constant state of tension and anxiety which never allows married people to become complacent. They are always forced to choose. In this way we emulate the anxiety which is such an important ingredient of adultery and is largely responsible for its ongoing attractiveness. Parties to an adulterous affair have no security. They know that what they are doing is wrong and they also know how much they are risking because of the affair. They are therefore forced to reconsider the appeal of their lover constantly: to weigh them against their spouse, their homes, their children, and to decide that their lover is so special that they simply cannot be separated from them. In essence, adultery involves a constant state of reappraisal. But this weighing in the balance leads an adulterous husband or wife to be constantly reminded of how special their lover truly is. They must choose their lover daily and re-commit themselves to the affair.

In marriage we have the same thing. Because of the natural attraction to other men and women, husbands and wives are forced to make the same choices. And every time they choose each other and decide to remain loyal and focused, they bring added excitement and passion into their marriages.

CHAPTER NINE

BORED WITH SEX: THE LOSS OF PASSION IN RELATIONSHIPS

ADULTERY THRIVES ON SECRECY, MODESTY AND MYSTIQUE

*'I am happy now that Charles calls on my bedchamber less
frequently than of old. As it is, I now endure but two calls a
week and when I hear his steps outside my door I lie down on my
bed, close my eyes, [ready myself for sex], and think of
England.'*
Lady Alice Hillingdon, *Journal* (1912)

A COUPLE WHOSE wedding ceremony I conducted invited
family and close friends to their beautiful bridal suite in
the elegant Claridges Hotel for drinks after their wedding reception. After about an hour, I started saying in a loud voice, 'Boy,
is it late, and am I tired! I guess we'd all better be going now.'
And turning to one of the guests, I said, 'Aren't you coming,
too?' People began to take the hint. It was, after all, this couple's
wedding night, and we all had to scram. But just as everybody
was leaving, the bride, who was very beautiful, began to cry:
'Oh, please don't go yet. I can't believe the wedding is over.' Her
new husband tried to comfort her. 'What's wrong, darling?' With
tears rolling down her cheeks, she said, 'I don't want to take off
my wedding dress.' Of course, she meant that she loved being a
bride and couldn't believe that the most special moment of her

life was now over. But how do you think her husband felt hearing this? You see, this couple had been living together for two years prior to the wedding. They separated just one day before the wedding. How new or special was their wedding night bound to be?

One of the greatest fallacies ever advanced in the history of human relationships, which is actually increasing with the passage of time, is that people simply cannot become bored with sex. Here, I don't only mean bored with the same sexual partner, which undoubtedly we are prepared to admit. Rather, I mean bored with sex in general. Ours is such an oversexed society that we think we can never get enough of it. This is a far cry from the truth. People are becoming increasingly bored with sex, and it is principally the oversexing of society that is responsible for the decline in sexual interest generally, and in marriage in particular.

Recently, two students who had been going out together for over half a year, and who seemed to be quite serious about their relationship, broke it off abruptly. As I am quite friendly with them, they candidly replied to my question when I asked why it had petered out: 'We quite literally *screwed* the life out of our relationship. We had sex at every possible moment, several times a day. It's just not exciting any more. We don't seem to have much more to look forward to.'

All around the world, the jury is back and the verdict is in: people are getting bored with sex. From magazines to movies, flesh and erotica are out, while dressing and subtlety are back in fashion. It seems that we have all suffered a dreaded sexual disease that is a more potent turn-off than any health considerations or fear of AIDS: we're being bored to death by sex. In Britain the porno magazines are dressing their models in order to sell copies. *The Sunday Times* reported that *Penthouse* magazine, 'the men's magazine that was the first to bare all, is asking its models to put their clothes back on. Skin, it seems, is no longer "in".'[1]

What has led to this sudden exercise in modesty? Could it be the Christian 'decade of evangelism', or the Jewish call for a 'decade of renewal'? Is it a general return to a more puritanical era and ethos? No, nothing quite as profound as that. It is simply a business decision. *The Sunday Times* went on to say: 'The plunging sales of "girlie" magazines have led to a catharsis in Britain's publishing industry . . . Penthouse once boasted 500,000 readers; now it claims 120,000 a month . . . The number of naked women is being reduced in favour of serious features . . .' They feel that they will actually gain more subscribers if they dress their models with clothes . . . Is this possible? This *is* a pornographic magazine, isn't it? Can someone please tell me just what the heck is going on?

At the outset of the sexual revolution, it was assumed that the more sex poured into a society, the more explicitly people dressed, and the more easy sex became to obtain, the greater the interest would be. The younger generation felt that their intrinsic sexual selves had been stifled under a mountain of arcane Victorian sexual restrictions and American puritanical sexual codes. It was their belief that by removing these restrictions which were designed only to repress their sexuality, real harmony, peace, and pleasure would be theirs for the taking. There can be no denying that the sexual revolution was thus, at least in part, a radical response to the repression many felt was prevalent in sexual matters. I for one sympathize with this view and reject repression as damaging in virtually every respect. But instead of society adopting the option of sexual focus on a specific target, they instead elected to be as carefree, irresponsible and reckless in sex as they were in shopping and spending money. Of course, this ran completely contrary to everything we knew about every other area of life. In life, like in adultery, it is specifically the scarcity of things that make them precious. If the streets were lined with diamonds they would be as worthless as granite stone. What the progenitors of the sexual revolution did not foresee is that sex is like so many other areas of life: it can suffer from overkill. Yes, ladies and gentlemen, the unthinkable is true: people can become just as bored with sex as they can with anything else. There can be no question that a dramatic increase in sexual explicitness of society leads, not to a greater, but to a lesser interest in sex, and a general decrease in human eroticism.

Casual Sex

Society has become so complacent about sex. Its explicitness has caused sex to lose its mystique. A wife catches her husband with another woman and he apologizes, but cannot understand why she is so hurt. 'It was just sex. I didn't love her.' Just sex! *Just* sex!! Yes, just sex. Because sex has become totally casual, and therefore a husband can equate it with washing a woman's car. Nothing serious in that either.

One of the great challenges of modern day living is to re-establish the parameters that separate the casual from the intense. Life needs centres of intensity. Human undertaking and affairs must be understood not just as casual and arbitrary, but rather as purposeful and meaningful. It is purpose that makes things passionate and intense. Humans can never be really passionate about things which they believe to be accidental or arbitrary. When you are given money unearned, when it comes accidentally, like by way of winning a lottery, you are never as respectful or mindful of that money as you would be if it had come through hard work. If a man or woman truly believed that their spouse was chosen for them by heaven, and that their marriage was preordained, they would be very passionate about making it work. But in today's prevailing climate, where so many people speak of having accidentally married the 'wrong' person, how can they be excited about making their marriages special? Lack of purpose sucks out the intensity from our marriages and makes them casual. Our attitude becomes, 'If it works out, then great. And if not, then there's always something or somebody else.'

I met a student who was very intelligent, but also slightly immature. He was eighteen years old and he had been very sheltered by his mother. He came to the L'Chaim Society on Friday nights and became very friendly with a girl. They used to go for drinks and to plays together and eventually started going to her room and talking late into the night. This happened numerous times, but he was naive about the ways of the world and didn't quite comprehend that there was something romantic happening. He thought it was just a friendship until one night when, in the midst of a conversation about a film they had seen, the girl began to unbutton her blouse right in front of his eyes, just as naturally as she was speaking to him.

The student came to me the next day as white as a sheet. I asked him what had happened to make him look so grim; did a relative die, God forbid, or did he lose his best friend? He said no, something far worse. Almost in a daze he said, 'I always dreamed what it would be like to be with a woman for the first time, it was something mysterious and inviting, which I very much looked forward to. Last night it was all stolen from me. When for the first time a young woman undressed in front of me, it was in a totally casual way. I believed that it was going to be passionate, electric, exciting, intense. It ended up being almost accidental. She did it for me, but it didn't feel natural.' Then in a most uncharacteristic display of anger, he pounded his fist on the table and shouted, '*It was so damn casual.*' The student felt that he had been cheated, and that the line which separates the casual from the intense was somehow blurred that evening. And the first truly intense experience that he was meant to have became something commonplace.

The most intense thing known to human beings is sexual intimacy with another person. Nothing could make our blood flow faster, our heart beat quicker, or our flesh prickle with greater expectation. Sexuality is central to all human passion; indeed, it is the very source, veritably the mother of all passions. In today's society however, where sex is often practised in a spirit of total non-commitment, people can undertake those same moments and feel that nothing has happened; as if nothing special had come between them.

Modesty Preserves Intimacy

Judaism has long advocated the need for modesty in society: in the way people dress, in the way people speak, even in the way people think. While many thought that the purpose of the laws concerning modesty was to prevent sinful thoughts, they were wrong. Modesty is necessary to preserve *intimacy*, not to prevent sin. Modesty was not made for the benefit of the person who wants to sin, just as laws were not made for people who want to commit crimes. Modesty has to do with something much more subtle. There is an old question, 'Do you lock your house to keep people out, or to protect what is on the inside?' Similarly, should a person act and dress modestly in order to prevent intrusion from outside, or to preserve and maintain what is inside: the delicate and precious ability to have and maintain an intimate relationship?

An intimate moment is one in which two individuals invite one another into their private space. Not just a private room, but *a private part of themselves*. If every bit of ourselves has already become public property through lack of modesty, what part of us is left cordoned off and preserved for an intimate moment? The current lack of emphasis on modesty has meant that our intimate selves have become like a secret told to too many people. It still may be exciting news, and a lot of people may be interested in hearing it. But in no way is it personal or private. After a while it becomes stale and boring, however sensational it was to begin with because intensity and passion thrive specifically on those things which are sometimes hidden or obscured, and must therefore be discovered and renewed. The human body is meant to be explored within marriage. That is what makes the body a treasure instead of a public playground.

When Sex Becomes Commonplace, Romance Vanishes

In an earlier generation there were many expressions of love outside the bedroom. This was the meaning of romance. A couple would hold hands, dance together or cuddle. In today's society non-involved men and women kiss and hug even as a form of greeting, and total strangers dance together at parties: what is left to a couple as an expression of affection besides the bedroom? And we are quickly becoming desensitized even to that.

After a very hectic term of our University Society's events in the October and November of 1990, I took my family to Amsterdam for a weekend. On Saturday, the Jewish Sabbath, we were staying in a hotel room overlooking a very busy shopping arcade. I decided to put my theory to the test: in this, probably the most sexually explicit city in the world, had people's sense of romance been deadened? After all, what meaning could holding hands have when sex is so readily available? Why waste time when people can go straight for the kill? I watched the people below for four hours, searching continually for couples who were holding hands. Did the romantics still exist? In all that time I saw only five. To my mind, there is an absolute correlation between the degree of explicitness and the lack of romance. Will something as simple yet romantic as holding hands have any excitement in a city where one can see exposed flesh in every shop-front? And why waste time on petty romance when you can go straight for the kill and immediately have sex? Unfortunately, it is not only the holding of hands that will suffer in such a city. When the threshold of excitement is constantly lifted, it soon reaches the point where we become immune even where male and female sexual organs are concerned. This is exactly what happens in a city like Amsterdam. Men sit in bars watching women perform the most explicitly sexual acts with not a stitch of clothing on. And are they excited about it? No! *They are bored to death.* As they watch, they turn to the waitress to order more beer and after a few minutes start talking business or sports once again. It is too explicit, too open. And yes we *can* become bored of sex.

Now that sex has become a sort of casual interaction that can happen even with people we are not serious about, later when we do care for someone and we want to bond with them, we find that the strong and potent sexual attraction which is necessary to keep couples together has been dulled and deadened. When you add too much water to glue it won't stick. So it is with our sexuality.

A recent article in *Newsweek* magazine told of a long-running French nudist colony which was now undergoing a rebellion by its young. Many of the parents who served as founding members of the colony were troubled that they were not able to impart their tradition of naturalism to their children. The reporter quoted one of the girls explaining why, unlike her parents, she was wearing a bathing suit on the beach: 'If I don't put on clothes,' she said, 'the boys don't even look at me.' I know of countless American friends who come to the topless European beaches, which are outlawed in the United States, and feel the same way. For the first few days their heads are like radar towers, scrutinizing every mammary gland that passes. After a few days, however, seeing how many stones they can skip on the surface of the sea becomes more interesting. It seems that attraction can be greater when the person is partially hidden from view than when openly displayed. This is because modesty is what makes intimacy possible.

Here we find the solution to why so many couples are breaking up and how it is possible to one day fall out of love even after years of marriage. In a society where modesty is treated as a nuisance and an imposition, we quickly become desensitized to our spouse and must look elsewhere to find passion. No wonder then that study after study cites sexual boredom as the leading cause for infidelity in marriage as well as for divorce. Let's face it: the average woman or man is not looking to destroy their marriage, ruin their lives, or hurt their spouse by engaging in an extramarital affair. Rather, they are just looking for a little bit of excitement or attention, excitement that they would not be searching for outside of marriage if they found it within marriage. Baltimore psychologist Shirley Glass cites the astonishing statistic that 75 per cent of men say that sexual excitement is a justifiable reason to stray, as compared to 53 per cent of women. The women prefer falling in love as a justifiable reason, with 77 per cent agreeing that love justifies an extramarital dalliance, as opposed to 43 per cent of the men who agreed.[2]

We have to stop looking at unfaithful partners as merely evil, cunning, and duplicitous. They do not set out to be mean or hurtful. All they want is passion. And when people don't find it with their spouses, they look for it with someone else. While this of course does not in any way justify or excuse their actions, it does help us understand the problem so that we can deal with it.

Be Careful Not to Let Your Sexual Steam Leak Out

In his book *Doesn't Anyone Blush Anymore*, Manis Friedman tells this steamboat story. Soon after the steamboat was invented, a captain brought his boat down a river and stopped at one of the small villages in Europe to show it off. He was fascinated by his new toy, and tried repeatedly to impress the simple peasants with the loud boom of his foghorn. Over and over again, the captain stoked the engines, got up a big head of steam and sounded the horn. But when the time came to show how the boat ran, it wouldn't budge. He had used up all his steam on the foghorn.

If we waste our sexual energy wherever we go, letting it leak out wherever we roam, we are left without any when we need it. If we are sexual when it doesn't count, we will have no steam left when it does. If we dress in an explicit and provocative way when we are not in a sexual situation, then our bodies may not pose the same erotic attraction necessary later to create a sexual situation.

According to Jewish thought, a healthy society in which marriage and intimacy can flourish is one which is completely alert sexually. This means a society which knows that if women *and men* don't dress modestly, they will soon become desensitized and less attractive to one another. A healthy society is one in which men and women, whilst socializing and being a part of the outside world, put up a curtain which separates their inner selves from everyone else. This gives them the ability to have times when that curtain is lifted to allow someone else to enter their private space for intimate purposes. Immediately afterwards they replace that curtain. We must therefore seek to reconstruct the borders that once existed in society's dress and behaviour and to create again the kind of sensitive environment that once kept our grandparents romantically married until a ripe old age. If we do not, we risk continuing with our current inability to attach ourselves to people.

The Insatiable Generation

Let's face it. This generation is insatiable. People are just not satisfied with their spouses, with their jobs, with their cars, and certainly not with their sex lives. And this in turn is because we are all bored. If there is one common denominator which sums up modern life it is total and utter boredom. People are bored with everything: television, films, sex. The fact that we need to have so many different partners shows how dulled we really are. When you give human beings things that have no content they quickly get sick of it. Often, the only excitement that monogamous partners get is to watch erotic films in their bedrooms to keep them stimulated. And now, with things such as the Playboy Channel, one need not even go out to the video shop to remain interested in sex. They have a constant stream of images pouring into their home. What they don't realize however is that every time a synthetic image is used as a sexual outlet it detracts from the passion and intensity of their own married lives.

The average US home watches four hours of television per day. The major question that this statistic used to lead to was, 'How much time, then, does that leave for human beings to actually talk to one another?' But the question now that we have incessant pornography on television is, 'With all the watching we do of other people having sex, how much time or interest does that leave the average husband and wife for the same sort of thing?'

The number one cause for divorce today is not financial problems or parental intervention, as it was in the 1950s and 1960s, but sexual boredom. You are divorced because you are bored with each other. You have fallen out of love. You are no longer passionate about one another. You don't necessarily miss or think about each other when you are away from one another, and even when you are together in bed you think about someone else in order to be stimulated. You either find an adulterous partner or you get out of the marriage. Passion can only be preserved through newness. Anything which is new is special to us. Conversely, anything to which we are exposed incessantly, without modification or change, becomes boring and passionless. What one needs in a relationship like marriage is passionate excitement and newness. In an age lacking in modesty one cannot have newness. We have seen it all, done it all, and nothing much is new.

In his best-selling book on the state of modern-day education, *The Closing of the American Mind*, Alan Bloom writes about how teenagers' 'easy sex' dulls them to the possibility of a passionate life: 'A significant number of students used to arrive at the university physically and spiritually virginal, expecting to lose their innocence there. Their lust was mixed into everything they thought and did. They were painfully aware that they wanted something but were not quite sure exactly what it was.' He alleges too that now they begin having sex at such a young age they arrive at university slightly less enthusiastic, and highly more cynical about their studies and about life in general. Their Eros has been satisfied and they are therefore not as lusty for life.

Overexposure Dulls Passion

I was sitting with a couple whom I did not know all that well, at whose wedding I was to officiate in Oxford. I told the two of them, Jewish law advocates that husband and wife dress and act modestly with one another. If you are not preparing for a sexual or intimate encounter, a wife should be wearing a nightgown and the husband pyjamas, not always parading around the bedroom nude. Nothing upset the prospective bridegroom as much as that comment. He was furious that I was telling them how to conduct their private lives and found this to be very offensive. He was prepared to accept that Judaism had the right to make demands on our public lives. But to encroach upon people's private lives was absolutely wrong. I responded: 'Look, you can discard this advice and insist, as you have been, that how you conduct your intimate married life is your business only, and no one has the right to offer any advice. But by doing this, you run the risk of the nightmare scenario. You are so exposed to each other's bodies for such long periods of time that one day your wife will arrive home, you will be reading the newspaper, she will undress and you will *still be reading the newspaper*.' Judaism insists that husbands and wives don't parade around each other naked, not for any puritanical reasons, but so that they don't become bored with one another. Overexposure leads to dullness. Modesty on the other hand leads to newness, discovery and the ability to be excited about the subject.

Separation and Renewal Leads to Passion in Marriage . . .

People are bored with sex and nudity in films because they are presented with it continually. For this same reason we are also bored with our spouses and feel forced to find excitement in extramarital dalliances and cheap one-night stands, that leave us feeling degraded and 'just not right'. The monotony that exists in today's monogamous relationships leads us into thinking that it is time for someone new. If we are immodest we have already explored everything that could be new to us. If social modesty was preserved we would have a situation where people are always looking forward to discovering one another.

The moral is this: we must be very serious about our sexuality. The many laws which religions such as Judaism have instituted for modesty were meant not to restrict and limit human sexuality, but to *focus* it. This focus enables us to lead long, stable, fulfilling lives in the very old institution of marriage and never abandon the viability of monogamy, the possibility which it offers for a relationship with passion and close loving kindness and familiarity existing side by side. There must be a sense of mystery and discovery to keep a marriage special.

Madonna's latest 'bare-all' film, *Body of Evidence* (which I purposely avoided) has the absurd story line that she murders her boyfriend through sexual intercourse. But even the most explicit sexual scenery in the entire world was not going to save this film, which only attracted small crowds and bad reviews. Doesn't she realize? People are no longer interested. They are bored with sex. They have reached saturation point. Meanwhile, films such as Disney's *The Jungle Book* and *The Lion King*, cartoons in which the only unclothed characters are the animals of the wild, have been packing houses with viewers of all ages. The same is true of other Disney animated features that have grossed far more in earnings than the sexual romp movies which have failed. Incredibly, it seems that sex has suddenly become impotent. Or is it merely a case of severe over [s]exposure?

In a society where there is no separation between sexual explicitness and modesty, where there is no distinction between constant revelation and occasional concealment, people lose interest in all things sexual. We become immune to all erotica, and the magic that human sexuality is meant to spin becomes dull and ordinary.

The part of England in which I live is usually rainy and cold. People are therefore clothed fairly warmly and pretty much all over for most of the year. But then there are some summer months where the weather is warm, sometimes even hot, and people then dress very scantily and explicitly. When this first happens, you can see everybody eyeing each other up, and there is a sexually charged atmosphere in the air. I remember once on a hot Saturday afternoon that had come after a long period of cold I was walking home from synagogue with an Oxford student. He was so taken by this new form of Oxford dress, and so obviously obsessed with seeing every part of every newly exposed woman's body, that he quite literally walked into a street lamp. Being that the laws of the Sabbath, which prohibit travelling in a motor vehicle, may be broken in a life-threatening situation, I suggested to my friend that although it was the Sabbath he was permitted to take a taxi home instead of walking, for fear that he otherwise might walk straight into a bus! The fine weather continued and two weeks later I was walking with the same student; he was now completely engrossed in our conversation, despite the various exposed shapes and curves which passed us by. Why? Because he was now incessantly exposed to it, people had been dressing this way for a few weeks, and there was nothing new. He was bored already, as was everybody else. Of course next summer they will be out in force once again to see the latest fashions, but only because they will have had a hiatus of so many months.

The Sexual Society

The same is true on a collective level. In the same way that a candle that burns too brightly consumes its wick and splutters out, a society which has no respect for modesty and is sexually over-explicit consumes the sexual passion of its members. The result is the utter demise of our sexual interests, which spells disaster for all intimate relationships. There is simply no physical relationship that can thrive without passion. Therefore, the society which we help to nurture must, of necessity, encourage modesty in dress, speech, and action. By expressing our sexuality in conformity with simple laws of modesty, which above all maintains that human sexuality be manifest only in an intimate setting, and only with an individual who has demonstrated their love for us through solid commitment, we ensure that the candle which represents our sexual selves always burns brightest, and is not exhausted by heat that is too intense, leaving us limp and unmoved after our sexuality has already peaked and climaxed. We simply cannot create a society that is healthy and passionate sexually which peaks at a constant rate. We can be overexposed sexually and be left with no sexual interest. And it is imperative for our marriages and indeed for all human relationships that we remain passionately interested in the one member of the opposite sex with whom we have chosen to live our lives, rather than searching for novelty in the form of a new sexual partner.

Modesty, therefore, is one of the principal avenues by which we can turn our marriages into illicit affairs. One of the great secrets of adultery is that two lovers never grow bored with each other since they are never over-exposed to one another. They don't live together or share the same bedroom and they only undress in front of one another when they wish to have sex. Thus, they always cherish each other's bodies. In marriage it should be no different with husbands and wives choosing to undress only with the intention of creating moments of passion and intimacy.

SOURCES — CHAPTER NINE

1. 11 April 1993
2. Bonnie Eaker Well, *Adultery: The Forgivable Sin*, 1993
3. Alan Bloom, *The Closing of the American Mind*, 1987

CHAPTER TEN

THE CENTRALITY OF
SEX TO HUMAN
RELATIONSHIPS

ADULTERY INVOLVES INTENSE FOCUS

HAVING ESTABLISHED that monogamy runs completely against the grain of human nature, we may now understand the centrality of sex in marriage and the need for couples to have the most passionate intimate lives possible (a) if they are to remain together at all, and (b) if they are to remain faithful to one another within marriage. The whole purpose in this book of using adultery to rekindle passion in marriage is only important if you truly understand how important a good sex life is to marriage. But nowadays, people don't like hearing this. Most people today certainly feel that sex is not one of the loftier pursuits of man, and is even somewhat degrading. When I tell my students at Oxford that once upon a time people actually married because they couldn't have sex any other way – in other words, they married for sex – they look at me in horror and astonishment. A student stood up during a lecture I gave and said, 'Of all the superficial, silly things I have ever heard, to tell us we should marry for sex. My God!' I rose and I thumped my hand on the desk and shouted (for effect), 'Superficial and silly? That's what sex is for you? Of course that's what it has become. The Jewish religion sees sex as the ultimate form of knowledge and union. In the Bible and the Hebrew language, there isn't even a word for "sex". The word for "sex" is "knowing", as in "And Adam *came to know* his wife, Eve."' Sex, therefore is the ultimate form of human knowledge and intimacy, not some fleshly physical pastime.

The problem is that today sex is not a form of knowledge; it is not even an intense experience. You can have sex with a woman, see her on the street the next day, smile and keep on walking. Sex has become far too casual. That is why we are so engulfed and overcome by boredom. That is why our lives lack so much passion and our hearts are bereft of fire. A society that cannot appreciate the sublimity and enormous power of sex is doomed to a permanent state of casualness.

Sex is the most intense experience we have in life, the thing that we all look forward to most. It has the power to dominate all human affairs and make everything appear insignificant in its presence. If a husband and wife have a good sex life, then the fact that dinner isn't ready on time isn't nearly as important. The things that people argue about, and destroy their marriages over, are not as important. Hence the reason why *the* key to a successful marriage is to look upon and treat your spouse like your lover. Only passion has the power to drown and cancel out all the other petty squabbles of life.

Couples Who End Up Being Best Friends

At one of my classes on human relationships, a participant became very irate. It was a man. He asked me if I was trying to say that the only thing in marriage was sex. I replied that while I am sure that it is not the *only* thing, it is the *most important* thing. Unquestionably, it is the one area of life that you reserve specifically for marriage. He reacted with hostility to my response and in my experience it is often the case that people react with disdain to the idea of the centrality of sex in marriage. Let me therefore repeat: sex is certainly not the only important thing in marriage. But it is what changes a friendship into a marriage. You are not husband and wife when you share a home or apartment. You are similarly not husband and wife when you merely share a bedroom. You may then be only roommates. You are specifically husband and wife when you share *the same bed* and enjoy intimate moments of loving.

A major trend in the United States is the celibate marriage. The celibate marriage is built on the idea that no marriage can really preserve its passion and that makes people hung up on the sexual problems in their relationships. So, who needs sex in marriage at all? Just focus on the really important things in marriage, like going to art galleries together, discussing Vivaldi, listening to music, baking bread, talking, relating, communicating.

But that's what you do with everybody else. That's not marriage. Marriage is sharing one bed. It's becoming one flesh. It's having children together. Sex is definitely the most important element of a marriage at least in its early and intermediate stages. A couple who grow older and still feel very close and loving even in old age have engendered that closeness by virtue of the passion they shared earlier in life. Sex in general is the only thing that can truly keep a man and woman together over a long period of time. And a good sex life in particular is the only thing that will guarantee that they remain faithful to one another. No other activity known to man has the power of combating the unnaturalness of marriage, and nothing other than sex is therefore strong enough to serve as an adhesive between husband and wife. In a celibate marriage, or a marriage where there is no passionate sexual life, the husband and wife might be best friends, and they might feel closer to one another than they do to any other person on earth. Nevertheless, they are not truly bonded as husband and wife ought to be. We might say that they are just really close. They haven't left the domain of the casual and entered into the realm of the intense, which is what marriage is all about and what the word relationship, which conveys nought but a vague idea of association, cannot give.

Adultery Glorifies Sex

The power of adultery is that it glorifies sex and that is the reason why, unlike marriage, it has always retained its attractiveness. Entertain no misconception. *Adultery is about the pursuit of great sex.* Adultery is attractive because you enter into a relationship in which you are first and foremost a sexual being, with the right to indulge yourself in sexual gratification and shirk all other responsibilities. This may explain why a high incidence of female adultery occurs specifically among housewives. A wife feels that she is having an affair with someone who is not interested in her for her cooking or her home-making abilities, but purely because she is a sexual being. The lover is interested in her as a *woman*, not as a servant. In adultery, a man is made to feel that he is not just a provider or a businessman, but primarily a man and a sexual creature. The attractiveness of an affair is sex alone. People have a need to feel erotic and adultery caters to that need. It is not about shared interests or aspirations. It is not about having children. The excitement of sex which extramarital affairs can provide is enough for people to risk their family, career, future and their security. They are suddenly reminded that life isn't only about being overwhelmed or consumed by daily chores.

There is so much to learn from adultery. If this could be translated into the context of marriage, then a couple would be reminded that they married each other because once upon a time they were sexually attracted to each other and powerfully in love and they will do something about it. Couples must cordon off time from their lives to have an illicit affair – *with each other*. Marriage must also serve as an erotic enterprise. They must make time to get away from the kids, the house, and their jobs, a few times a week, just as two lovers would do, and ensure that they have the most passionate sexual moments together. Rarely do we hear of couples who had a very good and healthy sex life ending up divorcing.

Achieving Sexual Focus

One of the things I argue most vehemently for is that couples should keep their sexual and intimate lives together happy, passionate and comfortable. This can be achieved in a number of ways. The first thing I would urge is that couples get rid of the television sets from their bedrooms, immediately. There is no greater distraction to focusing and concentrating on each other than having a television. The men have to compete against the likes of Tom Cruise, Mel Gibson, Arnold Schwarzenegger, the women against Madonna, Michele Pfeiffer and Margaret Thatcher. That is one problem. But even if it's a Donald Duck cartoon, why should you bring such a terrible distraction into your bedroom where you should be focusing on each other? I truly believe that a television in a couple's bedroom has a direct bearing on the deterioration in their marriage.

I was once speaking to a world renowned social anthropologist who came to our house. He is single, and I asked him why he hadn't married. He said that he hadn't found the right woman. I asked why not, and he told me how during three years of research in the Philippines he had a number of Polynesian girlfriends and once you have been with a Polynesian woman you can never go back to a Western woman. I asked why. He replied that it was because Polynesian women have nothing in life. They are so poverty stricken, they don't know how to do anything *but one thing*. They are so good at that that when you come back to the West where women are distracted by so many other things it's not as exciting. Admittedly, this statement is somewhat sexist and narrow, but the essence of his point may indeed be true. Western couples who have VCRs and cable TV probably end up having far less sexual relations. I know this outlook is certainly not politically correct. But the verbal constipation of today's sex and marriage therapists who tell us how to improve our sexual life can be greatly simplified: *minimize distractions from your sex life. Make sex the principal form of recreation and entertainment you engage in; not television and videos.*

Husbands and wives who have nothing else to do in their bedroom have a good time together. They don't just sit and watch television together. They enjoy each other's company. In the same way that pornography represents something which separates the husband and wife because it means focusing on the images that you are seeing and not on each other, TV viewing means we are focusing on some artificial stimulation or artificial entertainment when we could be entertained by one another.

Overemphasis of the Sexual?

I recognize that one of the objections which can be made towards this entire thesis as outlined in this chapter is that it might overemphasize the role of the sexual in every marriage, to the exclusion of perhaps equally important lines of communication. This only allows me to re-emphasize my point. Often I hear complaints from husbands and wives who begin to drift apart from one another, or men and women who go out with each other and won't get married, that they are 'incompatible'. But the only essential form of compatibility necessary for marriage is that he be male and she be female. And this attraction as male and female should not be made subservient or subordinate to any other ancillary, external interests. If this fact is allowed to manifest itself in all its glory, then it will easily supersede and overcome any incompatibilities which might exist. The interest of a man being with a woman and the interest of a woman being with a man is so much greater than whether or not you share common interests.

I know that by now the reader will be raising his or her eyebrows in disbelief. How naive can this crazy Rabbi be? Isn't compatibility at least as important, if not more important, than sexual attraction?

If it were true that other things such as compatibility or commonality of interests were as important as sex then women would stay with women and men would stay with men, because no woman will ever be understood as well by a man as she is understood by another woman. Logic would dictate that men would gravitate towards men, and women would gravitate towards women. Homosexuality is far more logical than heterosexuality. If commonality of interests is paramount, and if what you naturally share in common with another human being becomes the overriding concern in marriage, then we should remain all our days with members of the same sex.

The fact that a woman is willing to leave the confines of her female circle to spend all of her life with a man and share his bed, amidst his male centred interests, and the fact that a man is willing to live life with a woman, is a most unnatural statement. He is only doing it *because she is a woman and he is attracted to her*. She is doing it *because he is a man and she is attracted to him*, not because of the common interests they share. The most important ingredient in every marriage and every relationship is not mutual interests, but *very strong attraction*. What is the principal attraction they have to one another? Is it that they have things in common? They both love literature? Do they marry because of that? No: he is a man and she is a woman. Everything else is insignificant in comparison to that one fact.

Whenever I make the argument publicly that sex is the central ingredient of every marriage, I am inevitably asked,

'Well, what about couples who are too old for sex or physically incapacitated so that they can have no sexual relations. Are they not as close as another married couple?' My response to this is to say that they can be just as close, even after their sex life has ended due to advanced years, as a young married couple with an active sex life. But their closeness is due to the fact that for many years they did have sex together and they were exclusive sexual partners. The closeness they enjoy in old age is directly related to their sexual lives together which preceded this current state. That they are lovers in their old age is due to the fact that they did things that lovers do in their youth. It was not only their many years together and their many shared experiences that contributed to their current unity. Rather, it was primarily their sharing the same bed together for so many years which created such a strong bond that it continues even after the sexual side of their marriage has ceased. An active, vibrant, and fulfilling sexual life together induces a close and enduring state of unity between husband and wife which lasts throughout marriage.

CHAPTER ELEVEN

JEALOUSY IS ESSENTIAL IN EVERY MARRIAGE

ADULTERY IS ABOUT INTENSE JEALOUSY

WE'VE SAID that marriage thrives when a husband and wife make their spouse their only sexual outlet. The focus of sexuality on one person alone makes them very exciting. But another word for intense sexual focus is jealousy. Jealousy overwhelms us and becomes an obsession. The word itself is synonymous with intense focus. In Chapter 5 I made the case that one of the ten commandments of adultery is intense jealousy. Indeed, jealousy is one of the most intense emotions known to man and is as harmful as it is beneficial. Just think of the degree of intensity of emotion which could bring this about: 'Many sociological and criminological studies show that there is a significant correlation between pathological jealousy and homicide. Recent FBI statistics show that around 25,000 murders are committed every year in the United States. Of those that are solved, just over one-third (34.5 per cent) of all the victims were spouses, mistresses, lovers, or rivals of the offenders, with real or suspected sexual infidelity a major precipitating factor.'[1] Can one imagine just how powerful sexual jealousy is that it accounts for one-third of all solved murders in the United States per year! Now imagine what intensity of passion we might have in our marriages if we would turn that jealousy to our advantage and use it as an aphrodisiac in marriage. In this chapter you'll see how.

Your Spouse is More Desirable Than You Think

What can be done to preserve the passion in a marriage? The solution begins with a thorough understanding of the problem.

One of the things that perplexes me most about married people, primarily husbands, who begin to lose interest in their wives, sometimes to business pursuits and other times by focusing attention on other women, is just how attractive and desirable their own partners are. In so many cases, other men would die for the woman that the husband is ignoring. Conversely, the woman whom the husband now pursues and risks utter destruction for is in no way comparable to his wife; not in beauty and not in personality. What has happened and how can the interest be reclaimed?

This answer is simple and straightforward. Although their spouse is very desirable and attractive, *they have forgotten it*. It seems that at times a man's wife can be attractive to everyone but the husband himself. This in itself is not so surprising. As we can become immune to the beauty of our homes, our fortune at having a good job, and living in a rich democratic Western country, we can become indifferent to the people who mean the most to us. As time wears on, we begin to take them for granted. After daily exposure and achieving a feeling of closeness, we sometimes no longer feel the need to impress them, or work to earn their trust, love and confidence, which we feel we already have.

And then something happens. Because of continued neglect, the offended party will have a greater desire to socialize with men or women outside the marriage. Other men also begin to exhibit a greater interest in a woman who they see feels neglected. Every man loves catering to a damsel in distress. The husband notices, and now he wishes to reclaim what is his. He begins to redevelop a previously lost interest in his wife, and things begin to get exciting again. He understands that he can no longer take her for granted, because she is exhibiting a new independence. Basically, what she is saying to him is this: I can get along without you. If you ignore me, I will ignore you. And maybe both of us will still find happiness.

It is not only the fact that he may lose her that causes him to work to re-seduce his wife. Her new-found independence is also exciting and sexy to him. It shows him that she is not as boring as he thought. She is a desirable woman who requires love and attention. Moreover, she needs to feel erotic. She is a sexy being. She has sexual needs that need to be filled, and if her husband won't address them, then she'll find someone who will. In short, she is a temptress. And whereas before he was convinced that, just as he was not interested in his wife, no one else would be either, now he discovers that she is highly desirable and can find hundreds of men to share the night with her. In fact, the moment she shows herself to be available, she has many eager suitors. That this is true is evidenced by what I said earlier, that 78 per cent of husbands who had been unfaithful were convinced, when asked, that their wives were not having affairs even though they were. My wife, they thought, is not interested in sex. And nobody would be interested in her.

The same applies to women of course. I sat once with a famous writer discussing this book. She has also written books on relationships, and we were comparing notes and findings. I spoke to her extensively about my firm belief that passion can be restored into monogamous relationships, and that it was all in the mind. She disagreed vehemently and told me that I was absolutely wrong. Suddenly, she came out with a confession. 'I had an affair,' she said. 'I was married for six years. I loved my husband, but the sex was terrible. I worked in a bookstore at the time, and a man came in one day, and we just hit it off. The two years of my affair with him were the most exciting of my life and actually did much to destroy my marriage. Not because my husband ever found out — he didn't. But because after the excitement I experienced in those two years, and the sensuousness of my lover, my husband simply could not compare. He was a dull bore. I still love him, but I know that now I can never really be excited by him, in comparison to the man I knew.'

But why wasn't it in the mind? Because this was different, she insisted. Her husband simply 'lacked the equipment'. She maintained that he was not nearly as well endowed as her lover. Thus, with all the goodwill in the world, and notwithstanding whatever effort he made, he would still be lacking physiologically.

'Did your husband also have an affair?' I asked. 'After all, if you were running around with someone else, surely he would have felt the sexual depletion in his life and the deterioration of your interest in him. Did he do anything about it?' 'No,' she answered. 'He's simply not the type. He probably didn't notice anything anyway, because he's not that interested in sex.'

Just two weeks later she called to tell me that her life was shaken to the core. She had discovered that her husband had indeed been carrying on an affair over the last year. She had been tipped off by the woman's husband, and she drove around to the woman's place of work and confronted his mistress, who she discovered was very attractive. Her husband's mistress admitted to the affair, and told her at length how she did not desire to be a homebreaker, and hoped that the wife would forgive her. But what could she do? She found the woman's husband the sexiest, most passionate man alive and did not feel that she could give him up. To her he was irresistible.

In the end, her husband decided to return to his wife, and their marriage continues till today, albeit with outstanding problems still seeking resolution. But the point had been proven. So much for lacking the right equipment. So much for being a bore. And so much for not being the kind of man who would ever be interested in an affair. Perhaps if she had recognized all these things about her husband prior to her own affair, she might have salvaged the core and innocence of her marriage. In the event, not being fully aware of his potential, she found passion elsewhere and in the process lost her husband to another woman.

The first step, therefore, in restoring passion in every marriage is to know that: (a) all sexuality is in the mind and can therefore be controlled, and (b) each and every married spouse has the potential to commit adultery, which is indicative of the fact that we are all sexual beings and are thus all innately passionate and exciting.

Jealousy Rekindles Passion

What has happened here is very simple. Whereas before he was not completely aware of, had become desensitized to, something very special that he possessed, circumstances have forced him to take notice. He now remembers that indeed he is married to an attractive woman, a woman whom other men can only envy him for. By attractive, I don't only mean physically attractive. A beautiful person is someone who embodies beautiful character traits. It may be that one begins to notice how loving, caring, and kind one's spouse is. But whatever it is that the spouse begins to notice, it is *jealousy* that reminds them. They are jealous that their spouse is showing an interest in someone else and that other people are expressing a desire to have them. There are few emotions which are as painful. It is taken as a total rejection of everything that one stands for when the person one is married to develops a need to be entertained or flattered by someone outside the marriage. But it cannot be helped. Everyone needs to feel loved.

Did you ever have the experience when rummaging through old clothes which one wishes to discard and donate to a charity, one chances upon an old outfit which has lost its appeal. A close friend who is helping you sift through the old clothing notices the outfit and says that it is lovely, and that if you are throwing it out anyway, they would like to keep it. Suddenly, you're not so sure that you want to get rid of it anymore. Your friend's appreciation for the garment has reawakened your own interest in it as well. But why? Just a moment ago you were adamant that you didn't want it. You were going to throw it out! Ah! But that wasn't because it didn't suit you. You wanted to get rid of it because to you it was *old*, and you had become used to it and bored of it. But to your friend it is brand new. And their excitement about it, coupled with their desire to take it away from you and make it their own, reminds you of just how nice it really is. And suddenly you want it back.

The same applies to becoming weary and bored with one's spouse. The moment someone else manifests an interest in them

We must expend every effort to constantly realize and be reminded of how precious the people with whom we are fortunate enough to share our lives really are. Although jealousy is usually destructive and serves to create unnecessary tension in a marriage, it can also be turned to good. Rather than waiting for the breakdown of a marriage in which each partner begins to scan the horizon for someone else to provide stimulating company, one must induce a perpetual state of jealousy. This in turn will enforce a state in which each spouse will do everything within their ability to continually please and impress their partner, so that they can keep them and have them remain fully in love with them.

Now, don't confuse jealousy with unfaithfulness or being untrustworthy. No marriage could last without a husband and wife being fully confident that their spouse will always remain devoted and loyal. If a wife had to really worry about what her husband was doing out late at night, and if a husband had to be concerned about whom his wife was thinking about as they made love together, both would be driven to insanity, or at the very least, would be miserable. By jealousy in marriage I do not mean that each partner *consciously* seeks to make their partner jealous, or flirts with other people at cocktail parties and the like. This is a desperate action that will cause nothing but pain and acrimony, and as such is destructive to husband and wife alike. Rather, a husband and wife should always be cognizant of the interest shown them by other men and women, even when they are not looking to receive it. The fact is that other men will stare at your wife, and other women will look admiringly at your husband. Be aware of these glances and compliments. Look for them; be conscious of them. Strangers who do not suffer from familiarity with your spouse see them as a woman, and as a man, and they are drawn to them. When you notice this make an effort to re-seduce your spouse so that they are not taken by or drawn to these attractions. But my central thesis in this book is not that we should focus on adultery itself (which hopefully our spouses are never guilty of), but rather on its *possibility*. Every married person should be always aware of the fact that at any moment even your most loving spouse is fully capable of committing adultery and finding a lover. No sense of dedication and devotion to marriage, not even strong religious conviction and a wish to remain loyal to the marital vow, can deter them once things are set in motion. The reason: because well before they define themselves as a husband or a wife, they are first and foremost a man and a woman. Imbedded within them is the *potential* for adultery, and within this potential is the awareness on the part of all external observers that the person to whom you are married, and who you might easily take for granted, is wanted by other people. Others appreciate their sexiness and attractiveness, even if you don't. And as you watch and realize that this best friend of yours who is speaking innocently to your wife is still very much aware of how lovely and attractive she is, a spirit of jealousy should awaken in your bosom as you endeavour to secure your wife's devotion to you, amidst this paying of homage by another man, because you are passionate and excited about her at all times.

Likewise, I believe that it is absolutely healthy that when a husband is sitting at home waiting for his wife he should have to worry about where she is and who she is meeting. When he doesn't worry about things like that it is because he is convinced (a) his wife is not the type to have an affair, meaning she's boring and non-sexual, and (b) no man is interested in her enough for her to have an affair. Every husband and wife should always be consumed with doubt that maybe their spouse is having an affair. This will ensure that (a) they always think about their spouse instead of feeling smug and secure and having the free time to devote to contemplating sexual affairs with others, and (b) their blood will pump with excitement when they are reunited with their spouse, who is a sexy and seductive being.

If a husband goes away on a business trip all the while concerned and worried about what his wife is doing back at home, whom she is seeing, what she is doing at nights, he will spend his time calling her, telling her he loves her and checking up on her instead of pursuing one-night stands. But if he feels smug and secure about his wife's fidelity then he doesn't feel drawn to his wife from that great distance and he feels himself free to pursue extramarital sex. In the same situation if the wife at home is wondering who her husband is seeing while he is away she is manifesting the type of jealousy which binds couples together. We must induce the kind of state where at all times and at all moments we feel drawn to our spouse. When we feel attached then we don't feel free or even desire to seduce others. No wonder then, as I have already said, the great majority of husbands and wives who are having an affair are simultaneously convinced that their spouse is not. They're convinced that their spouse is not sexual and lacks any erotic dimension.

Jealousy Is Like Fire: Destructive But Absolutely Necessary

Ancient Jewish teaching has some negative things to say about jealousy. The Talmud advises that a husband should never become too jealous, since this will only lead to anger and bring tension into the marriage. Jealousy can cause one spouse to treat the other insensitively and constantly question their innocence. Being overly jealous of one's spouse can also lead them to feel claustrophobic, and they might purposely rebel against their imprisonment. All people need their freedom in a relationship. Nevertheless, the understanding that jealousy might lead a man directly into another woman's arms, or vice versa, has often been misconstrued as meaning that there should never be any jealousy over one's spouse. Books that describe in detail the sexual permissiveness that raged in the 1960s, such as Gay Talese's *Thy Neighbour's Wife*, are united in proclaiming how so many couples in that explosive era felt themselves to be enlightened because they could transcend 'petty' jealousies and willingly give over their spouses to other sexual partners, and even watch. The celebrated philosopher Bertrand Russell had a similar arrangement with his wife whereby each could have any lover they wished and they would even tell each other about it afterwards. Justifying this strange arrangement he wrote: 'A man or woman who has been thwarted sexually is apt to be full of envy; this generally takes the form of moral condemnation of the more fortunate.'[2] But such ideas are not only unholy, but vapid and stupid. How foolish! A lack of jealousy betrays a lack of love. We all seek to protect those things which we love, and desire that they always remain attached to us. And would these same 'enlightened' free advocates of open marriage also exchange their children as willingly as they exchange their spouse? If one of your best friends told you that they liked your child more than their own, and would it be all right to swap, is it enlightened to exchange? If we love someone, we seek to protect and possess.

This is also why open marriages, whereby husbands and wives seek to transcend jealousy, always fail miserably and lead to much heartache and misery. Russell did not believe in jealousy. However, when his wife Dora had a child by another man he left her, later commenting: 'My capacity for forgiveness, and what might be called Christian love, was not equal to the demands I was making on it . . . I was blinded by theory.'[3] Their daughter Kathleen Tait pithily remarked about her parents' strange marriage, 'Calling jealousy deplorable had not freed them from it . . . both found it hard to admit that the ideal had been destroyed by the old-fashioned evils of jealousy and infidelity.'[4] Similarly, Gay Talese describes the reaction of one husband who had been persuaded to indulge in open marriage upon discovering that his wife had had sex with the advocate: 'Convinced that the balance and order of his life had been destroyed, a vengeful John Bullaro quietly plotted the murder of John Williamson and also contemplated his own suicide . . .'[5]

In the book of Proverbs, King Solomon declares that 'one thing opposite the other did God create'. This encapsulates a very profound Jewish thought, namely that everything in life has both a good, positive dimension and an evil, negative dimension. Good things can be used for evil purposes, and bad things can be used for good purposes. Witness the fact that in the Bible God is constantly referred to as being a jealous God, as in 'your God is a jealous God'. This certainly suggests a positive connotation to the phenomenon of jealousy. The marriage relationship between a man and woman is meant to reflect the relationship that exists between God and the Jewish people in general, and God and man in particular. The proof that God is possessive of the Jewish people and loves them is that He is jealous of them, and cannot tolerate their worshipping foreign gods and idols.

The same is true of a husband and wife. Jealousy can be very positive and is actually a weathervane to measure the sexual attraction, life, and possessiveness that still exists within a marriage. A husband who isn't jealous of his wife's smothering stares at another man has either cast his eyes on another woman himself, and is happy for the licence to chase his new prey, or at the very least has already reconciled himself to the demise of his marriage. The same applies to a wife.

Then there are those things which one does not share with anyone, such as one's most intimate thoughts. The same is true, of course, and infinitely more so, of one's spouse. A spouse that does not feel a profound sense of hurt when they witness an interest being expressed by their husband and wife in another man or woman must question the degree of their love and the state of their relationship.

The rule to remember is this: most of us are jealous without even knowing it, and we must seek to expose this feeling in ways beneficial to the marriage. This does not mean that we should force our spouses into compromising situations with other men or women in order to fire our jealousy. It does mean that we should constantly think about the desirability of our own spouse to other people, and carefully observe the appreciation shown of our wife's femininity, and our husband's masculinity. When, for instance, a husband looks at a very pretty woman and thinks to himself how lucky her husband is to have this woman as a wife and instantly feels attracted to her, upon pondering such thoughts the husband should immediately think to himself that the same thought is probably going through countless other men's minds when they see his own wife.

How Jealousy Works

Rachel, who was a friend of mine, left her husband after one year of marriage. By her own admission he was an extremely caring, considerate, and loving husband. But, she said, he was a total bore. 'We have nothing in common. I love going out, he loves staying at home. I love drinking and partying and need always to be around people, he loves quiet evenings with the two of us alone.' I was trying to keep the marriage together. 'Is the sentiment you are expressing subjective? Is it personal to you?' I asked. 'NO,' she said. 'He has no close friends. To be frank, no one really likes him. Everyone finds him a complete and utter bore.'

Her husband was a man for whom I had a lot of respect. He was not boring, so much as very studious and serious, an academic who specialized in Egyptology. I invited him to Oxford to discuss his predicament, and at the same time asked him to deliver a lecture at our weekly Sabbath dinner which is attended by about ninety students. The students loved him and found him fascinating, and being young and handsome, there was more than one young lady who went over to speak to him about his subject after he had concluded. The next week, his estranged wife came to my office, and when I deliberately told some of the students who were present that this was the wife of the man who had lectured the previous week, a few of them went over to her to tell her what a remarkable lecture he delivered, and how great an expert he is in his subject. Two of the young women said to her, 'Oh! He was fascinating.' She couldn't believe that they were talking about the same man. It took other women finding him interesting and attractive to convince her that he was.

An almost identical story took place with Alan, another close friend, who had been going out with the same woman for two years, but could not bring himself to propose. His girlfriend, Julie, asked if they could come down together for the weekend so we could discuss the matter together. She is a celebrated BBC political correspondent, well known to all who listen to the radio, and I asked her if she would speak to the students about her work. On the way down from London, he insulted her terribly by insinuating, as he had told me directly, that his problem was that he just did not find her physically attractive enough. 'I guess she is all right-looking,' he told me, 'but certainly not beautiful.' She arrived in tears and refused to sit near him at the large table which was filled with people. She sat inbetween two young men, both of whom had heard of her, and both of whom felt very privileged to enjoy her conversation through the evening. It became clear halfway through the evening that Thomas, on her right, who was a dashing and highly intelligent American Rhodes scholar, was very interested in her and, without knowing that she had come down with someone else, asked if he might drive all the way to London to take her out to dinner. As this went on, Alan was growing incensed. He noticed that every time Julie bent over, Thomas followed every contour of her body (every one else noticed it as well). While Julie certainly was not flirtatious and did not make a conscious effort to make Alan jealous, she still had Thomas, a young man very popular among the Oxford women, in her thrall. This radically changed Alan's thinking about Julie's attractiveness and the next night, when the Sabbath was over, he proposed to her. Six months later they were married (and to this day seem very happy).

I told Alan after the wedding that the secret of his retaining passion in his marriage is always to recall that evening, and to see the attractive woman in his wife.

Putting Jealousy to Work within Marriage

I've explained that the reason jealousy can excite passion in a marriage is that one partner is suddenly reminded that their spouse is not merely a husband or wife but is also a sexually desired and desirable man or woman. If we could go beyond looking at our husbands or wives in a mundane sense and see them instead as sexual partners, sexual beings, then we could prevent our marriages from growing stale. If we could treat our spouses as though they were new then we would always see the relationship as new and we would always be forced to retain our spouses' attraction by winning them over constantly, and by showing them undying attention and affection.

Note that in the Bible there is not a word for 'wife'. It simply doesn't exist. Rather, the expression which is always used to convey the idea of a wife is this: 'The *woman* of'; but never does it say the *wife* of. And the reason is because a woman never becomes a wife. She always remains a *woman*. Even after you marry her there is no guarantee that she will remain faithful and loyal. She is a woman, not a wife. And whereas one might be able to rely on the faithfulness of a wife, one cannot trust a sensual woman to remain loyal. The only woman that remains loyal to her husband is the one who is constantly seduced by her husband and is treated in a loving and caring way. *No woman ever becomes a wife.*

When you first begin to date you're on your best behaviour, trying to impress the guy or girl you've taken out, trying your best to win their affections and attention and to make sure you look attractive for them, and this makes it exciting. Your mind, your emotions, your language and your eloquence are all engaged in trying to win the affections and favours of this person you're out to impress. But as time goes on, it becomes accepted that as you are already married they no longer have to be impressed or invited into your life. When someone else comes along, the excitement returns and the hunt is on again. However, if one is continually aware that the *potential for adultery* exists, then one will constantly be engaged in winning over the affections of one's spouse.

Therefore adultery does have a positive element as a possibility, at least; it is not purely negative. If the concept of adultery did not exist then we might take our husbands and wives for granted. But if the person remembers that at any time the marriage partner could choose to go outside the marriage to find sex, excitement, passion and romance elsewhere then he will not be able to take them for granted and therefore the feeling of newness will remain. Just as before we convince someone to marry us we are well aware that they need to be impressed with us, because they have so many other suitors to whom they can turn, the same applies even after marriage. The potential for adultery exists in each and every one of us, throughout our married life. And we must do our utmost to satisfy the legitimate sexual and loving needs of our spouse, if they are not to turn elsewhere to find them.

It is through utilizing jealousy, therefore, that we can further make our marriages into an illicit affair. Every man or woman involved in an adulterous affair lives in an intense state of jealousy since they cannot dominate their lover completely, and they know that their lover has a second life of which they are not a part. We must work to induce this same state of jealousy in marriage.

SOURCES — CHAPTER ELEVEN

1. Robert L Barker, *The Green-Eyed Marriage*, 1987
2. Bertrand Russell, *Why I am Not a Christian*, 1957
3. Bertrand Russell, *Autobiography*, Vol 1, 1967
4. Kathleen Tait, *My Father Bertrand Russell*, 1976
5. Gay Talese, *Thy Neighbour's Wife*, 1981

CHAPTER TWELVE

TRUST IN MARRIAGE

ADULTERY IS ABOUT TRUST

In the man, jealous aggression tends to concentrate on the partner. The woman more frequently extends the aggression to the rival and third parties!
Daniel Lagache, *La Jalousie Amoureuse* (1947)

'THE POSSIBILITY of adultery', as I have called it throughout this book, is a double-edged sword and in this respect the methods which I have advocated to use the possibility of adultery to remind us that our spouses are sexual beings, and thus to recapture the passion and excitement in our marriages and relationships, trap us in a powerful and very hurtful Catch 22. On the one hand, we need jealousy and the recognition of the sexual attractiveness of our spouses in order to maintain ongoing newness in our relationships since this forces us to win their attention every day of the year. On the other hand, this process leads to hurt and pain as we re-examine our own sexual appeal, and wonder what it is that our spouses see in others that we may not possess, whether we are their equals, and finally, how serious and deeply felt is their attraction to the other.

The Catch 22 of Jealousy

Gay Talese tells the true story of John Bullaro, a man who, feeling bored with his wife, persuaded her to engage in open marriage, thus granting him the licence of taking multiple sexual partners. His wife at first hesitated. But after watching her husband take numerous women to bed, she finally consented and submitted to another man. This experience had a profound effect upon him. To be sure, it made her once again into a sexually desirable wife. But it also caused him to lose her. 'Bullaro felt for the first time in his marriage that Judith was no longer his . . . Though she was cheerful and dutiful around the house, and kindly towards the children, she seemed preoccupied with her private thoughts, and at night instead of going to bed with him she stayed up late reading . . . Suddenly and ironically, she was becoming the kind of woman he had long idealised in his fantasies – the daring carefree woman he had searched for . . . the impulsive, sexually liberated woman . . .'[1]

The major problem with the plan advocated above, effective as it might be, of using jealousy to recapture the passion in a marriage, is that it entails the spouse who harbours the jealousy experiencing deep pain as well. As we begin to recognize how our spouses are deeply desirable to members of the opposite sex, how they too are naturally sexually attracted to other men and women, and that attraction increases exponentially commensurate with the degree to which they feel unappreciated or ignored, we cannot help but feel terribly hurt as well. As we come to terms with our own inability to have our spouse focus all their sexual attention and energy exclusively on us, we may simultaneously entertain a fear that we are being judged in the process, being compared to other men and women, and found wanting. Maybe we are not as handsome, maybe we are not as sexy, maybe we are not as loving. From there it is but a short step to actually fearing losing our spouse, as we are discarded in favour of someone better. This terrible fear can become a self-fulfilling prophecy, since the spouse loses confidence in him/herself and is no longer as sexually alive or attractive.

The problems caused by the terrible 'Catch 22' of marriage

are real and beg for resolution. On the one hand, a marriage, in its most complete and exciting form, involves partners who are aware of their sexuality and their attractiveness to other men and women. Their sexuality would naturally pull them in a direction outside of the marriage, thus necessitating their spouses' constant attention so that they might be retained, and remain 'won over' and totally devoted to their spouses. This is the method I have been advocating throughout the book as the surest possible means by which to mentally perceive your spouse as exciting and new. On the other hand, this state of affairs leads to an inevitable state of jealousy which, while exciting, passionate and even necessary, can also be so painful that it can remove the will to live from a man or woman. It eats away at the necessary trust which must exist in every marriage in order to make it a viable enterprise.

I do not know of any easy solution to this dilemma. One might even argue that this tension drawn from unresolved conflict – on the one hand wanting to possess our spouses sexually completely, and on the other, wanting them to be sexy and desirable in general, and by extension to others – is necessary to maintain a healthy and impassioned intimacy. Perhaps the very creativity in our sex life is derived from this unresolved conflict. We could argue that it is this struggle itself which ensures that our sex life will never become stale and complacent, but always alive and refreshing. How could it? We are constantly hovering between two extremes.

There will be those who argue that the rule suggested in this chapter is too constraining to live by. Why after all, if my spouse is overly jealous, should I have to suffer? The instinctive reaction is, 'let them grow up a bit, instead of my life being infringed upon. I can't live feeling imprisoned.' (This is a sentiment expressed primarily by men.)

The Oxford University L'Chaim Society of which I am director is supported in its entirety by private donations. Some of its supporters are prominent international businessmen, with hundreds of employees working for them. I was once privy to an argument that ensued between two of my closest married friends over the issue of hiring a secretary. The husband was happy for his principal assistant of ten years when she got married to an American and moved to the States, but was very sad to lose her. His wife also worked in the business, in charge of their publicity and public relations department. Together they scoured all the employment agencies in search of a suitable replacement. One day, they thought they found the perfect replacement. A woman's CV that seemed too good to be true came through the fax machine. In subsequent interviews with Henry, she proved to be the perfect candidate whom they thought they would never find. He wanted to hire her instantly.

But his wife objected, and told him under no circumstances would she allow him to hire her. The woman was young, very attractive, and dressed highly seductively. In her first interview she even came with one of the middle buttons in her blouse open, thus exposing her bra. The wife insisted that she knew that type of woman, and that she had left her button undone intentionally. The man and his wife had a huge fight over the matter. She called me in tears and in the midst of the conversation he grabbed the telephone and told me that he is a generous husband and father, allowing for his wife's extravagant tastes. 'But someone's got to pay all these bills, Shmuley, and I need an efficient assistant. This woman is perfect, and I am not prepared to give her up just because of my wife's insane jealousies.' He was adamant. 'Let my wife go and see a psychiatrist. I am not giving up this secretary.'

Of all the irrational elements to be found within the behaviour of a spouse, jealousy is the most troublesome of all. I have met many husbands and wives who find themselves utterly unable to deal with their spouse's jealousy. They treat it as something which betrays a deep character flaw in their spouse, something which they must 'work at, or it will destroy our marriage'. They rarely consider the possibility that perhaps, regardless of whether or not their spouse is justified in insisting that they not speak to 'so and so', maybe they should abstain, just to preserve the peace of the marriage, and to accommodate their spouse and make them happy. No, this jealousy has got to change and their husband/wife will just have to accept it.

The very serious flaw in this thinking is that it will not change. I have never yet encountered a case history where a seriously jealous spouse has changed their attitude toward their partner's interactions with certain individuals. The fact is that the confident and flirtatious way that some men and women speak to our spouse, and the way in which our spouse responds to them, just rubs us the wrong way, and it always will. Worse still, the attitude that 'my spouse is being irrational and therefore I will not accommodate them' is predicated on the idea that we are not obliged to accommodate their seemingly irrational wishes. It betrays a belief that one must conform to the desires of one's spouse only so long as they make sense. What you must do in this situation is think back and ask yourself why it is that your spouse feels so insecure. Have you hurt them significantly in the past? Have you had an affair? And if you haven't, maybe you have shown too much attention to someone in the past that gave your spouse good cause to be jealous. Or maybe there wasn't any stranger in particular on whom you concentrated but just generally neglected your spouse. In the final analysis, a spouse will not be overly jealous unless you have given them ample cause for worry, or alternatively, destroyed, or failed to nurture the confidence they have in themselves. You may not have shown your own spouse *enough* attention. Maybe they feel neglected and unloved. Maybe they feel that *to you* they are no longer attractive, and thus are made to feel insecure by any close association you have with a member of the opposite sex. No man or woman who feels passionately in love with their spouse, and that their spouse positively adores them will feel overly jealous by the presence of a stranger. Jealousy, like most human emotions, is governed by the rules of cause and effect, and something, however subtle, is causing your spouse to be uncontrollably jealous.

I also firmly advocate that the jealousies of our spouse must be accommodated, tied as they are to their essential masculinity and femininity. Your husband is jealous of the close association you have with your driving instructor because your husband is a man. Don't ask him why. That's the way men are. If you think he's being irrational, then discuss it with him. Try and make him see your point of view. But if he won't, then find a different instructor. Your husband, along with his seemingly irrational desires, should come first.

Similarly, I told my friend in the above situation, your wife's jealousy obviously results from her being your wife. That's the way some women are. She wants you to herself and feels insecure when you will be spending more time in your office with a woman who she feels does not respect your marital commitments than you will be spending at home with her. To be sure, your business is important. But your wife is *more* important. Accommodate her on this request and she will show you everlasting appreciation. But don't tell her to stifle her essential femininity and the natural love, and hence jealousy, which she feels towards her husband. Jealousy as we have said in the foregoing chapters is essential to marriage and so is trust. Your wife must trust you in order to love you. Without this there can be no passion.

Every husband and wife knows that there are few things as sexy and rejuvenating to a marriage, yet also as deeply painful, as to watch one's spouse become the object of desire to a member of the opposite sex or to be interested in an unfamiliar member of the opposite sex. Yet, it is also a fact that when this attraction begins to manifest itself the hurt and pain can be unbearable and there is nothing as painful in the entire world. It is not adultery that is hurting us but the *possibility of adultery* inherent in every marriage, since every marriage is comprised not just of husbands and wives, but of two sexual beings with innate sexual needs.

But we must learn to thrive upon this tension and contradiction. If one stops to think for just a brief moment, one will immediately conclude that these two contradictory emotions must always act against one another, opposing each other. When we are married, on the one hand, we cannot become so complacent about the feelings, emotions, and sexual needs of our spouse that we believe we possess them entirely, and can thus take them for granted. On the contrary, we must feel in the fifteenth year of marriage, the way we felt on the fifteenth day of dating: that if we do not treat our partner well, they will leave us and find someone else. The bond of marriage is tenuous and is offset by our powerful sexual instincts which are manifest specifically in the face of neglect. On the other hand, marriage cannot exist if there is no strong bond created between husband and wife and if they are constantly flirting with other men and women, and contemplating sexual affairs with them. A balance is necessary, whereby they are not so much 'ours' that we take them for granted, but they are not so distant that we lose them to someone else in thought, speech, or action.

The Bond of Trust

The healthiest resolution to this paradox and problem is that of trust. So long as we know, not just believe, but know, in the core of our being, that our spouse loves us and will always remain loyal and faithful, then we can remain fully aware of the sexual attraction they pose to others outside of the marriage, and how they themselves are naturally attracted to others, without fearing that the marriage will be compromised by this attraction. It is imperative, therefore, to root out all forms of adultery from our midst. I realize this is easier said than done, but it is vital if we are to instil faith and trust in our marriages, and not become insanely jealous, devouring each other in the process. With trust we gain the best of both worlds: the constant attraction posed by the knowledge that the people we are married to are wonderfully attractive to all who see them, coupled with the flattery that amidst that desirability to others they choose to remain steadfastly loyal to us, in every way.

This is what adulterous lovers enjoy. Amidst the tenuous and unpredictable state of their relationship, they trust each other with their compromising secrets even more than they trust their own spouse. This incredible trust helps them to maintain a passionate and devoted atmosphere of attraction. Marriage deserves no less. Put your spouse first in all matters. Make them feel that they never have to worry about you being interested in someone else. The result will be that they give themselves over to you completely and you will help make your marriage into an illicit affair.

SOURCES — CHAPTER TWELVE

1. Gay Talese, *Thy Neighbour's Wife*, 1981

CHAPTER THIRTEEN

MARRIED COUPLES: PARTNERS OR LOVERS?

ADULTERY IS ABOUT ATTRACTION

'When we are alone in our bedroom, with our bodies pressed firmly against each other, we rarely talk about the weather or where to go for dinner.'

M Y FRIENDS Jeffrey and Susie Goldstein are happily married. However, he loves football. His wife seems to have no interest in the sport whatsoever. The same thing applies in my own marriage. I used to devote a lot of time to sports but Debbie is not interested. I love video games, Debbie is convinced they are immature. Why would a woman marry a man whose passion is football? Why not marry someone who has the same natural or socialized interests as yourself?

Take a look at courting or dating with a view to marriage. What people seem to search for most is compatibility. They maintain that if you have nothing in common, no commonality of interests, then your marriage will be a disaster. People tell me all the time that they are in the midst of going out with someone but, although they are in love, they refuse to marry the person in question because 'we simply don't have enough in common. We'll run out of things to talk about.' They are attracted to someone, but they fear that their marriage together will be doomed. They have nothing in common. In this scenario, I usually tell the man or woman in question that if you are correct, and compatibility is all-important, then it is best to marry someone of the same sex. Women have more naturally in common with women and vice versa. If marriage should be predicated first and foremost on the commonality of interests and compatibility then men should marry men and women should marry women. Heterosexuality is totally illogical. It is irrational. Why should you love someone who is the opposite?

Attraction versus Common Interests

Let's look at a scenario: boys and girls attend the same nursery. At first they are all happy to play with each other. Then they begin to grow up. By the time they get to junior school the boys are always playing with the boys. They are rumbling on the floor and pretending to shoot each other. It is undoubtedly true that by this time little girls have more in common with other little girls than boys. In his book, *The New Sexual Revolution*, Robert Peel offers impressive and seemingly incontrovertible evidence from various scientific studies that a boy's attraction to dump-trucks and guns, and a girl's to dolls and playhouses, are innate and not socially conditioned. Thus, children gravitate toward members of the same sex since they innately enjoy the same activities together. As they grow older and mature, however, they begin reaching across the divide. Sexual attraction begins to supersede common interests, boys find themselves searching for a girlfriend rather than just spending time with other boys, while the need to look attractive assumes great importance to girls. In their pubescent years, suddenly, their attraction to the opposite sex assumes a permanent and predominant role over the common interests they share with members of their own sex. Thus, a man and woman find themselves spending the great majority of their time with husbands, boyfriends, and wives, rather than with friends of the same sex.

This is a very important point to absorb, because one of the fundamental reasons for the tremendous breakdown in marriage today and the dramatic rise in infidelity is that we have called the wrong shots. We've drawn the wrong conclusions. We have made commonality of interests more important than attraction. *Stated in other words, one of the principal reasons for the loss of passion in marriage is that we look upon our spouse first and foremost as a partner sharing our interests in life, rather than our lover.* This same mistake is not repeated in adultery, where lovers treat each other like sweethearts. We must return to the time in our lives when we saw in our spouse a sexual partner, rather than someone with whom we share so much in common. I have said earlier and I will say it again: in marriage you are meant to be lovers not music or botany lovers.

The irrefutable truth is that we get married because of attraction and the most important thing in marriage is sexual attraction. Commonality of interests is completely subordinate to the idea of attraction. We have put commonality of interests on a par with attraction, and we are therefore divorcing more and more because no common interest is sufficiently strong to keep a man and a woman together over a significant length of time. Sexual attraction, however, one of the most potent forces known to man, has that power. When I interviewed Shere Hite at the Oxford Union, she told me that the single most important finding of her report on male sexuality was the discovery that over 80 per cent of men do not marry the women they are most passionately in love with. Rather, they pass over the woman to whom they are most attracted in favour of the woman they have the most in common with. Unfortunately for them, those who do so also statistically stand the highest rate of divorce. Men and women are *not* attracted to one another because they have similar interests, but because they feel sexual magnetism that draws them irresistibly towards each other.

The Differences Between the Sexes Preserve Their Attraction

Once you begin to focus on the necessity of attraction, you understand why Judaism defined different roles and modes of dress for men and women. It was not, as has been constantly suggested, to imprison women, or to make them subordinate to men. It was to preserve the attraction between the sexes. Men and women were given alternative roles. Judaism maintains that men and women should never come to the point where they are best friends. An attraction should always remain. They should never be deadened to each other's sexuality. They should never be immune to the simple and powerful fact that they are different, which constitutes the reason for their attraction. Nowadays, when I tell men that the most important ingredient in a relationship is attraction, they dispute my claim. They speak of numerous women to whom they are not attracted in the slightest, and who are just very good friends. But is this progress? Is a society where men cannot emotionally discern the difference between men and women healthy? Is it productive to blur the line that separates the sexes? The whole idea of attraction is that you are not like each other. You are different. Those who are perceived as the most enlightened in society today are those who combat with all their might the belief, and sometimes even the evidence, that men and women differ in anything but their physiology.

When my wife's Chassidic Jewish girlfriends come to Oxford, looking modestly feminine with their long sleeves and long skirts, the male students ask if they can take them out. I always say, they're Chassidic, I doubt they'll date unless you're serious about getting married. But why the sudden attraction? These are girls who are brought up in an environment totally different to the average Oxford student. So why are the men consistently interested in them? *Because they look different.* They dress in a very feminine way. They look like women. And that's the attraction. Would the men be prepared to marry them? Probably not, they would say, they are not from the same background, they don't have a university degree, they're too religious, and so on. But their femininity is still very appealing, in the same way that stark masculinity in the form of a male stripper, or a strong athlete can be very attractive.

Friendship and Marriage; Friendship in Marriage

In Judaism, the laws that separate the sexes were designed not to preserve modesty, but to preserve *the distinctions* between men and women. What woman would be flattered to hear that their male friends are not remotely sexually interested in them, or don't even notice that they are female? There was a student at Oxford who was engaged to be married and had her closest male friend come to visit her from the United States. They went, with the other fiancé's permission, on a trip to a different city. They shared a hotel room, although they had separate beds. I said to both of them, 'The two of you are engaged. Why did you allow such a stupid thing?' She replied, 'My fiancé trusts me and this person is my closest friend. We weren't going to do anything.' But is this flattering? Do you want to know that you are undesirable to another person, your male friend? Is it good that in our society, men and women have become immune to each other's sexuality?

One of our L'Chaim Society committee members was the kind of girl whom all of the men would come to talk to about their emotional problems. She was every guy's best friend, but never anyone's girlfriend. She walked into my office one day and closed the door, saying she wanted to tell me about something she was upset about. I told her to open the door, for it is a Jewish law that a man and woman who are not married cannot be secluded together in a room. 'I'm a married man and you are single so we can't be in a room with a closed door,' I told her. She started to cry. I asked her what the matter was. It is a law, I am not trying to offend you. She said, 'I'm not crying because you offended me, but because that is the most beautiful thing that anyone has ever told me. You are the first person who ever treated me like a woman.' Most men who had looked upon her had made her feel as if they were looking at another man instead of a woman. Everyone desires to be attractive.

There is nothing flattering about being deadened to a man or woman's sexual appeal. It is fine for men and women to be friends but they have to do so in a modest environment, where they don't have to overlook natural attraction to the point of immunity. Pretending that your female friends are not attractive is not complimentary. There are reasons for the centrality of modest dress in the Jewish religion, specifically women wearing feminine garb as opposed to clothing indistinguishable from a man's. You are not supposed to be the same. It doesn't mean women should be subordinate to men, but that they should retain their essential differences. I believe that husbands should not become best friends with other women and wives with other men, not only because it may be improper, but because it is still sending the wrong signals even if nothing happens. It means that you are not seeing other people as women and men. It can't be healthy for a marriage. Remember, marriage thrives on the differences, and hence the attraction, between men and women. Two lovers in an adulterous affair might not share anything in common. One might love museums, the other mud-wrestling. They might be as different as the sun and the moon. But they still long to be together and share the same bed because they are consumed by sexual fire and passion. Which just goes to show the extent to which sexual attraction, not common interests, is important in marriage.

When husbands and wives are having difficulties in their marriages, and they are not sexually interested in one another, they often don't address the problem directly. They will go to a cinema, a play, or a concert together. Is that why you got married, because you both love music? There is no passion in your marriage because you haven't seen enough of Tom Cruise lately? All the other elements are subordinate to the attraction between male and female. Forget the damned film. Do something about your love life. Don't go shopping together. Do as two lovers would. Go to the most luxurious hotel room, jump into the jacuzzi together and light your spouse's fire. Give them a sensual massage that will send them to the moon. But don't just sit and listen to the London Philharmonic Orchestra together. You are lovers, plain and simple. Not *culture* lovers. I maintain that if a husband and wife devoted just half as much time to their sexual encounters as they do to their mutual social calendars, they would have the greatest marriage on earth.

Of course, commonality of interest is important. You like to sit on beaches together. But recognize that these activities are ancillary to your marriage, not central. Two lovers committing adultery spend most of their time either in the hotel room or looking forward to going to the hotel room, not the art gallery. Don't convince yourself for a moment that because you both love sitting on the back of a horse you will therefore stay together forever. The essential differences which separate the male and female have to exist. There have to be certain things which separate the sexes at all times. You will never be infatuated or in love with someone because you are compatible. That's all rubbish. You might do business with them, you might go on trips with them. But you won't share their bed every single night because of that. You will do so because of attraction and attraction only. It is not just physical. Spiritual or emotional attraction is a desire for feminine warmth or masculine warmth. Women and men are different and the total of the differences helps to preserve their gravitation towards each other.

What is Attraction?

What is beautiful? When a man and woman are sitting together in a crowded room, and he looks at her and she blushes. That is what attraction is. It is like a magnet, displaying its power even from a distance. I think it is wonderful that men and women pray in separate spaces in the synagogue. Why? We have to create a sexual society, where men and women *do* feel attracted to one another and this is achieved when a certain degree of distance and separation, hence mystique, is maintained. The only way that you can wake up to the same face for the rest of your life without getting bored is if that attraction remains. Could you share the same room and life with your best friend? Wouldn't it get tedious? Why do we need to have more than one friend? Because we grow tired of the same person over and over again. But the same is not true of an exciting sexual companion. This is why, whereas we feel we need more than one friend, and sometimes many, the same is not true about having a spouse. If it is fiery and passionate, we are more than content with just one.

The key to marriage is to be reminded at all times that the husband you are married to is not simply a husband but a *man*, your wife not simply a wife but a *woman*. It is to be reminded of the femininity and masculinity of the genders at all times. In essence, the secret to a thriving marriage is the ability always to see the man in your husband and the woman in your wife.

The greatest proof of this is that when you are engaged in an intimate act with your spouse, you are not conversing and you are sharing little in common. The only thing you are doing is celebrating that one of you is male and the other female, and therefore you both have favours to offer each other.

CHAPTER FOURTEEN

NOURISHING A MARRIAGE

ADULTERY BOOSTS THE EGO; AS SUCH IT IS AN ACT OF RE-CREATION

IN ONE OF its most significant and famous pronouncements, the Bible maintains that God created man in His own image. From time immemorial, theologians of all denominations have debated what exactly this means. To me the application of this teaching is in everyday life, and its meaning is clear: in the same way that God is a Creator, so is man. Just as God creates and takes life, man, too, is endowed with that power, and I don't mean by having children or committing murder. Every time we show someone extravagant attention and affection, we make them feel important, and we really and truly 'create them' and bring them to life. Those who are ignored or unloved feel as though they are not alive. Our emotions, then, have the power to elicit an identical response. And when a husband shows his wife that to him she is the sexiest woman in the world, this is what she truly becomes. She thinks of herself as a highly attractive and desirable woman, and acts the part. She starts dressing better, carrying herself better, and attracts the stares of all the men around her.

It is no wonder then that nearly all the books on adultery which I have read point out that one of the leading signs in detecting your partner's infidelity is if they suddenly dress much better than ever before, and have found renewed confidence in themselves. The books also point out that this applies particularly to women. In other words, their husbands were ignoring them, so they didn't care how they looked and how they carried themselves. But suddenly they have a lover who finds them alluring and attractive, wants to have sex with them, and they thus begin to live and act the part. And even their husbands notice and find them more attractive.

Conversely, when he fools around with other women, even if his wife is the world's most beautiful woman, her looks will go to pot. Adultery is the quickest form of murder because you show someone that they don't matter. Their feelings and hurt are of no consequence to you, and also you have traded them in for someone you obviously find more attractive and alluring. To you, then, it is as if your spouse is dead.

The same applies in marriage. You must believe and accept that lurking deep within each and every husband and wife is a passionate, sensual, and sexy being. If the person you are married to has a heart in their breast that beats, and if they are not in a coma, then they also have a hidden, rudimentary fire burning in their hearts, waiting to be uncovered. For those who do not appear overtly so (and with the passage of time we naturally become bored with even the most beautiful and handsome partner), this must be brought to the fore by the incredible love, affection, and desire which only you can show your spouse. When you show them that you think they are sexy and appealing, then they will dress that way and act that way.

The ultimate definition of love, I believe, is one person ascribing significance and totally enhancing the existence of another human being through their affection for them. When you love someone, their wishes become your wishes, their delights become your delights, their pleasures become your pleasures. Anything else is not love but selfishness. Love gives us the ability to put ourselves second to someone else, to make ourselves number two, thus defying our essential human nature to be selfish and to put ourselves first.

If you live on this planet ninety years, but no one ever takes notice of you, it is as if you do not exist. And neither do you feel as if you are ever really alive. The ultimate negation of another person's existence is to ignore them. Conversely, the ultimate affirmation of their existence is to love and take notice of them. And commensurate with the degree of love which they are shown is the amount of confidence they will have.

This is the enormous power of love. Through loving someone intensely we can call forth their existence from nothingness, playing the role of creator, bringing them to life. And by cheating on them and in effect ignoring them, we play the role of a creator who takes life. Whereas love enhances and uplifts our spouse's existence, adultery degrades and destroys it. There is no simpler or more profound way of putting it. This simple truth captures the essence of adultery and why it constitutes the most serious breach of the marital bond.

The opposite extreme of ignoring your spouse is showing them extravagant love by always attempting to accommodate their every wish, even when it may not make sense to you. Extravagant love means always seeking to fulfil every desire your spouse makes which itself induces a state of passionate desire on the part of the one receiving the love.

The Problem With Marriage

Upon assuming my responsibilities in Oxford as Rabbi at the age of twenty-one, I was convinced that the greatest challenge to marriage was the simple difficulty of two people, each accustomed to their own way of life, now sharing that life with another person, making room for one another, and somehow accommodating each other's aspirations. But as time developed, I began to understand that the real problem was sexual. Why was it, after all, that when people dated before marriage they were far more willing to bend and give in to one another, just in order to impress each other? Why did they make it such an important point to curb their tempers and always be considerate? And why was it so much more difficult after marriage? The answer of course is that after they are married, they are usually less interested in impressing each other, and thus do not make so great an effort. Stated in other words, and using an all too familiar cliché, when living and sharing a life together, a husband and wife can take each other for granted. They may not look forward to the love and sexual favours that they once wished to discover, and thus do not make a commensurate effort to win those favours.

Human sexuality is one of the most beautiful and satisfying activities known to man. It is magnificent in marriage to have a couple give up all the petty arguments in life and just learn to get along, in order that they may spend all their days in each other's arms, rather than bicker and fight. Is there indeed anyone reading this book who can explain why a husband or wife would rather argue over dinner not being ready, and refuse to apologize after an outburst, thereby ending up spending the night in separate bedrooms, rather than falling into each other's embrace and experiencing an evening of love and bliss? The only explanation can be that sometimes we just do not value that embrace and that act of love enough. If we desired sex with our spouse badly enough, we would do anything to get it. And because we forget its sublimity and refuse to recognize that it is far more beautiful and precious than anything which the couple can be arguing about, we continue in our stubborn ways, fighting instead of making up. Hence the need for passion. Witness the most common complaint that an aggrieved wife has of her husband: 'Why are you showing that other woman all the attention and not me? Why do you apologize to her and not me? Why do you buy her gifts, and not me?' The answer of course is that he unfortunately is bored with of you. And until he gets his head together and undertakes the steps necessary to restore sexual interest and passion in his married life, he will continue to show his mistress and potential lovers the attention that normally would be reserved for his wife.

The conclusion that can be drawn from this point is that far from sex being our enemy, it is our friend, and must be used to our advantage. The same cause for adultery, namely a desire for passion and sex, can also be used as the main pretext for a husband and wife to begin to treat one another, once again, with love, caring and honesty.

The Essential Elements of a Relationship

Let us examine this in more detail. There are four ingredients and recognitions essential to every thriving relationship: firstly that the person we are married to is not just a spouse or a person, but a *sexual being*. Second, that they have sexual needs and crave to be desired. Thirdly, that they are sexually attractive to other people who will risk all to have an affair with them. And finally, bringing all these things together, that they are not so much under our spell and control as we once thought. We must strive hard to retain their attention and affection, and if we do not, since they are sexual beings, we will lose them. The same manner in which we were forced to impress and charm them in order to have them marry us in the first place, must be used in order to have them remain married and sexually loyal to us at all times. It is the essential attraction in marriage that keeps husbands and wives interested in each other.

All these considerations bring back the chase, the excitement, the mystery to a monogamous relationship and ensure that it never becomes stale or boring. The rule to remember is that the reason why men, primarily, commit adultery is because they search for newness, and women are unfaithful because they feel neglected and unloved. The solution to both is always to promote and maintain sexual attraction even at the expense of common interests.

Fulfilling Every Need

Any husband or wife who is a decent person and loves the person they are married to is perfectly willing to fulfil each and every desire of their spouse, within reason. However, there is one important proviso to this willingness: the request has to make sense. Let's face it, if your partner asked you to go out late at night to buy food you might well refuse. If, however, your partner explained that the news had reported that a terrible snow blizzard was about to hit your part of the country, and it would be difficult if not impossible to venture out of the home for the next three days, you would hop in your car straight away. Humans, it seems, need rational and intelligible reasons to motivate them, and even loving human relationships are not immune from this need. The problem with this need for logical motivation in marriage arises when your husband or wife, by virtue of the fact that as male and female they are different to you, simply cannot explain in a way that is intelligible *to you* why something is important, even though *to them* it is important.

Let me give you an example of what I mean. Consider a couple who marry. She tells her husband how much she loves flowers and asks him, if he plans to buy her anything, to please put flowers at the top of his list. He replies that flowers die quickly. 'I can't understand why you're insisting on me buying things with such a short life span; they're a waste of money!' He agrees to buy her silk clothing and sparkling jewellery instead. She grows angry and insists that he cannot love her until he does what she has asked. He then demands that at the very least she should explain herself to him, but she cannot. Where is the woman who can truly explain why women love flowers? Yet he insists that he cannot appreciate or respond to her request unless she can rationalize it for him. In the meantime, he continues to buy her even more expensive gifts, and she continues to be miserable.

Why do women love flowers? After all, they do die very quickly. Certainly they are colourful and radiant. But an emerald, pretty clothing, or a beautiful painting possess these same qualities, and they last so much longer! Why then should women insist specifically on flowers? Not one person I have asked has ever been able to answer this question adequately. And in truth it doesn't have to be answered. To me, the fact that women love flowers is part of the feminine mystique. That is what makes them women, and that is what makes them different, and hence attractive to men. If she loved pickup trucks or computers she might not pose the same attraction.

But the husband who refuses to buy his wife flowers, insisting instead on purchasing longer-lasting gifts that she can remember and always keep, is making a two-fold mistake. The first part is only a mistake because of the specific context of his being in a relationship. The true meaning of a relationship is that one accepts and entertains the wishes and the desires of the other partner. If you choose to fulfil only those desires of your partner that make sense to you, then your relationship is a *de facto* relationship with yourself. There is no room for a partner to exist as him or herself in such a relationship, since only when they comply with the wishes and understanding of the first partner are they and their desires taken seriously. Being in a relationship means being responsive to the needs of the other person with whom you share the relationship. It means trying your best to please the person you say you love. It doesn't mean doing what you *think* will please them, amidst their incessant protestations. In a relationship you first listen, and then you give.

This could be understood in another way: a relationship is

about two people making room in their lives for each other. In the fullest sense, this means another person, not just a clone of yourself. If there is nothing in your life which gives space to another person, if you cannot generate the sensitivity or discipline to merely execute another's most basic needs as they express them, then for all practical purposes you are not involved in a genuine relationship. Although you and your spouse may share the same house, and you may even have had children together, you are still as distant as the sun and the moon: there is no real harmony or correspondence, even though the view we have from earth may show up superficial similarities. If this is the case, you are not genuinely looking for another person with whom to share your life, but rather you are looking to duplicate or, in mathematical terms, to square yourself. One man and his doppelganger do not constitute a relationship.

However, the second mistake that the husband makes is far more significant. When he only carries out those wishes of his wife that make sense, or alternatively when he says that he will do whatever she wants as long as she explains herself, he is insisting that he be connected only to her intellectual, rational side. Her deeper, truer self not only remains a mystery to him, but forever remains a domain with which he has no association. In the simplest sense of the word, *he is not married to all of his wife*. In fact, he is not joined to the part of her which is most attractive: her womanhood. He connects himself only with the part of her which he can understand and appreciates, but rashly neglects the part which makes a far more holistic statement of the whole person that his wife really is.

There is an essential femininity in his wife which, since he is male, he will never understand: thus it will always remain undisclosed to him. It is that femininity which expresses itself in the kind of things that he cannot appreciate; in this example, flowers. She cannot explain those desires for the same reason that she cannot truly explain what it means to be female as opposed to male. It is a quintessential point of existence, not a revealed or expressed mode of behaviour. Thus, there is nothing she can possibly do that can convey to her husband her intrinsic desire. He is not her, therefore there is a part of her that he will never understand. It completely transcends logic, *but this does not invalidate its importance*. On the contrary, this is what creates the differences between male and female, and hence sustains their attraction.

The *Woman* in Your Wife; The *Man* in Your Husband

When the husband insists on an explanation, or insists that he will only purchase those things for her which he can also appreciate, he renders it impossible to be truly married to the woman in his wife. He may be married to the part of her which is the same in all humans, her capacity for emotion and intellect, but the part of her which should most attract and stimulate him, her femininity and womanhood, is something which he has dismissed completely.

It is clear that this man's relationship with his wife is at best superficial, and at worst merely comparable to any relationship he has with his other friends, barring the sexual element. He is attempting to create her in his own image, not that of God, and dismisses her intrinsic identity as a separate person. In other words by telling her that she doesn't know what she wants, or insisting that her demands are foolish or don't make sense, he refuses to acknowledge her independence as a human being.

When he actually fulfils her every desire, whether or not he understands it, he ensures that he is connected with her innermost self. Only now is he married to his wife in her entirety, which also encompasses the part of her which is essentially different to him, i.e., the woman in his wife. Of course, the above is just an example from many that we can draw upon. The point is that in each relationship there will always be at least one attribute of one's partner which will forever remain an enigma to oneself.

What man would want a wife who is exactly like a man, and what woman would stay married to a man who was identical to her in every respect? Denying your husband or wife's right to be different, by refusing to accommodate, or even mocking (what appears to you to be) the irrational requests they make, and which are tied up to their very masculinity or femininity, in the long-term will end up diminishing the attraction which we have for our spouse.

Remember, your wife is never your wife. She is a woman to whom you are married. Therefore, don't take her loyalty or fidelity for granted. She has sexual needs and poses a deep sexual attraction to others. You ignore this at your own peril. Rather, seize upon the fact that your wife is a woman and devote yourself to her totally, make sure that she is sexually satisfied, lest she begin to look elsewhere for love and affection. Likewise remember, your husband is not just a breadwinner and father – he is the man you married and you must cherish him or lose him. Show your spouse extravagant love. Show them overwhelming interest, to constantly boost their confidence. Show them through tangible action that they have nothing to fear from people outside the marriage. Show your spouse how attracted and interested you are *in them*, how beautiful or handsome you find them. Prove to them, that you remain fully focused on your spouse. Even if you are forced *to go to an extreme* for a duration of time in terms of behaving unnaturally and avoiding conversation with other men or women, do it. In the final analysis this extreme is beneficial to you as well. It helps you sedate your desire for strangers outside the marriage and focus all your attention on your spouse. Your spouse will feel loved and special and confident and trustful in your relationship.

Feeding Marriage

Marriage is a hungry animal, and needs to be fed constantly. Marriage is like our stomachs that need constantly to be filled. One must pour an inexhaustible supply of love, affection, attention, caring and understanding into this magical brew. And just as one does not merely eat and thereby become satisfied, no one walks under a canopy and just emerges *married*. Marriage is a vibrant and electric institution. It is alive. And one must monitor its pulse constantly, if it is not to die.

CHAPTER FIFTEEN

RESTORING PASSION
IN MARRIAGE

ADULTERY IS ABOUT PASSION

Having learned from adultery the absolute centrality of sexual attraction and passion for a successful marriage, we now must ask a serious and sober question. Can passion really be maintained within a monogamous relationship, or will my writing this book prove an exercise in futility?

All too many people think that the jury is already in with a definite settlement. While marriage can provide support and security, it cannot maintain its excitement. Every week here in Oxford I hold a debate on some important social or religious issue, in front of a student audience. When I once made the case for the necessity of marriage, they conceded that my arguments had been convincing, and one student stood up and said, 'Yeah, I guess it is worthwhile to *sacrifice* passion for the sake of stability.' Every one of the students present agreed with this sentiment. And that shocked me. *Sacrifice what for what?* What was he on about? Why is there a natural assumption that having many sexual partners is more passionate and more exciting than having a single sexual partner with whom one is really and truly in love? It seems incredible that contemporary society at once accepts the importance of marriage, above and beyond that of affairs and extramarital sex, but at the same time feels that it is still a sacrifice and that one would be having a far better time bedding as many people as possible.

This is truly one of the greatest fallacies and must be refuted. Rediscovering passion in sexual relations involves not so much a change in partner as a change in attitude. We equate passion with newness, and finding a new partner will almost certainly result in very passionate sex. But it is a shortcut that has no permanence. Pursuing this path will just lead a man or woman to become bored with their new lover as well after a short space of time and search for an even newer partner. Adultery is at best a temporary solution to the problem of passion because the same quality of 'monotony through familiarity' is bound to be visited upon one's new partner. For a permanent resolution to the problem of boredom, we must search for something new *in* our partner, on a regular basis.

The Dullness of the Marriage Bed

It's probably safe to assume that when couples first marry they enjoy a passionate and satisfying sex life together. But as time goes by they invariably begin either to lose sexual interest in each other or at the very least, the longevity of their marriage gives rise to sameness and monotony. It seems that monogamy involves what I called earlier an unavoidable Catch 22. The more familiar, the more accustomed one becomes to one's spouse, which in itself is desirable in every marriage, the more the passion seems to wear off. Every marriage must have trust and love, which of course build up with time, in order to flourish and succeed. But the longer a man and woman live with each other, the less they try to impress each other. Whereas before he would shower before they made love and would do his best to please his wife, now he just jumps into bed, does his 'slam, bam, thank you ma'am,' routine, and then takes out a good book, or just turns over and falls asleep. This view seems largely borne out by the overwhelming statistic that by far the highest rate of infidelity in marriage, among both men and women, occurs after five years of marriage.

Is having sex with the same partner over a long time a preordained ticket to erotic boredom? Here are comments from three married men that may be of interest: '. . . I've been married sixteen years now and been completely faithful to my wife. I'd have to say, in all candour, that our sexual relationship now is much better than it was when we were first married. To me, the trick has been to be creative about our sex lives – not with whips and chains, or gymnastic positions – but with keeping away from routines; and staying attuned to one another's needs. For instance, we've learned to spend a lot of time giving each other sensual massages as part of our foreplay. It's an almost incredible, tantalizing delight . . .'[1]

Less positively, a forty-four-year-old man says: 'Let's face it, my wife isn't as attractive as she once was, she's let her body go to pot, and her idea of good sex is [coitus] twice a week. It's like she's doing me a favour. Is it any wonder I say our sex life is boring?. . . So I go to a classy hooker once a month as my way of getting even . . .'

A forty-nine-year-old man: 'Although I've been happily married for twenty-seven years, I've certainly noticed a definite deterioration in our sex life. We get along really well, we do more together now than we ever did, but sex is the one area in our lives where we seem in such a rut. I'm not sure who's to blame for it, since I think we're both involved, but I guess we've both given up too easily, accepting a lousy sex life as given. I'm not proud to admit it, but the way I've coped with this for years is by having occasional affairs. At least that way I feel like I can still turn someone on.'

The last two accounts surely seem damaging for they portray

an all too common scenario of events. But even if this scenario is typical, is it unavoidable and incurable? Are all marriages destined for some adulterous fate because it is simply too difficult, perhaps even inhuman and unrealistic, to maintain passion over long stretches of time with the same sexual partner? The answer is, of course not. And as the gentleman quoted above noted, such an attitude is a cop out. Only lazy and uncreative people will lose passion in their marriage and take the easy way out by finding excitement with someone else, until, inevitably, their laziness and superficiality lead them to become bored with this partner too.

The Excitement of Novelty

There can be no question that sexual passion is associated with newness. Indeed there can be nothing in life which is special and attractive unless it appears novel and original at all times. Who ever thought that the same sexual routine all the time could possibly be interesting? But all the same, why do so many people fall for the vapid and regrettably commonplace belief that newness means having a new sexual partner? Why shouldn't newness mean that we never allow the special kind of sex that can only result from being in love to be demeaned by allowing it to become monotonous? Are any of us really so unthinking or juvenile as to assume that newness can only be found in a new face and new flesh, rather than in new methods and creativity? Or even better, in seeing our spouse in a new way? Earlier I told the story of a husband who used his creative genius to convince his wife that he was another man, and who while she was blindfolded engaged in the most exciting intimate encounter with her, something that he had previously thought himself incapable of. And even though the encounter was of only a single night's duration, the mere memories of that erotic night caused him to see his wife in a completely new light. She had been transformed in his eyes from being a complacent mother and housewife into a fiery woman who would stop at nothing for sexual and erotic gratification. His wife had finally come alive for him *in his mind*, a place where his erotic feelings for her had been previously dead. Can we too not use our own imagination to create these erotic possibilities?

The Art of Erotic Surrender

Even the most secular sex therapists agree that capitulating to monotony in marriage is ridiculous and avoids the central issue. These therapists are unanimous in advising that the most satisfying sexual gratification is found not in new people, but rather in never allowing ourselves to go down the path of monotony and sexual boredom through an accepted routine. 'Don't let sex become routine. For too many couples, sexual dissatisfaction is a direct reflection of boredom resulting from an absence of variation or creativity in their sexual interaction. To avoid too much "sameness" in sex, don't always try to get amorous at the same time of day, change the scenery on occasion (for instance try sex some place other than your bedroom whether it means checking into a hotel for a night or sending the kids to sleep at friends' homes so you can make love in front of the living room fireplace), and vary the action.'[2]

The therapists in question then go on to list many important variations which are beyond the scope of this book but are very important both conceptually and practically. Without going into any great detail a few will be mentioned because they are of great significance. They include introducing new options into one's sexual interactions, such as experimenting with sensual massage, and new types of sexual activity which have never been tried before, experimenting with different positions and foreplay, changing venues such as going to hotels and using the car, and so on. But having read tens of books on similar subjects in preparation for this book, I can tell you that often this advice can itself suffocate creativity and stultify the emotions. In earlier chapters, we have introduced what I believe to be the ultimate means by which to reinvigorate monogamous relationships. With reference to the specific issue of restoring passion in marriage, however, my own personal immediate advice is this: do unto your wife whatever you would do if you had wished to seduce your secretary, business assistant or airline stewardess. Do unto your husband what you would do to that sexy fellow lawyer if you had wanted him to think you a sex goddess. Surely you have ideas as to how you would win them over to you, and how you would pleasure them. Let your own sexual creativity be manifest. Make your marriage into an illicit affair. Your wife's opinion of your sexual virility is no less important than the woman next door.

Perhaps most importantly, we must remember that human sexuality is not an entity on its own, but is a natural outcome of a loving and romantic relationship. Therefore, the greatest way to enhance one's sexual life is not to try to implement new sexual positions and techniques, but to bring far greater romance into everyday life. Preserving romance is an ongoing challenge, which bids us focus on those small, non-sexual interactions of affection, which sadly have lost their centrality in contemporary society. For example, how many people today write love letters to their spouse? And how many buy flowers for absolutely no reason other than a sign of affection for the woman or man whom they love? These gestures aren't just ceremonial. They make a recipient feel loved and appreciated. There can be no question that the extravagant love and attention which we show our loved one has a direct bearing on the passionate feelings which ensue at bedtime. As Masters and Johnson say, 'It is no surprise that as we fall into non-romantic complacency in our relationships, our sexual interests and passions are apt to dwindle, too.'[4]

Restoring Romance

Today's generation is incredibly superficial. Synthetic images of violence and explicit sex on television and in film form the dominant part of our culture. The result is that we have lost the ability to be genuinely entertained by things which are deep and meaningful. A romantic is seen by today's society as an antiquated, naive fool. We don't understand why he or she would waste their time on serenading the opposite sex with a guitar, or writing them poems. How silly! Isn't the only important thing to get right down to it, to have sex? How many men actually aspire to romance? Too few. Why should they waste time on romance when sex can be had with a far less caring attitude? They are far more interested in 'scoring'. Even foreplay can be seen by many of this generation, especially by men, as a necessary evil in order to seduce our partners. She won't do it otherwise so you may as well kiss and hug her. But after that *action*!

This is one of the reasons why, remarkably, sex suddenly becomes so boring after so short a space of time. It has no underpinning. It has no framework. It has no depth, and it has no structure. Nothing without depth is really interesting. We master it far too quickly, and then it is time to move on to something else. Take for example two kinds of toys, a toy gun and a computer. One bores us after just fifteen minutes, the other can occupy our time and imagination for years to come. The reason: because there is so much more to a computer; it is so much more intricate and has so much more depth than a mere piece of plastic. Because it has depth, it always presents us with something new to discover: a new piece of software, or a new way to design beautiful images in a drawing package. And how much more entertaining is a human being, possessor of infinite depth.

The same applies to married couples. If we see nothing in our spouse but their flesh, if married couples focus purely on their sexual lives outside a romantic framework, they will undoubtedly get bored with each other quickly. If they cannot enjoy conversation, if they do not see the magic of sharing a life with another human being, a creature of limitless depth, then their partner presents nothing new to discover. We get bored terribly quickly because we 'master' them at the same speed. How many inches of flesh does a person have? Are we really going to be excited by seeing the same thing day after day? But when we peer into each other's soul, if we can be inspired by the infinite beauty possessed by our spouse, inspired enough to write and sing to them about that process of discovery, then how can we possibly become bored? The marriage then becomes a journey, embarked upon with the express purpose of reaching new heights together, as we explore the range of human drama and character.

Today's generation is a superficial one because all we see or perceive are those things which lie on the surface. We thus have no real idea of love. It becomes commonplace that even if a husband has the most devoted wife, one who sits by his side when he is ill, answers the phone with glee every time she hears his voice on the other end and turns the world over just to make him happy, he still finds it easy to compare his wife to the woman with the better figure sitting next to him on the aeroplane and find his wife lacking. Appearances are everything; love, devotion, and commitment are nothing. This is the reason that so many otherwise loyal spouses are prepared to commit adultery. They judge things primarily on appearances, and then talk themselves

into the fact that they are so deprived that they have a right –
no, *an obligation* – to bring some excitement and satisfaction into
their lives. 'I need it, I deserve it,' they tell themselves.

The women whose husbands have cheated will often express
their hurt and horror upon discovering their husbands' indis-
cretions by citing their loyalty and then questioning how their
husbands could have done this. How could your husband have
committed adultery amidst the loyalty and devotion you have
always shown him? Simple! Those factors did not count for
anything in his decision to be unfaithful. In fact, they did not
even arise in his mind. He simply saw something he liked, felt he
had to have it, subliminally compared it to what he had already,
found it new and therefore more attractive, and just went for
it. How could it be any different, in a society that does not
promote loyalty, love and devotion as supreme values, but rather
physical beauty and sexual attraction? Values cannot exist in a
vacuum. You are the same wife who sat there watching Madonna
and Demi Moore, lying half naked on the screen, together with
your husband when the two of you were in bed together. You
watched as they became his heroes (and yours for that matter).
So why does this all surprise you so much now?

The Erotic Effect of Desire

In her little red book about sexual passion *How to Satisfy a Woman
Every Time*, author Naura Hayden includes a chapter entitled,
'The Joy of Marriage'. In it, she tells the story of her friend,
Helen Gurley Brown,

> a truly beautiful woman, inside and out, and loaded with sex
> appeal. I'll never forget a couple of years ago when we both
> were on the same plane from New York to Los Angeles. She
> got up to stretch her legs, and every man on the plane craned

his neck to watch her as she reached for her bag, and then headed for the restroom. When I saw her later in Los Angeles at the baggage claim, I told her of all the men eyeing her, and asked her how does she keep so sexy all the time? She gave me a great reply which I could *never* forget. Helen said she feels so much love from her husband, David, and that it is with her all the time, and it makes her *feel* sexy all the time. Wow! Now *there's* a great love affair *and* a great marriage.

This is a terrific story, demonstrating my point aptly. Here is a husband who actually *loves* his wife. He loves her so much, and presumably demonstrates it so readily in thought, speech, and action, that his wife *becomes* physically attractive as a result. Stated in other words, whereas modern-day society believes that physical attraction is the instigator of real love, and that it is how you look that is all-important, this story shows that the opposite is true. Real love on a deep level is so powerful that it *creates* an aesthetic reality. Not only that, but it creates a situation in which the appeal of aesthetic beauty will never wear off because that appeal is anchored in something far deeper and far more penetrating than something that only exists on the surface. If every single one of us loved our spouse in the manner described above, then they would feel absolutely desirable, and would look, dress and behave accordingly. We would watch them transform before our eyes from being merely a complacent, ordinary and bored-looking man or woman, into the most conspicuous sex object, radiating appeal.

The point is that any couple who feel that their intimate life together has become monotonous or boring face a choice: they can either admit defeat and accept that their life together will never be passionate, and at that point either live without passion or find extramarital sexual partners, or they can fight back. There are wonderful techniques which they can employ which will serve to change the situation. We have explored some very important ones. But the most important factor is a couple's wish to make their marriage work. Don't take harmful shortcuts. Forget about what you could be doing with the man next door. Concentrate on what you're going to do with the man who shares your life.

The Infinite Erotic Experiment of Marriage

The march of life and every passing experience can breed one of two responses: we can either be bored and adopt the 'seen it all, done it all' philosophy. Or we can truly learn from our experiences and adapt them to suit our needs. The man quoted above who says his sex life with his wife is now better than ever did not see sixteen years with the same wife as sixteen years of doing the same boring thing all the time. Rather, he saw it as sixteen years in which to experiment with a new and exciting variety of sexual possibilities with the woman he loved most. The long duration of his marriage was not seen by him as a monotonous imprisonment. Rather, it gave him sixteen years of experimentation with the same lover whom he saw in a totally novel light with each new experience they shared. But the experience has got to be *new*. Use your imagination in marriage. Become a marital artist.

We are all capable of the same, as long as we master the way in which we look at our spouse and always focus on the sexual possibilities which they constantly present. We must see our spouse as an open door sexually, rather than focus on the sexual experiences which we have already had with them, which appear to be a closed door. This may indeed be the house that we live in, but the opportunities for construction and decoration are endless.

SOURCES — CHAPTER FIFTEEN

1. Masters & Johnson, *Sex and Human Loving*, 1985
2. ibid.
3. ibid.
4. ibid.

CHAPTER SIXTEEN

AVOIDING TEMPTATION

'People ask me, Do you ever get crushes on the men you work with? And the truth, which I usually find ways not to say, is yes, often, don't you? All these men and women running around America in their grey suits in the boardroom, in the television commercials where the woman in the meeting utters the topper: I think they're all half in love with each other and have trouble recognising it, never mind admitting it, because it is potentially dangerous, and awkward, or painful, never mind politically incorrect.'

Peggy Noonan, chief speech-writer to Ronald Reagan, *What I Saw at the Revolution*

A CLOSE FRIEND of mine had just become engaged to a wonderful girl. She had it all – intelligence, unusual beauty, the gift of music, sweetness and femininity – he felt incredibly lucky and showed her the utmost appreciation. She really was something special. However, it was only a short time before he began to see her unusual gifts as somewhat of a curse. For he was not the only one to whom she appealed. Virtually every man she met found her desirable as well. As she worked in an academic work group, she spent many long hours with men who flirted innocently with her, and others who went as far as inviting her out and even writing her love letters. Naturally, she found all this wonderfully flattering, but her fiancé would have none of it. Angry as hell after yet another argument with her over the subject and her refusal to distance herself from men who posed as courtiers, he came to see me. He demanded that she remove herself from all the men who were overly attracted to her. Her defence was that she loved him with all her heart and would never contemplate doing anything to hurt him. What possible harm, therefore, could arise from her getting on with her academic work together with men who worshipped her? So long as she had no interest in them, what could possibly happen?

Funnily enough, I have encountered this scenario frequently in my time counselling students and married couples. One partner will begin to attract an admirer or admirers, to the other partner's great jealousy and consternation. The admired spouse will refuse to disassociate themselves from their admirer either because they feel it is innocent, or because they work together, or because they simply find it impossible to extricate themselves from the situation. Often, the admired spouse will even be resentful of their spouse's 'misplaced' jealousy, finding it unfairly imprisoning. They will also take great offence at the implication that they might not be faithful.

Beruriah and Rabbi Meir

The Talmud relates the story of Beruriah, the wife of the great luminary Rabbi Meir, one of the most famous Jewish sages of all time. It should be mentioned that Beruriah was equally famous and can be called one of the most celebrated women in Jewish history, and certainly the best known woman of the Talmudic era. She was renowned for her devout piety, goodness, and even her scholarship and erudition, which was unusual for a woman in that period. Amidst all these unparalleled qualities, however, ironically she met a humiliating and tragic end. Here is her story as the Talmud relates it.

> Rabbi Meir fled to Bavel. Some say it was a result of the
> episode involving his wife Beruriah. Once, she ridiculed that

which the Sages said that women are *suggestible*. Rabbi Meir said to her: 'By your life, someday you will acknowledge the truth of their words.' Rabbi Meir appointed one of his students to try to seduce her. It took a long time, but he was very persistent, and she finally agreed. When she found out that it was all a charade orchestrated by Rabbi Meir she strangled herself. Not expecting such a turn of events, Rabbi Meir fled to Bavel out of shame and grief.[1]

The point of the story is not to demonstrate the 'suggestibility' of women, nor the propensity of even the strongest willed or righteous women to be seduced. Rather, the point of the story is to demonstrate the suggestibility of all *humans*, and how none of us is immune to flattery, love and attention. Because far from being a weakness, this is one of the most sublime human virtues.

In fact, the Talmud does not spare even the reputation of Rabbi Meir himself, of whom we find the following story.

Rabbi Meir used to ridicule people who sinned, because he felt that it was not that difficult to overcome the evil inclination. One day Satan, who is the source of the evil inclination, appeared to Rabbi Meir in the guise of a beautiful woman standing on the other side of a river. There were no boats available for crossing the river, only a rope bridge. Rabbi Meir grabbed onto the rope and started making his way across the river. When Rabbi Meir had gone halfway across the river his evil inclination released him from its grip.

Satan said to Rabbi Meir: 'Were it not proclaimed in the heavens to take heed of Rabbi Meir and his Torah, I would have reduced you to two small heaps of remains.'[2]

In telling us that even the great Rabbi Meir exerted every effort to reach the beautiful woman on the other side of the river who was forbidden to him, the Talmud does not seek to emphasize his weakness, but his *humanity*. There is nothing wrong with being attracted to other people and responding to their affections. Indeed, if we did not react this way, we wouldn't be soft or vulnerable enough to exist within a loving relationship. The only thing wrong with reciprocating a stranger's affections is the fact that you are married and have commitments.

There is No Crime in Wanting to Share Somebody's Bed

This reaction to another's affections is not a fault. Is there anything wrong with being responsive to human emotion or warmth, or with the desire to be loved? We apply to women who are promiscuous the most degrading terms, yet what is the crime in wanting to be held and loved by another human being? What is the crime in wanting to share physical closeness with a caring and loving partner? (If anything the crime is that those who are promiscuous deny themselves the essential ability to experience a unique and intimate relationship with their one chosen beloved.) Wouldn't we complain even more about someone who was so cold that they were totally unresponsive to any love and emotion shown to them?

Beruriah was like any other man or woman on this planet whose emotions are healthy. When shown extravagant emotion and attention by a member of the opposite sex, she couldn't help but respond, and neither could Rabbi Meir. I would argue that it is far more of a problem if someone does *not* respond at all to the affection shown to them by a member of the opposite sex. Think about it for a moment and be honest with yourself. Amidst the jealousy that is created upon seeing your spouse sexually interested in another, would you prefer it if they were immune to the rest of the world sexually? Would you prefer a dispassionate partner in life, and someone who is completely unattractive to others? As far as married people are concerned, the only thing wrong with being responsive to the affections and emotions of a stranger is that it contradicts the marriage and penetrates the inner circle of activities and emotions which should be reserved exclusively for the married partner. In this respect, as I have said earlier, while the *possibility* of adultery is healthy and guarantees the sexual passion in every marriage, the *act* of adultery itself is totally destructive, bringing unimaginable pain and bitterness in its wake.

If it is healthy, even proper and desirable to be responsive to the attentions of another human being, and perhaps even self-destructive not to respond, then how can we remain loyal in thought, speech and action to the one we love? How can two opposites coexist? On the one hand repressing our sexuality is unhealthy, and being fully cognizant of the attraction we pose to others is positive and leads to excitement in marriage. But on the other, actually committing adultery destroys everything in one fell swoop that we had hoped to achieve in marriage!

Control is not Heroic; Sex is Best out of Control

The answer is never to put ourselves into the kind of situation where we will be forced to fight our natural, healthy emotions; never to find oneself in an intimate environment with a member of the opposite sex that is not our spouse, in which a natural attraction can begin to develop, which we really don't desire, and which we will be forced to resist. It is not healthy to resist or be forced to repress strong sexual urges. Thus, we should only seclude ourselves, for example, with our spouse. Endure the same seclusion with a good friend of the opposite sex, and it might conjure up sexual sentiments which one will then be forced to repress. Contrary to popular thinking, you're no hero if you can control your sexual urge. Sexual instinct is not meant to be controlled. Really exciting sex means losing control. Jewish laws vigorously maintain that a man and a woman who are not married should not be secluded together, and should not allow themselves to be put into situations in which they will have to resist. Having to resist one's sexual urge will create an environment where sex is a conscious effort and demands control, thus diminishing the real passion of sex which occurs only when one's senses, emotions and libido put them on auto-pilot.

Those who would argue that they have nothing to fear because, as in the case of the beautiful fiancée above, they are so overwhelmingly in love with their spouse, are not only failing to be completely honest with themselves and denying the fundamental responsiveness of human nature, but are also actually harming themselves. Humans are not designed to be unresponsive or totally apathetic to the warmth and love shown them by another human being. And if we do achieve this apathy, who is to say that we have progressed in life? Is stifling our essential humanity beneficial? Rather, we must seek to be in the kind of environment that doesn't serve as a test for our integrity, but rather cultivates our ability to remain focused and trained on our spouses, and to show them the same degree of devotion which they show to us.

A Jew prays daily to his Creator, 'Master, do not bring me to grave tests.' Yet this generation seems convinced that it can turn itself on and off sexually like a light switch. Apart from the fact that this is highly improbable, there is also the problem that the whole beauty of sex is its spontaneity. Sexual relations and arousal should come naturally and automatically, and not be subject to human will or approval, lest we risk compromising our passion. A passionate person is someone who responds to romantic moments and the nuances of life in a flash, and not just when they consciously decide to do so. Anything else is contrived and mechanical.

Of course, compromising situations will arise now and then even if one makes endeavours to steadfastly avoid them, and I am not suggesting, therefore, that we should have no control over our sexual selves, and succumb to every passion the moment it arises. Make no mistake. I am not writing a book in favour of adultery. Indeed, all sexual relations must be subject to human will and there must always be a conscious decision involved. Anything else will lead to an attitude of condoning date rape or any rape for that matter where the man can just say, 'Well, I was in this situation and my spontaneity and passion got the better of me,' or any other situation where people 'excuse' their infidelity with the pathetic explanation that 'It just happened'.

So while it is much easier, and better, to avoid such situations in the first place, the fact is that tempting situations will occasionally arise and people must be able to exercise self-control. Even within a marriage there must be times when one partner does not want to have sex when the other does, and again the one who does must restrain themselves out of consideration for the other. In fact, this is a very important law within Judaism: there can be no sex in marriage unless it is undertaken willingly, even joyfully, by both husband and wife. But at the very least one must seek to minimize those occasions so as not to stifle or diminish one's sexual urge. The trick is never to get oneself entangled into a situation where one will be forced to suppress one's sexuality. Repression is not healthy.

Simple Interactions Lead to Affairs

The statement that we must not allow ourselves to enter into compromising situations is not prudish, but a compliment. It means that we always have the ability to excite, and to be excited. People always find us interesting and attractive. And it is a recognition of this innate sexuality possessed by us all, which serves as our most basic defining characteristic, which must be safeguarded and protected, if we are not to squander our sexuality and destroy our marriages. Countless books chronicle how the overwhelming number of affairs between men and women began with innocent, yet admittedly compromising situations, in which the original intention of the two parties was never to have an affair. In her book about female infidelity, *Tempted Women*, Carol Botwin records many such real-life cases in which wives found their private lives in upheaval as a result of seemingly innocent liaisons:

'A group of us from the office went to a birthday party for a co-worker. My boss and I danced. Just the touch of his hand on my neck drove me wild. That night our affair started.'

Another woman relates how her affair started, not just in innocent, but seemingly virtuous circumstances: 'It all began when we met at Church. We were both very unhappy in our marriages. One day at a social gathering we started talking and one thing led to another.'

And yet another woman relates very similar circumstances: 'We began sharing problems and became the best of friends. All of a sudden we both felt that our friendship was changing into something more. Three months later we wound up in bed.'

Should men and women then be hermits? Should women refrain from working because of the possibility of meeting romantic men with whom they will have an affair? Should men and women stay locked up at home, in a modern-day version of a chastity belt? And should we seek to limit the natural and innocent interaction between men and women because of their propensity to allow a casual interaction to develop into a full-blown affair?

Of course not. As I have emphasized and re-emphasized throughout this book, even if it would be practical to separate the sexes, Judaism does not condone, nor does it believe in, a psychology of repression. Rather, our interactions can remain exactly the same, and men and women can interact in an innocent way. The secret, however, is modesty. Firstly, we must dress modestly. A man or woman who dresses provocatively is making a statement that they desire to be noticed. And while it is fine to be noticed, it is a different statement when we want to be noticed sexually. Dressing in an overtly sexual manner is a proclamation that amidst our various personality traits, it is our sexuality which we want people to notice first and foremost.

Secondly, and more importantly, we must speak and behave modestly. This means refraining from overt sexual discussions with colleagues. It also means not speaking too personally about our intimate lives with men and women to whom we are not married. Unless we are totally deadened sexually, *speaking about sex gets us excited about sex*. By encouraging or initiating discussion about our sex lives, we are unwittingly, and perhaps innocently, issuing an invitation to outsiders to join in our personal life. We are also telling them that we desire that they be exposed to our intimate selves, and that we are somewhat dependent on them in areas which are the exclusive right and property of our spouses. Marriage is only sacred if it is intimate and personal. Refrain from making it a public affair. Ask any husband or wife how flattered they would be if they discovered that their spouse was divulging the most intimate details of their personal lives to friends at the office. They would be mortified, and that's the way it should be. Because it is not only the sex in a marriage which is private. It is the marriage in its entirety which flourishes under the necessary blockade of privacy.

But modest behaviour also means not staring at a colleague with the kind of look that will tell them you are definitely interested in them and find them stimulating. Even if you feel it, don't show it. It means not overly complimenting your employee or co-worker to the point where they must question why it is that they have suddenly become your obsession. The same is also true of going for drinks together in isolation or even with other co-workers, enjoying another man or woman's company in a non-working environment, for this affords the opportunity to just enjoy the other person as a man or a woman. An ancient Jewish aphorism declares that the difference between a wise man and a clever man is this: a wise man is someone who will never allow himself to get muddled into a situation from which a clever man is smart enough to extricate himself. Remember that always in your associations with the opposite sex. People are not like Teflon but velcro. Male and female are naturally drawn to one another and naturally stick. Therefore, keep some distance.

Modesty in Thought

Of course, the two premises above are predicated on the most important premise of all: thinking modestly. If we fantasize about our colleagues and see them in a sexual light, or if we look at them sexually, it is inevitable that, first, we will give ourselves away and they will know exactly what we are thinking, because these things cannot be hidden completely. Second, we will eventually, and perhaps inevitably begin to act upon this longing, and if we don't, then we will damage ourselves through repression. Modesty of thought is the most urgent and most important guarantee that we will remain steadfastly loyal to our spouse, sexually satisfied with them, and will avoid an adulterous affair at all cost. It also means that we won't be tempted to think about someone else when we are in bed with our husband or wife. In all our social interactions with men and women, it is not sufficient to just refrain from having sexual affairs, we must not fantasize about them either. Apart from the fact that it is a great abuse to look at people and immediately see them for only one thing, to create them as sexual objects, devoid of all human emotion and responsiveness, the only way to have real passion in monogamy is to focus all our sexuality, especially our thoughts, on our spouse. And if you absolutely feel the need to fantasize in order to generate personal excitement when you are in bed with your spouse, then fantasize about *your spouse* in an erotic situation.

Our Spouse is a Man or a Woman. Everyone Else is a Human

The rule is simple, yet far more difficult to enact in real life. The manner in which we perceive the men and women to whom we are married should be first and foremost sexual. It is imperative that we see our spouses first as sexual beings, and only thereafter as people. Stated in other words, your wife should be a woman to you before she is a human being. Her femininity should dominate her personality so that you always maintain not just your respect and love for her, but your instinctive attraction. And you should notice her body and sexuality as much, if not more, than any other feature. This leads to a relationship which maintains its passion always.

But people to whom we are not married should be *people* to us, first and foremost, even though we are not immune to their sexuality and we realize that they are also either male or female. If a man has a female co-worker, he may respect her intelligence and her capacity for efficient and thorough task execution. But he should not dwell on her charm as a woman, although she may possess much. He must focus on her as a person, not as a woman. And although they may have a close working relationship and enjoy each other's company immensely, they must still keep their distance. A husband should not focus on his co-worker's legs or bust, but on her personality and humanity. He must see her in the generic. Not female, but human. With his wife, it should be the opposite. She must be first a *woman* to him.

Part of the distance which we must enforce is to ensure that we minimize all forms of physical contact, which can immediately lead us to becoming aware of the attraction posed by the person in question. In his opus, *War and Peace*, Tolstoy describes how Count Pierre Bezhukhov gets trapped into marrying a woman whom he knew was wrong for him. Basically, it involved this transition from person to woman. Once he studied her in all her femininity, he was hooked.

> He half rose meaning to go round, but the aunt handed him the snuff-box, passing it across Helene's back. Helene bent forward to make room, and looked round with a smile. She was, as she always did for evening parties, wearing a gown cut in the fashion of the day, very low back and front. Her bosom, which always reminded Pierre of marble, was so close to him that his short-sighted eyes could not but perceive the living charm of her neck and shoulders, so near to his lips that he need only stop a little to have touched them. He was conscious of the warmth of her body, of the smell of perfume, and heard the slight creak of her corset as she breathed. He saw not her marble beauty forming a single whole with her gown, but all at once having seen this, his eyes refused to see her in any other way, just as we cannot reinstate illusion that has been explained.

A thirty-three-year-old secretary in New England who had an affair with a co-worker describes a modern-day equivalent to Tolstoy's tale: 'He bent over in front of me to fix my typewriter, and I couldn't resist his body.'

In fact, it is safe to assume that the danger light is on the moment we leave the realm of seeing our friends as people, and begin to focus on their specifically masculine or feminine virtues. A woman who ended up having an affair with her college professor describes the affair as coming about like this: 'I never intended to have an affair. My lover is my former college professor who shares my love of literature. We started this relationship very innocently, by having lunch after class and discussing the class. I found him to be caring, sensitive, under-standing, and very sexy.'[3] It was specifically this transition from a professional relationship and appreciation for literature, and discussing that literature, to noticing his caring and sensitivity as a man, that led to the affair.

Another woman explains a very similar occurrence: 'I was trying to adjust to the death of my father and remarriage of my mother. My boss understood my feelings of confusion and readjustment. He listened. He showed me he cared by doing little "romantic" things for me – flowers, tapes, notes. I responded although I am married. No one had ever done these things for me before, and things like that mean *everything* to me. I didn't mean to fall in love with him, but I did.'[4]

The Importance of Distance

This means that we must carefully monitor the friendships we have with members of the opposite sex. I know that even raising the matter in this book will cause readers to roll their eyes back as they assume that this is yet another example of religious prudishness. I know that my students at Oxford become irate if ever I should mention that male and female friendships must have borders if they are to remain healthy and not run down the sexual path. The students protest: 'Come on, do you really think that people do nothing but think about sex? Can't you accept that a man can have a female friend and not think about her in a sexual way?' And I respond: 'Of course I agree that a man can have a female friend. But I am realistic enough to know that this friendship will not last unless they keep some kind of distance, establish some sort of boundary which recognizes that they are still a man and a woman with the potential for attraction. In fact, it would be a mutual insult if there were no need for distance. It would basically mean that neither was attractive.'

I have argued throughout this book that in order for relationships to be reinvigorated, husbands and wives must take the steps necessary to cultivate their sexual selves. This means that it is not at all a put-down to accuse someone that they are always thinking about sex. Remember, we are all innately sexual beings, and the objective here is not to repress our sexuality, but rather to focus it on one outlet: our spouse. In a study conducted by Dr Shanor, it was reported that the average man under forty thinks of sex six times per hour. But the average married couple has sex 1.5 times per week.[5] So, according to Dr Shanor a man thinks of sex over 600 times for each time he has it, which just goes to show how important it is to concentrate one's thoughts on one's spouse. Go ahead and think about sex as much as you want. But make sure that the object of your desires always is your spouse.

It is perfectly legitimate for married men and women to have close friendships with members of the opposite sex, even when, as is inevitable, they are fully aware of each other's sexuality. But there is a big difference between close and intense. We must endeavour our best to ensure that the friendship does not develop into a dependency. In the case of wives who have an affair, this is especially true. Whereas many studies indicate that for husbands who commit adultery, it is sex which precedes a relationship with a lover and any emotional entanglement will come later, if at all, in women the sequence is reversed. Eighty-two per cent of those who responded to *Woman* magazine's office affairs survey stressed the *friendship* they had found with their lovers. It was the starting point and glue of the affair. 'Most women who have affairs start by having an intimate friendship with a male, which gradually leads to an emotional involvement.'

A mother and housewife who had an affair in her mid-forties asserts, 'I got involved with someone at work through our daily telephone contact. We found out that we had a lot in common and we liked each other's personalities. We were good friends over the phone before we ever met each other. After we met it was many, many months before anything of a sexual nature occurred. I became more and more attracted to him over time, until finally the emotional attachment and physical attraction became so strong it was too difficult not to get involved sexually.'

Similarly, Barbara, a teacher, describes how she started her affair with Bruce, a colleague: 'We spent a great deal of time together. Having the same work made it real, real interesting. We had lots to talk about. We were friends first, then the friendship developed into a sexual relationship. It was just something I slid into. We always ended up together and one day we decided to go a little bit further with this relationship.'

We must all be honest enough with ourselves to discern when we are beginning to become romantically or sexually interested with someone outside the marriage. We must distinguish between a professional relationship and an obsession. Once we begin to find ourselves making petty excuses to see this colleague or friend, to be with them and work alongside them, once we discover that we are discussing each other and our lives, far more than we are discussing work or general topics, then problems are developing and we must seek to be separated from this person, even at the risk of losing our jobs and damaging our careers, until the attraction can subside, at which point we can resume a more normal and healthy friendship, as once existed.

Rabbi Chiya is Tempted

The Talmud tells the story of Rabbi Chiya, the son of Rav Ashi, who would prostrate himself during prayer and say: 'May the Merciful One save us from the evil inclination.'

One day his wife heard him saying this and wondered, 'Many years have already passed since we have stopped having relations because of old age: why then is he so worried about his evil inclination?' Once, while he was studying in the garden, his wife disguised herself and started walking back and forth in front of him. He asked her: 'Who are you?' She replied, 'I am Chasuda (a prostitute who was well known in the vicinity), and I have only today returned to this town. He asked her to lie with him, and she said, 'Only if you bring me the small branch that is at the top of the palm tree.' He clambered up to the top of the tree and brought her the branch. Later, when he returned home, he saw that his wife was stoking up the fires in the oven. Feeling despondent about what he had done, he started to climb into the oven so that he would die. His wife stopped him, asking, 'What is going on?' He related the entire incident to her, and she told him, 'That woman was none other than I.' Inconsolable, he said, 'I did not know this at the time, and my intention was to do a forbidden act. Therefore, I still deserve to be punished.' It was said that for the rest of his life Rabbi Chiya, the son of Ashi, was distressed by that incident and that eventually he died of the heartache.[6]

The point of the story is not to teach us of the fallibility of the great sage. Nor is it the Talmud's wish to express the humanity of its heroes, as some have sought to suggest. Rather, the mistake the sage made was to allow himself to enter into a situation where he could be rendered susceptible. As soon as he heard that the woman in question was a prostitute, he should have distanced himself from her because their association could only lead to one thing. She wasn't there to talk, and they weren't going to become friends. So too, if we begin to feel that a friendship is leading down the slippery slope of emotional dependency, then we must cease any and all contact immediately with the person in question, even if it will hurt their feelings and paint us in a bad light. The security of our marriage and the happiness of our spouse precedes every other individual consideration, and no marriage can really last until this principle is taken seriously and we are prepared to sacrifice other things in its implementation.

Can You Have Close Friends of the Opposite Sex?

A close friend of mine married late in life. Although he loved his wife dearly, he was already settled in his course in life, and had many friends, a not inconsiderable number of whom his wife objected to. One such friend was a woman the same age as her husband, who had been friends with him for many years. About six months after their marriage, the husband insisted that he was going to Cannes, on the French Riviera, with this woman friend. His wife was flabbergasted and I was called in. She simply could not believe that her husband was planning to go away for the weekend with a female friend. But he, for his part, couldn't understand what all the fuss was about. 'Look, Shmuley,' he told me, 'I have known this girl for ten years. We are close friends and the friendship has always been platonic. I can control myself. I just don't want the friendship to collapse, so I'm going to spend some quality time with her. And we're not going to stay in the same room together.'

I told him, 'Andy, this is wrong. And not because I believe that something will happen. I believe you when you say that nothing will. It's wrong because when a man and a woman go away together, alone, for a weekend, something *should* happen. The very fact that one is male and one is female, and they are secluded, should be exciting and stimulating. Are you proud of the fact that you have deadened yourself sexually to women, or even this one woman? And how about your friend? What if she was in this room and she heard you saying how you did not find her attractive, were not turned on by her, and thus there was nothing to worry about. Would she be happy, or would she feel offended? Can she possibly be flattered when you tell her, "I can go away with you for a weekend and nothing will happen because I am completely oblivious to the woman in you, and for me it is just like going away for a weekend with a man?" That's why it is wrong. Because you are not supposed to put yourself into situations in which the only way out, and the only way in which you can preserve your fidelity to your wife, is by turning yourself off sexually.'

About two months later I was delivering a series of lectures to eighteen-year-old High School students. I told them this story, and my friend's arguments. I asked them what their opinion was. I was startled to discover that out of a group of forty, thirty-eight students said that there was nothing wrong with him going away for the weekend with this woman. Their reasoning was that there is nothing wrong with men and women being good friends. In fact, they told me, they applauded his maturity and sexual liberation. His action meant he respected women and didn't just see them as sexual objects.

'Give me a break,' I told them. 'It is one thing to say that a woman does not want to be treated *exclusively* like a sex object. It is quite another thing to say that women are actually happy when their sexuality and their intrinsic femininity, their very womanhood, is completely overlooked. That's rubbish. Far from being a compliment, telling someone that they are not attractive as a man or woman is *the* biggest insult.' Conversely, the fact that we must all be on our guard against committing adultery and the fact that none of us is safe and all are susceptible to it is a compliment to us. It means that we are all attractive, sensual creatures whose inner passion is alive and well. But it also means that we must always be on our guard against things getting out of hand.

Real marriage means being devoted in thought, speech and action to one's spouse, at all times and in all circumstances. Most of all, it means being devoted even in the subtle nuances of love, and in the predicaments in which one finds oneself. Fidelity in marriage is not only expressed by not going to bed with someone else, but also by not sharing any of those special secluded moments, which are so important to a marriage, with someone else. At all times, what a husband or wife should consider in their interactions with members of the opposite sex is this: if their spouse were watching them at this moment, would they be happy or angry? Would they feel pride, or would they feel humiliation? Would their love increase or diminish? And, most of all, would they object to our behaviour?

A married friend of mine was at the beach when an attractive young woman whom he didn't know just walked up to him and asked if he wouldn't mind administering suntan lotion on her back, shoulders and legs. 'Sure,' he said, and happily complied.

'How could you?' I asked him.

'Come on, Shmuley,' he said. 'Stop being such a religious prude.'

'Well,' I said, 'if there really is nothing wrong with what you did, then I assume you wouldn't mind my telling your wife about this insignificant little episode.'

And at this he balked, and admitted that had his wife been there with him, he wouldn't have done it. So why did he? 'If I said no, I would have offended her. Her intentions were completely innocent.'

'Maybe,' I said, 'but why don't you think of your wife's feelings before this stranger of a woman? It was not this woman at the beach to whom you undertook real obligations, but the woman who is sitting and waiting for you at home.'

Real love and respect in marriage means treating your spouse as though they are always present, and acting accordingly. It is where people are courageous enough to employ this rule at all times that happy marriages are found.

It is also by implementing many of the suggestions contained in this chapter that I believe society can finally rid itself of the ambiguities surrounding accusations of sexual harassment and especially date rape. If there was general respect within society for the principle that a couple only seclude themselves in private settings as a prelude to a sexual situation rather than merely as a casual social interaction then there would be no confusion about what happens later, if indeed the act did lead to sex. At the moment no lines are drawn and there is out-and-out confusion.

SOURCES — CHAPTER SIXTEEN

1. Avod a Zarah 18b
2. Kedushin 80b
3. Carol Botwin, *Tempted Women*, 1994
4. ibid.
5. Dr Shanor, *Why Men Are The Way They Are*, 1990
6. Babylonian, Talmud, Kedushin, 80b

CHAPTER SEVENTEEN

THE PAIN OF ADULTERY

'When Harold told me he was leaving home to move in with a woman he'd met at his office, I just collapsed. I simply could not believe it . . . Whenever I did have to go out to get some necessity or other, I was so paranoid I thought everybody was staring at me, thinking "poor, pathetic thing; no wonder her husband dumped her."'
How to Get Him Back from the Other Woman

O N A SPEAKING tour of North America I asked a group of Jewish women to think how they would feel if they discovered that their husband had an affair. Understandably, most said that they would be extremely hurt, and many went as far as to state that their whole world would collapse. The men in the audience were less vocal on the subject, but basically expressed the same sentiment. Because I wanted them to explore the underlying meaning of marriage, I asked the women exactly why they would be hurt. The answer seems obvious, but it leads to a better understanding of what marriage is all about. The consensus was that an affair would mean that their husband loved or was infatuated with somebody else, and that was the ultimate form of rejection. To have your husband commit adultery with someone, they said, was to be discarded like so much useless waste.

Fair enough. But what if it wasn't a long-standing affair, just a one-night stand while he was on a business trip? He obviously did not love the woman involved. He did it merely because he felt the urge, knowing full well that he loved his wife, and this was just a form of adventurism or sexual release, perhaps to cure the pangs of loneliness, or perhaps a brief quest for danger and excitement. In short, the husband thought it was no big deal. Would they still be hurt?

They said yes, most definitely. But I wanted to know why. I shaved away circumstances from the scenario that might distract our attention from the real reason why we find infidelity unacceptable: 'Why would you be upset? He did not love her, so you can't feel rejected. Suppose he even says that while the whole thing was going on, he was thinking about his wife! And it just happened to be that you, his wife, were not around, so what was he to do? And you also can't say that it means that he is attracted to other women and that's painful. First of all, because every spouse is somewhat attracted to people outside their marriage, although of course they may not do anything about it. Secondly, perhaps you, the wife, are far more attractive. What then? He only committed a sexual act with this other woman because his wife was not around and, for all intents and purposes, it appears that he had no other motive and he is telling the truth. So why be upset at all?' Here suddenly the audience was at pains to respond to the question. It's as if all married people react with revulsion to the thought of their spouse having an affair. But they don't quite know why.

We must seek to understand the deep, almost indescribable pain felt by a spouse upon discovering the marital infidelity of a partner. As I write this chapter two outrageous controversies are raging; one here in England and the other across the Atlantic. In Britain, the Conservative government has been rocked by the discovery that two of its ministers committed blatant acts of infidelity. One, the junior Transport Minister, was discovered to have had five mistresses, one of which affairs is said to have continued for over ten years. When his, by all accounts, devoted and loving wife discovered the affair, she took her husband's double-barrelled hunting rifle and blew off her own head. How can we account for the magnitude of pain and humiliation that will lead a wife to abandon her children and family in this most gruesome way?

At the same time, the famous Lorena Bobbit trial is raging in the US. A young Ecuadorian woman is being tried for cutting off the penis of her former Marine husband. After committing this act, she drove off in a rage from her home, reached a road intersection, and cast the penis, which she was still clutching, into the gutter. She claims that incessant abuse and marital rape on the part of her husband led her to a temporary state of intense and insane rage in which she dismembered her husband in response to all the pain and heartache he had caused her. Of particular note is her contention that her husband showed her lists of women with whom he had had sex. This is said to have been the final, most devastating part in the whole gory affair, that sparked off her wild spree. How crushed must this woman have felt from bearing witness in the most mocking way to her husband's infidelity, that she, a normal woman and wife, with no previous history of violence or emotional instability, should be led to this savage act? How can we account for these tragic stories?

The most profound reason why a wife (or husband, of course) is upset by infidelity is this: her husband, something which belonged to her, was used, even abused, by someone else. By doing so, the spouse who was not present was made to feel that they did not exist.

Most people would get upset if someone, even a friend, used their car without permission. Yet, if they asked, we might happily allow them to use it, as well as many other possessions. But then there are those things which are so personal and so private that we would not allow anyone to use them. For example, one's wedding ring is not the kind of thing that one ever feels comfortable about lending out. It is too personal, too private, to be given to someone else to use. The same may be said, for example, of one's bedroom. (One of the little things in life which irks me greatly is when married couples allow people to come into their bedroom, especially when it is part of a tour of the house.) But how much more so when it comes to one's husband or wife! When they share an intimate experience with someone else, we feel violated, just as if someone had used our most intimate object for their personal use.

This is the only plausible reason I see for the deep sense of hurt people feel when they discover that their spouses have engaged in compromising activities outside of marriage. We feel we possess our spouses; they belong to us, and they should not be 'used' by anyone else. We feel outraged when our house is burgled. It is one of the most frustrating things that can happen to us. Having worked hard to afford certain possessions, and to create a pleasant home, we feel abused and violated when a perfect stranger comes along, takes away our treasures and wrecks our home. And this is how we feel when confronted with infidelity, but the feeling of loss and hurt goes right to the core of our being.

In other words, the real crime and hurt associated with someone taking your car without your permission has little to do with the fact that the actual car was taken. It may be brought back complete and as good as before. The thief might even have filled the tank up with petrol. So why are you angry? *Because you were not asked!* The act of taking the car without you being asked belittles you and makes you seem insignificant. The person who takes it acts as if the car had no owner. The extreme outrage we feel when our possessions are used without our permission really has little to do with the object itself, and has everything to do with ourselves. *It is not the object that has been violated. We* have been violated. We weren't asked. We were treated as if we were not important enough to ask. We were treated as if we were insignificant, and as if we did not exist.

A car is only an insignificant part of our possessions, but a cheating spouse is the ultimate statement of our non-existence and insignificance. Marriage is a total statement of what we are and to what we aspire. We make the great sacrifices, endure the most extreme inconveniences, lay out vast sums of money, expend great emotional effort, all to make our spouse love us and remain happy with us. In short, we put all of ourselves into our marriage (unlike our cars), so that when our spouses betray us and have an affair with someone else, even if it is just a brief encounter not to be repeated, the hurt is indescribable and never to be forgotten. With that one action, our spouse, the one who is supposed to make us feel the *most* loved and the *most* significant, the one who is meant to make their universe revolve around us and treat us as if the sun has risen for our sake, has dismissed our existence in its entirety. By sharing the most intimate conversation, romance, and bedroom activities with a stranger, our spouse has compromised our existence completely by treating us as if we don't have to be asked, as if we were insignificant.

Humiliation is a Type of Murder

No wonder, then, that by far the overriding feeling associated with marital infidelity is *humiliation*, far more than pain, betrayal, or shock. The partner cheated against feels disgraced. In Judaism the biggest crime is to humiliate someone publicly. The reason that the Talmud declares that he who humiliates someone publicly loses their share in the world to come, and likens this act to killing, is that it is exactly so. The severity of the act of killing is that one person decides to negate the existence of the other in its entirety. There can be no greater crime, or statement of arrogance, than this. And the same is true of humiliating someone publicly. By humiliating them, one dismisses the existence of the other person by destroying their reputation and self-esteem. If you murder someone you incur a capital penalty, thereby losing your place in this world. But if you humiliate someone publicly, you lose your place in the world to come. You die an eternal death. It is a bigger sin to make someone *wish* they were dead than to make them dead. It is a far bigger sin to make someone a conscious participant in the act of their own murder.

The greatest form of humiliation, therefore, is adultery. When you commit adultery you are dismissing someone's existence in its entirety. You are saying that they couldn't compete. Your existence should be defined by your spouse's love. To love is to be a creator. By loving someone we call forth their existence from nothingness and make them feel that whether or not they will wake tomorrow morning actually makes a difference and will be felt by a significant number of people. To love then is to create someone anew. And to ignore someone is to consign them to insignificance and make them feel that if they die tomorrow no one will notice and no one will care. Adultery is the ultimate form of this rejection. Here is the same man who has spent his life, money, time and affection on you, dismissing you completely. He enjoys intimacy with another woman. He acts as if he has no wife. He pretends that you do not exist, that he is not married. What wife? He is saying that she doesn't exist.

A fascinating corollary which bears this point out – and which really caught my eye when I first saw it – is this: if a man is cheating on his wife and has a mistress, the mistress will be extremely upset to discover that he has a second mistress. Nearly all women who were serving as the lover or mistress of a married man said they would be furious if they discovered that they too were being cheated on. Some went as far as saying, 'I would kill him'. Yet on the other hand, paradoxically, the same women do not give a toss that this same man is having sexual liaisons with his own wife, perhaps even every night. They do not consider this as 'cheating'. To them, the wife is nothing. She is not even in competition. It is as though the wife does not even exist. The mistress can be devastatingly jealous of a third woman, but rarely of the wife. The reports that I have seen concur that roughly 80 per cent of women who serve as mistress to a married man would be 'very upset' if they discovered that the man was seeing yet another lover, and yet take no notice of the fact that he has a wife.

Is it not ironic that instead of the adulterous spouse feeling terrible remorse and humiliation for their act of betrayal, it is generally *the victim* who feels humiliated? Here we begin to see the magnitude of the crime of adultery, a crime in which the victim pays the highest price. Is there any other crime like this on the entire planet in which the victim experiences not only terrible hurt, and an outright negation of their entire existence, but also total humiliation? No wonder, then, that so many sinned-against spouses keep the unfaithfulness of their husband or wife a total secret. It reflects terribly on them that they were cheated on and in their own minds they feel inferior and inadequate.

Seen in this way, adultery represents the very antithesis of love, and not just in a practical sense. As explained above, adultery is the ultimate dismissal of someone else's existence. I say the ultimate, even amidst what may be construed as more heinous dismissals or crimes, such as murder, since in murder or other forms of violent crime the people usually hate each other. But in marriage, they claim and have taken vows to love each other.

The ultimate definition of love, I believe, is one person ascribing significance and totally enhancing the existence of another human being through their affection for them. When you love someone, their wishes become your wishes, their delights become your delights, their pleasures become your pleasures. Anything else is not love but selfishness. Love gives us the ability to put ourselves second to someone else, to make ourselves number two and even take pleasure in doing so, thus defying our essential human nature and survival-instinct to be selfish and to put ourselves first.

Playing the Role of Creator

If no one ever takes notice of you, it is as if you do not exist. You don't feel as if you are ever really alive. The ultimate negation of another person's existence is to ignore them. Conversely, the ultimate affirmation of their existence is to love and take notice of them. And commensurate with the degree of love which they are shown is the amount of confidence they will have and the degree to which they feel that they exist. A woman who feels that her husband is infatuated with her, and focuses all his attention on her, will feel more confident than the world's biggest supermodel. And the woman whose husband always cheats on her may easily succumb to suicide, since she feels ignored and as though she does not exist. I know of a woman who told me that after three years of marriage she had started to cut herself off in mid-sentence as if no one cared to hear her finish her statements.

This is the enormous power of love. Through loving someone intensely we can actually call forth their existence from nothingness, playing the role of creator, veritably bringing them to life. And by cheating on them and in effect ignoring them, we play the role of a destroyer who takes life. Whereas love enhances and uplifts our spouse's existence, adultery degrades and destroys it. There is no simpler or more profound way of putting it. This simple truth captures the essence of adultery and why it constitutes the most serious breach of the marital bond.

A Sense of Possession in Marriage

A wife must be allowed to feel that her husband is only *her* husband. And a husband must be allowed to feel that his wife is only *his* wife. This kind of attachment that develops between married couples is essential to the health and stability of every marriage, which will only last if both partners feel desirable and above all, confident.

Hence, one of the gravest sins in the entire Torah is to come between a husband and wife or wife and husband. For example, one must never embarrass a husband in front of his wife, or even cause him to look silly or misinformed.

I was told a story by a friend about a famed Rabbi who was hosting a young, newly married couple at his home for the Sabbath lunch. The young husband was trying to help set the table and moved the candlesticks which had been left on the table from the night before. His wife told him it was forbidden to move them on the Sabbath, since the Bible expressly prohibits the kindling or extinguishing of fire, and moving them might cause them to go out. 'How could you have been so silly?' the woman asked her husband. But the husband continued to move them, saying that since the candles were not burning, it was permitted to move them. At that point she turned to the great sage and said, 'Please tell my husband that I am right so that we can settle this argument. I can't believe that he doesn't know that they can't be moved.' The sage twisted his face, grabbed his beard and said, 'This is a most complicated legal question which I cannot rule on until I consult the sources at length.' The wife was flabbergasted. This was a clear case. How could the Rabbi be so mixed up? But she dropped the issue.

After the couple left, the Rabbi's wife asked him why he had behaved so strangely. 'Indeed,' she said, 'the young woman was correct. The candelabra could not be moved. So why didn't you respond to her protestation so that they could solve the issue?'

And the Rabbi answered simply, 'Because I would rather appear as an ignoramus than make a husband look foolish in front of his wife.'

The attachment between husband and wife goes to the very core of their beings. A husband belongs to his wife and vice versa, in a far deeper way than we can say of our other belongings. A car might lend us prestige and allow us to travel from point A to point B, and a house might shelter us from the cold and lend us dignity and a sense of permanence. But a spouse makes us feel whole, complete and loved, thus removing our existential loneliness. And therefore when they are used or lend themselves to use we feel personally violated, infinitely more so than with any physical object. Knowing that a spouse has committed adultery makes the spouse who remained faithful feel dirty. Just as one's car can be stolen, joyridden, and returned in pitiful condition, the same applies to one's spouse. But since one's husband or wife is part of oneself, the dirt created is felt inside. It is a violation of one's self.

From my personal experience in counselling men and women who discover that their spouse has been unfaithful, the thoughts expressed above are borne out by experience: again and again, the overriding emotion which they describe to me is one of humiliation. Yes, there is betrayal and there is a loss of trust, but what hurts the most is the humiliation.

These feelings of humiliation resound heavily in the personal statements of wives who have uncovered their husbands' infidelity and those of other men: 'Since I have been divorced I have been astounded at the number of married men who have expressed interest in me – the first was my ex-husband's best friend, who I regarded as a brother. I still can't believe the crassness of some men – how easily they disregard a sense of loyalty to their wives. Wives, I have a message for you – your husband is out hustling women. Those of us with self-respect are disgusted by him, and you should be too. Divorce him and get some self respect! I am thirty-eight, currently living with a male who is my best friend, but before that I lived for nine years of marriage with a sexist man until I found out what was going on.'[1]

The Attraction of Novelty

Coupled with this feeling of humiliation is a sense of being discarded and used, no longer fresh, exciting or invigorating. I remember once I was trying to sell a Colour Notebook computer. It was only seven months old and I advertised it as the top-of-the-line model available. It was not cheap, but, for a quick sale, I was selling it at a heavily discounted price. A student friend came in to inquire about it, and asked if he could send a fax to his father who knew much about computers. Without hesitation I allowed him to, knowing full well the quality of the item in question. Within an hour the fax came back to my office. It read: 'Marc, do not buy the computer. It is definitely not worth it. It has now been superseded by a newer model.' For the life of me, although this was only a computer, and one that I was trying to get rid of at that, I still felt personally humiliated by the fax. The bargain was not a bargain, not because it wasn't a terrific machine, and not because it wasn't a competitive price, but merely because there was now a newer, more up-to-date model. To be sure, this new model would cost a hefty lot more, but just to gain the new features, which were marginal at best, it is worthwhile discarding a great deal on the old.

Perhaps this is how a sinned-against spouse feels. Not only is there a sense of personal rejection, but rejection for a reason that they could never compete against. Every wife knows that among the many women that their husband will set eyes upon, most of them will have no great advantage over their wives. They are not necessarily smarter, more beautiful, glamorous, or even more sexy. But they are one thing that the wife could never again be: *new and untried.* They have a novelty value which the wife does not. And in nine cases out of ten, the attraction felt by the husband, and the excitement engendered by the affair, is for this reason alone. So how can a wife compete? Their every talent and very opinion of themselves lie strewn by the wayside, for they are competing in an arena where they cannot even enter the battle. They are powerless to alter the main reason for the other party's victory.

What makes this feeling of unfair competition even more painful is this absurd and clearly ironic suggestion: instead of the fact that I am his wife engendering and consolidating his loyalty, as it should, the reverse is true. Because I am his wife, and therefore he is used to me, I can never be as exciting, or indeed as forbidden, as a woman who is not his wife. It is almost as if the marriage itself is the reason for the infidelity. Hence, one of the wives' main reactions to an adulterous husband is this: 'It is my fault. Why was I so devoted to him? I shouldn't have run and done everything for him. I gave him the best years of my life, my youth, and his children, and this is what he does to me. I was too easy. I should have been a lot tougher. I should have played more hard to get.' Thus, adultery will initiate a cycle in which the wife, too, will be less loyal and devoted, and slowly the entire marriage begins to unravel.

After Adultery

There is a terrible confusion and confounding of the emotions in which innocent victims search their souls for collusion. It is an inescapable tragedy of adultery that the victim is left to feel the culprit, and is even more hurt than a remorseful husband after the event.

Telling your spouse that the adultery was no big deal makes things far worse; it utterly destroys and exposes the folly of the typical male defence of their infidelity: it was only sex, I didn't love her, it wasn't at all serious. Far from this claim lessening the pain of their spouse, it just adds insult to injury. The less serious it is, the more it shows that they completely dismissed the existence of their wife entirely. You see, if a husband was tormented and tortured over whether or not they were going to commit adultery, if they felt terrible remorse afterwards, instead of dismissing it as a trivial and passing event, at least then they would be showing that they took their wives into consideration and acted as if they did exist. But here, when they brush it off as nothing, they are making matters far worse. They are basically arguing that they *did not reckon at all* with the fact that they were married. It was no big deal. My wife never even came into my deliberations. I acted just as I would have done when I was single, when I didn't have to consider that I might be hurting someone. If it does happen, at the very least don't pretend that it was nothing. While to you it may just have been sex, and you think that you can go back to your wife in good conscience, to your wife it was serious indeed since you made her feel like she wasn't your wife at all.

In the *Hite Report*, a woman discusses the turmoil her husband's affairs brought into their life.

> Over a period of ten years, my husband had been unfaithful. We had gone through several crises, all over one woman, and with the help of marriage counsellors, ministers, realities, and friends, I had come through. Of a forgiving nature anyway – 'soft' – I wanted the children to have a united family atmosphere to grow up in. I believed my husband would grow out of his 'yearning' for another and accept his responsibilities to our

family. He didn't. In the end there was a complete breakdown. He started disappearing literally overnight 'just to sort things out'. I was 'only trying to help' and he was 'sorting things out'. In the end I couldn't take any more. My husband was always telling me that I didn't seem to need him as the other woman did. What he meant was that I managed without him – I had to – it wasn't that I wanted to.[2]

This is one of the reasons why after the adultery the marriage may never again be the same. The wife may never again be as loving or caring as she once was. This is not because she is still angry or vengeful or even because she is hurt. Rather, the reason is that she feels that it was her goodwill itself and her over-exertion to be a good wife which led to her husband's infidelity. But no more of that. She will make him spend more time earning her love, rather than seducing other women. Not to spite, but because she wants his emotions firmly fixed on herself rather than someone else.

The proof that the change which can be caused in a marriage following an adulterous affair comes about not of out of spite but from a genuine sense of hurt, humiliation and outrage can easily be established by the predominant feeling of love for the husband which still exists amidst the sense of hurt after the affair. 'I still love my husband very much, even though this other relationship he is involved in is hurting me deeply. I have never had a desire not to love him. I really don't think I could stop loving him.'

The First Marital Dispute in the Bible

To extend this line of thinking, it will be helpful to examine the first marital dispute in the Bible, recorded in Genesis 21:9. It is a fascinating story. Sarah and Abraham want children, but Sarah is barren. In an effort to ensure that Abraham has a son, she gives him her maidservant Hagar, a former Egyptian princess, to marry. Abraham therefore has a son through her: Ishmael, later father of the Arab peoples. But God has foretold through an angelic guest that Sarah will also have a child, and his name will be Isaac. Sure enough, this indeed happens, bringing great joy and happiness into their lives, and especially that of Sarah. However, something then goes very wrong. The Bible relates, 'And Sarah saw the son of Hagar the Egyptian, whom she had borne unto Abraham, making sport.' Sarah felt that Ishmael was having an adverse influence on her son Isaac, and she therefore commanded Abraham that he get rid of his son Ishmael. The Bible continues (v.10), 'Wherefore she said unto Abraham, "Cast out this bondwoman and her son, for he shall not be heir with my son Issac."' But Abraham was very unhappy at this; the Bible continues, 'This was very grievous unto the sight of Abraham, on account of his son.'

In this squabble, Sarah seems to put Abraham in a very difficult position; she asks him to cast out Ishmael, who, regardless of the fact that he was borne to him by the maidservant, is still his son. Even if he was being an adverse influence, one can only imagine the grief and conflict of loyalties that Abraham must have felt. At first glance it would appear that Sarah's request, although perhaps founded on some facts, is incredibly harsh and unreasonable. But in v.12 it is written that God suddenly intercedes on Sarah's behalf: 'God said unto Abraham, "Let it not be grievous in your eyes because of the lad, and because of the bondwoman; all that Sarah has said unto you, harken unto her voice, for in Isaac shall seed be called unto you."'

Abraham heeds God's advice, and we read that he 'rose early in the morning, took bread and a bottle of water and gave it to Hagar, putting them and the child on her shoulder, and sent her away, and she departed.'

What is fascinating about this story is not only the fact that

God deemed it necessary to intercede in this, the first recorded marital argument, but that furthermore he takes the side of Sarah, the wife. This is interesting, because the reason he takes her side seems to be, not necessarily that he thinks that she is right – her position seems very difficult to sustain, given that she herself had given Hagar to Abraham and told him to have a child with her – but that, regardless of whether she was right or wrong, the essential question was the peace and harmony of the marriage. In other words, for the sake of peace in a marriage it is not really important whether an aggrieved party is justly aggrieved or not. So long as they are upset, that is enough. And the most important thing is to end the argument as early as possible.

Harmony not Justice

This may be very difficult for us to understand, and indeed this story is, to modern thinking, one of the hardest to comprehend in the Bible. Our society is far more interested in justice, in the narrow sense of right and wrong, than it is in the pursuit of true justice, which entails the establishment of peace and harmony. We are always too ready and willing to start an argument, or to criticize someone dear to us when we feel that we have been wronged, and to feel that this injustice must be corrected. But here God says that we must always listen to our spouses, because what is most important is the preservation of the relationship, regardless of how difficult it may be to take heed of the other party and accord their opinion respect even when it may not make sense to us. The promotion of peace, love and harmony by far outweighs questions of right and wrong and our individual opinions.

Stated in other words, one of the greatest insults that can be paid from one spouse to another, and the greatest offence within a marriage, is to ignore the opinions of the other. It is to treat them as if they are unimportant; as though, because to us their opinion makes no sense, it is therefore not worth listening to. What this effectively says is that only when they are rational does their opinion have worth within the marriage; their intrinsic will is unimportant to us.

But we don't marry people in order to have them make sense. We marry them in order to love them and make them feel special. This is achieved first and foremost by never ignoring them or making them feel like idiots. Any marriage which proceeds along those lines is bound for certain failure. If one person feels that their opinion does not matter, then it is as if they do not exist. A relationship involves compromising one's own opinions, assumptions and positions, in order to accommodate those of the other party with whom one shares one's life and home.

The Adulterer: Adventurer or Nomad?

To commit adultery and to have affairs while married is to maintain, instead of a state of wholeness and completion, a state of nomadic indifference and wandering. The unfaithful partner will never be complete because he or she understands human sexuality in terms of a selfish desire for pleasure only, with whomever and wherever he or she so desires. They have no intention of accommodating the sensitivities of their spouse, and indeed display an indifference to their very existence. The adulterer has no permanent home, although he may have a wife, children and a house. Worse still, he has no other half. He does not really have his own bed, for his bed is wherever he makes it that evening. His life is but a brief thrill in the face of a passing wind. For him there is no warmth for half his heart is to be found elsewhere. He is like a man punctured, with all his love and warmth pouring out in different directions. Because it cannot be focused and directed toward one target, he cannot stay attached to one individual. Whereas a man or woman who remains faithful and loyal in marriage becomes stronger and stronger through the love shown them and through being synthesized with their other half, the adulterer is different: he is like a balloon losing air, becoming more and more diminished with the passage of time. Because his sexual steam escapes in useless directions, it cannot propel him toward his wife and family in a lasting and meaningful way. His life is not about love, but the opposite. He causes pain whenever and wherever he seeks and finds pleasure. Specifically in the area where he is meant to generate the most warmth, in his marital relations, he generates friction and heat. Every act of love is a stab in the heart to his other half. Now, instead of just him being punctured, he has punctured her life as well. Her former goodwill now oozes out slowly, and she finds every reason in the world to quarrel with her husband, even over the most petty problems. She has been transformed by her very own husband from a partner into an adversary.

Think about the level of contradiction in adultery. One partner in the marriage receives pleasure and excitement, while through the very same act hurt and pain is caused to, not just the husband or wife of this person, but to their other half. One literally acts in contradiction to oneself. One gains momentary happiness by permanently stabbing oneself in the heart.

One of the famous stories of the Bible is that of Esau, older brother of Jacob, who sells his birthright to his younger brother thereby squandering the privileges inherent therein. Why did he do it? Well, he was hungry. In fact, he was very hungry. What had he been doing that made him so hungry? He had had a very busy day, which included murdering a man, and stealing another man's wife – adultery.[2] This brief mention of Esau's adultery in the Bible is not incidental but actually central to the entire subject of adultery, because what it teaches us is that the adulterer is a nomad, as was Esau, a hunter, a man who lives from day to day, whose life has no permanence and who is entirely fly-by-night. Esau has no home and no bed. He has no dining room table. He is a hunter. He eats the beast of the field while in the field. The adulterer convinces himself that he is an explorer, but really he is a *wanderer*. He thinks to himself that really he is not doing anything radically wrong, just experimenting with other women and broadening his sexual experience and taste. He does not intend to harm his marriage. He will argue that he loves his wife, and what is so wrong with just a bit of excitement and pleasure on the side? What he does not realize is that his experimentation transforms him from a man of permanence to a man whose life is ephemeral. In the same way that the wanderer can never stay in one place, so too this man cannot stay connected to one woman. His life is totally unpredictable. To be sure, this lifestyle may indeed lead to passion, in the same way that the man of the jungle's life might be construed to be more exciting than that of the insurance salesman. But it is exciting precisely because of its lack of permanence. It is an illusion, and the adulterer hurts himself and destroys far more than he builds. But what is worse is that had they made the effort they could have had the same excitement in marriage, and even more. A married couple's sexual lives are the most special of all, far more than any extramarital affair could be, because, since they know their spouses so well and they are married to and trust each other, they have the added advantage of feeling completely comfortable with one another. Thus, they do not feel any pressure to 'perform' for one another in bed, they are not seeking to impress each other or demonstrate their sexual prowess. But, in every extramarital setting, since excitement is the *raison d'être* of the experience, there can never be the same degree of sensitivity since one is always conscious of how one is being 'rated'.

He has demonstrated that he has no home, that he has no wife, that he has no other half. He has also demonstrated that concomitant with his capacity for love and caring is a capacity for causing pain and selfishness. He will always remain incomplete until he begins to understand the profundity of his marriage and acts accordingly.

SOURCES — CHAPTER SEVENTEEN

1.   Midrash Rabbah su Genesis.
2.   Shere Hite, *Hite Report*, 1987

CHAPTER EIGHTEEN

ADULTERY OF THE MIND

But I have more respect for fantasy than that. You are what you dream . . . Because sex is all in the head . . . What did it matter that 'technically' I was faithful to Bennett? I was unfaithful to him at least ten times a week in my thoughts – and at least five of those times I was unfaithful to him when we were making love.
Erica Jong in *Fear of Flying* (expletives deleted)

SOME COUPLES are prepared to undertake the rigorous steps to restore ongoing sexual excitement in their relationships. Others, however, love taking shortcuts. What I have found from dozens of conversations is that by far the most common shortcut is fantasizing about another man or a woman, whom one finds very appealing, while in bed with one's spouse. This fantasy might be one's secretary or assistant, business associate, the milkman, or even the glamorous stars of the silver screen. Hey, if you can't actually take the person of your dreams to bed in real life, you can bring them into the matrimonial bed with the creative power of your imagination. If you can't literally be 'in bed with Madonna', the next best thing is to make your wife into Madonna. Many men and women to whom I spoke feel that at least this way they can bring much needed novelty and variety into their otherwise monotonous, monogamous sexual routine, without actually beong unfaithful or hurting the spouse they cherish.

Is this all right? Or does it do more harm than good? Is it worth replacing your spouse with the thoughts of another person if it brings immediate gratification in your sexual life?

Do you know what goes on in your spouse's mind when you make love? When the lights go out and you press against each other's flesh, are you sure that it is your face they are seeing? This question is closely related to the dilemma posed by the following occurrence. A few years ago I met a very friendly Jewish businessman who was happily married with children, but his wife was not Jewish. As time progressed he became more committed to his faith, and was anxious that his wife should begin to think seriously about conversion. She was not as interested as he was and needed some convincing. He suggested that I meet the two of them to talk about the subject. Throughout the meeting she remained somewhat hostile, although she has always been a very pleasant person. She feared that his Judaism would eventually come between her and her husband, and saw me as part of the problem.

But when we got onto the subject of Jewish marital laws, I mentioned that it is absolutely forbidden in Judaism for a husband to think about another woman while making love to his wife, and vice versa. Her eyes now swelled with tears and her attitude was completely turned around. You see, her husband was extremely handsome and charismatic and, although she trusted his *physical* fidelity to her completely, as she aged she just did not know what was going through his *mind*. True, she felt confident that he would forever remain loyal to her, but what about his thoughts? Was it the thought of one of his young employees that created passion in their bedroom? She told me, 'That law is the most beautiful thing I have ever heard. If this is what your religion is about, then I would like to become a Jewess right this very minute.'

Is a Fantasy Only a Fantasy?

Just a few days after this heartening event, I was studying with a lawyer friend as part of a weekly class. I related the gist of the above story and he was not at all sympathetic. 'I would not be offended,' he told me, 'if my wife thought of someone else when we made love. On the contrary, if that's the way she gets excited, then fine. It makes for greater passion in our marriage.'

'Yes,' I countered, 'but don't you feel that in such circumstances she would not be making love with *you*, but with a phantom, almost using you? Surely, it is not an experience which you are both sharing.'

But he was emphatic. 'What goes on in my wife's heart of hearts is her business. So long as she remains loyal and loving in all the areas that I can overtly discern, I'm happy.'

Perhaps. But from many of my experiences I have found people deeply troubled by the possibility of a spouse secretly harbouring a strong sexual attraction to other people in general, and to a specific individual in particular. Most people view this kind of attraction in two ways, both of which are negative. Firstly, they think it indicates a fault in themselves, either sexually, physically, intellectually, or emotionally; and secondly, they take it as almost a kind of infidelity; an adultery of the mind, as it were. In the words of one woman who described her exasperation to me: 'If I am attractive, then why does my husband need to look at other women? The answer can only be that I am not as attractive as other women are. Hence, every time he looks intently at an attractive woman, I feel as though my own femininity has been stabbed and I wonder if he fantasizes about her or me. I no longer feel like a woman.'

Here's another related question: is it OK to be turned on by men and women outside of the marriage, and then use the excitement generated by staring at them to bring passion into marriage?

Once I was walking with my wife and my brother in South Beach, the world-famous southern tip of Miami Beach, Florida, where I grew up. Today, it is the young people's capital of the world. Each night thousands of people revel, drink, and party there throughout all hours of the night. The setting and atmosphere is highly sexually charged and it goes without saying that a large percentage of the people are there to pick up or be picked up. I marvelled at the setting and said out loud that I did not know if this was the correct place for married couples to be. My brother, who is certainly not a rabbi, got upset. 'What's wrong with being here?' he asked me. 'There are many married couples who come here, and no doubt they do get turned on by many of the people who they see at the bars and walking up and down the strip. The women with low cut blouses and short skirts. The men with their glorious muscles bulging out from their tight tank-top shirts and tight jeans. But this is all very productive and good. Couples come here, they get excited and feel sexy. And they go home and make love. Do you have anything against that?' he asked.

I thought long and hard. On the one hand, what harm is done? The husband and wife are there together, and they are experiencing the sights together. As long as they go home together, as opposed to with someone else, if it brings passion into their marriage as a result of their night out, what harm has been done? On the contrary, this might even be said to have helped and enhanced their marriage! Far from focusing, therefore, on its pernicious effect, perhaps if it really is helpful we should encourage husbands and wives to entertain the thoughts of others while in the matrimonial bed?

The Sin of Stealing People's Goodwill

In his list of twenty-four of the most unforgivable crimes within the Jewish religion, for which 'God will not allow the person who commits such deeds to repent because of the gravity of his transgression', Maimonides, the great twelfth-century Jewish legalist and philosopher, lists none of those offences which society would say constitute the most heinous crimes. Included in his list are, for example, one who causes the masses to sin, one who hates admonishment because admonishment leads to repentance, and one who takes a share of a thief's gain. He who does that, does not know to whom the stolen articles belong, so he cannot repent properly by returning the items in question. Furthermore, by supporting his trade he serves as a reinforcement to the thief and causes him to sin. But one of the most fascinating offences which he lists, the severity of which defies all belief, is the offence of *stealing goodwill*.

What does stealing goodwill mean? One of the examples which Maimonides lists goes something like this: Jack has just received a raise at work and has therefore gone out and bought an expensive bottle of Dom Perignon champagne. Just as he arrives home with the intention of opening his bottle, he discovers that an old friend is calling on his doorstep. Jack hugs his friend, kisses him on the cheek, and tells him that he is ecstatically happy to see him, and that in his honour he will be opening an expensive bottle of Dom Perignon. He does, and by doing so he engenders a false sense of appreciation and love with his friend. He has misled and stolen his friend's goodwill by performing an insincere gesture. His friend, oblivious to the background of the bottle, will walk away with a false sense of his own importance in his long-lost acquaintance's eyes.

A Secret Breach of Trust

Adultery is not confined to a physically sexual affair or inter-course. For all intents and purposes, adultery takes place every time a man and woman who are married, but not to each other, create a strong emotional attachment and dependency on a member of the opposite sex to whom they are not married, even if they never lay a finger on each another. The reason is that this constitutes an abuse of the marriage. A couple get married not just to have sex together, but to grow dependent on one another to the point where they become synthesized as one unit, albeit in two bodies. You get married not only because you are in love, but because you want to feel needed. Notice how upset parents become when their children grow up, move out to college, and are no longer dependent on their parents. Any emotional depend-ency on inappropriate people outside of the marriage encroaches upon the ability of the couple to be welded together as one.

Taking this a step further, the ultimate abuse of a marriage, and the ultimate form of stealing goodwill is when a husband or wife goes to bed with their spouse, engages in intimate and even passionate behaviour, yet all the time thinks about somebody else. Not only is this a very severe form of abuse because it relegates one's spouse to the status of mere flesh and uses their body as mere friction in a manner which is really just one step away from masturbation, but it is wrong because it *steals* good-will. Your spouse enjoys a special moment with you, you endeavour to give them pleasure and they walk away with a deeper feeling of loving and attachment to you because of it, but it is an illusion, it is false. You didn't even think about them. In the realm of thought, you were somewhere else completely, with someone else completely. You have decapitated them and stuck someone else's head upon their shoulders. No wonder then that the code of Jewish law lists this offence as one of the most grievous sexual offences within Jewish law. And rightly so. Because we cannot take something as precious as our spouse, someone who is so devoted and loving towards us, and literally use their bodies for mere friction or what amounts to a form of masturbation. Nor can we insult them by showing that they don't excite us, while other people do.

Making passionate love to your wife when really you are thinking about someone else, or even being turned on by someone else and then making passionate love to your wife when really you should be turned on by them, is a serious breach of trust that, while it may never be discovered, severely erodes our innocence and purity. It is also one of the greatest forms of insult that we can offer to another human being, and one which people are not very likely to forgive or forget easily. It is very detectable and discernible. There isn't a single man or woman in the world who does not know if their spouse is millions of miles away while they are in bed. The love-making is different and a big gap, a great distance, is felt. It simply cannot be concealed. Replacing your spouse with thoughts of someone else in human sexual relations is a grave sin and should be avoided in the very same way that adultery should be avoided.

One of the beautiful things about sincerity is that it is immediately obvious. My favourite saying from the Talmud is this: those things which emanate from the heart penetrate the heart. And just as there can be no substitute for real emotion and truth, so too there can be no way of concealing lies and insincerity. Loving someone means making them feel like they are the foremost human on the planet, or at the very least, in your own personal life. And no matter how you slice it, whether we say sex must be accompanied by love, or whether we accept that sex can be for the purpose of pleasure only, there is still no one in the world who will feel comfortable about their bodies being used for friction. The reason is that it dehumanizes us. We no longer feel attractive and complete human beings, we feel like mere meat.

Perhaps an even better description would be that we feel like a headless trunk. Our bodies are being used by our spouse, but we have been beheaded. When our spouse closes their eyes, it is not in ecstasy but to escape from seeing us, to deny who they are with, and enter into a world of fantasy where someone other than ourselves is the real source of warmth and sexual excitement.

Therefore, thinking about another woman when you are in bed with your wife, or vice versa, is something always to be avoided, however difficult. There are those who would argue that sometimes it is truly necessary and that they cannot proceed in the act of making love without it. To them I respond, it is not love you are making, but a severe act of abuse. Furthermore, rather than drawing closer to your spouse as result of your love-making, you are being drawn further away. The rule we must remember is this: every romantic encounter in which we engage must be for the purpose of bringing us closer and closer to our spouse. Every sexual encounter must be for the purpose of creating a deeper and more lasting bond with our husband or wife. Thinking about someone else during marital relations creates dramatic distance between us and our spouse and pushes us, mentally, into the arms of someone else. When a couple are in bed together they should focus on one another, because the ultimate way of expressing real affection and love within marriage is through a special sexual encounter. We must not destroy that intimacy by mentally pulling other people into our bedrooms with us. Rather than use these shortcuts that bring short-term gains but long-term damages, it is far better to follow the advice set out in this and other books and work and learn to see the woman in your wife and the man in your husband and thereby retain passion constantly.

CHAPTER NINETEEN

AFTER ADULTERY: RESTORING TRUST

'My wife is a wonderful woman, but after twenty years of marriage she just doesn't light my fire the way she used to. So I dabble on the side. And who does it hurt anyway? I don't love any of them, and they're never really serious. My wife is the mother of my children and my companion for life. Why should she feel threatened by any of these temporary girlfriends?'

DOES THE MAN above sound strange to you? He shouldn't. All too many people are convinced of the same thing: they'll have adulterous affairs, maintaining the entire time that it has no effect on their marriage. In this chapter I will show you that it just isn't so. If a couple does survive an adulterous affair, and even if their love for each other grows as a result of working together through the difficult times to re-establish their marriage on a proper footing, this will not be without severe cost and sacrifice.

The first casualty of adultery is the most severe of all: that of trust. Even if an unfaithful husband or wife swear that they will never again be unfaithful, and even if they are completely forgiven by their spouse with heartfelt sincerity, still the act will never be *forgotten*, and will serve as a painful reminder to that spouse of what the person they are married to is capable of doing. Face it, if it happened once it could happen again and forgiving and forgetting are different things altogether. Adultery leads to a severe case of paranoia on the part of the offended spouse. Their self-confidence has been shattered. They see the infidelity on the part of their spouse as a grotesque act of abandonment and they feel discarded. They feel as though they have been weighed in the balance by their spouse against someone else and have come up wanting. Although this book attempts to analyse why it might have happened, and a trained therapist might do the same, no spouse will think along those lines. They will not want to hear stories of human nature, and that it is nothing serious since it can be construed as natural, or that their spouse's partner was uglier, less intelligent and less successful than they are. All they will feel is hurt, and all that they will think is that they were passed over for someone else. They couldn't care less whether or not this is true. Nothing hurts as much as adultery.

Fits of Paranoia

Coupled with the actual fact that an act of adultery has indeed been committed, it is inevitable that paranoia will set in. Every time the formerly adulterous partner is away from home their spouse will be anxious and nervous. What are they up to? I know that they swore it would never happen again. But it happened once before. Who are they meeting? These kinds of emotions will put severe strain on the marriage, because the spouse will be unusually nervous. They will speak to their partner in an unkind tone, and suspicions will be cast in all the wrong directions. This of course will lead to the partner feeling unfairly trapped, and that his spouse's insecurities are too deep to deal with. They may not be able to discuss their anxieties with their spouse, since they don't want to accuse their partner of something that may not even be happening, and look like insecure and paranoid wrecks. But in truth, it is the erring partner who has done this to them.

No one else. It was he or she who gave rise to the paranoia, but the sinned-against suffers from it. He takes offence at the many insinuations, but it is he who created them.

This will also invariably lead the spouse to accuse his partner of being irrational. The most innocent conversations will be suspected. Many arguments will ensue, and the errant spouse will find himself forced to lie to his spouse about innocent conversations, because his spouse does not see them as innocent. This is paranoia, and it is irrational but it is unavoidable and irreversible.

Thus a vicious cycle ensues, and instead of being honest as a result of the adulterous act, and a subsequent promise never to allow this to happen again, a breakdown of communications takes place. This is a shame, because one of the best ways to avoid adultery in marriage is for a husband and wife to have constant communication on the subject of sexual attraction to other men and women. They must be honest with one another. A husband must be able to come home and speak with his wife honestly and directly about the secretary with whom he fears he may be coming too close, and the wife about the business associate with whom she has been working on an important project and perhaps spending too much time with and allowing an unhealthy situation to develop. When these things can be discussed with total frankness and openness within a marriage, then not only can they be averted, but greater honesty and trust can be brought into the marriage. But what can one do here, when the once errant partner brings up the subject and his spouse immediately jumps down his throat?

The problem here, clearly, is that the trust in the marriage, upon which every good relationship is built, has been dealt a severe blow. How can confidence be restored? The essential fact that adultery has been committed cannot be denied. There is no way out. There may be paranoia, but as the famous American baseball player Yogi Berra once said, 'Just because you're paranoid doesn't mean that they are *not* out to get you.'

In Chapter 5 we mentioned that one of the hallmarks of an adulterous affair is trust. A spouse and their lover trust each other to tell no one about the affair, unless they both agree on disclosure. They trust each other not to make their sexual encounter only a one-night stand and to make the affair somewhat lasting, and not just 'to love them and leave them'. It is this immense trust which adulterous parties put in one another that serves to bind them to one another, and feel comfortably sexual with one another, amidst their very precarious situation. Their trust induces a sense of togetherness and closeness, as if it is just them against all the world. They understand that their actions might make them into pariahs, and they thus trust that even if they are rejected by everyone else, they still have each other to lean upon and rely on. They trust never to be abandoned by their lover, even when the heat is on.

Marriage must have at least this same degree of trust if it is to survive and flourish. A husband and wife need to feel completely comfortable with one another, confident that there are no secrets between them.

Love is Impossible if You Don't Respect Each Other

The loss of trust is coupled with another miserable consequence of adultery, namely, the loss of respect which one spouse has for the other in the wake of an act of infidelity. Of all the long-term effects of adultery, this is surely the most disastrous. Every marriage is predicated not just on love, but on an underlying layer of mutual respect and trust which is the foundation for an overlying layer of love. No wife can watch the husband she once respected as a loyal spouse and adoring father commit adultery without his stature being drastically reduced in her eyes. When she witnesses how every passing member of the opposite sex grabs his eye or how he flirts like an adolescent to the point of embarrassing himself she places him together with so many other 'dirty old men' who are not in the least bit impressive to her, because they are so weak and seem incapable of discipline and real commitment. The husband whom she once considered to be a paragon of virtue and conviction has been reduced to nothing more than quivering jelly in her eyes. She perceives him as being bereft of an ability to control his life and shape his own destiny. In the final analysis, sexual infidelity is all about weakness. It means giving in to impulsive and selfish yearnings without any recourse to how this submission will affect the lives of those whom we love most.

Inevitably, the average spouse will do their utmost to excuse and justify their infidelity by claiming neglect on the part of their spouse, often a lack of love and sensitivity, which they claim to have found in their lover. But while this may be true, it does not change the fact that they had a duty to their spouse to do something about that neglect. Their obligation within the marriage was to solve the problems within the marriage, rather than increasing the confusion and adding yet another complication. The operative rule always to remember is this: no problem in any marriage is solved by adding yet another complication or distraction. They committed adultery because they had no conviction and were frail. Can we look up to someone who puts personal pleasure above sensitivity to others, honesty, commitment, and decency? The answer is a resounding 'no'. One woman told me: 'At twenty-two one of my professors became very close to me. He told me constantly of how his wife didn't understand him and how cold she was to him. We almost started an affair, but I then met his wife. She was a beautiful mother of three with an idiot for a husband.'

I mentioned earlier that the overwhelming cause of female infidelity is neglect on the part of the husband. But still this can never serve as an excuse for adultery. Even if your husband is the world's biggest idiot, leave him, but don't commit adultery. Divorce will be a sad step, but far better than forcing yourself to become duplicitous and unfaithful. Perhaps if men and women deeply understood just how badly they were embarrassing themselves by displaying an inability to control their sexual selves, they might instead opt to preserve their dignity by remaining faithful to those who have done so much for them and who care for them most. Even better, they might choose the most difficult course of action, namely to work on solving their problems, rather than taking the easy way out with a lover, thereby creating even greater problems.

Why is respect so paramount in every relationship? For two reasons. The first has to do with the ephemeral quality of emotion. Whereas emotion is volatile, intellect is cool, calm and unchanging. While it is possible to transfer one's affections from apples to oranges, it will always be true that in a thriving relationship, both intellect and emotion are necessary. No couple could happily stay together for intellectual reasons alone. Without love, there exists no glue, no attraction strong enough to keep a man and woman bound to one another. Emotions are fly by night; they fluctuate with alarming regularity. The woman you love one moment you hate the next. The man you cannot live without one day, you cannot live with the next day, and so on.

But respect based on an intellectual and moral appreciation of one's spouse provides a bedrock into which emotion can be anchored, as well as a spring whence emotion may flow out. If a husband respects his wife, and if a wife looks up to her husband as a kind, decent and generous man, then the attraction they feel for each other will not easily come undone or fly away with the wind. In this scenario, they don't merely love each other. Rather, they have an undeniable *reason* to love each other; their love is based on more than the feeling of *being in love*. So even amidst a terrible argument, they cannot deny the love they have for each other because the reason for their attraction is not based on emotion alone, but on emotion supported by intellect. They share a life together for reasons that are tangible and glaringly apparent. A wife might be upset that her husband goes away on business and doesn't call for four days. But when she remembers how he sits every night helping the children to do their homework, and how he visits his elderly mother several times a week, she cannot remain angry for long for his regular actions serve as a powerful counter-balance to her current, transient state of displeasure.

The other reason why respect is so vital is that it ends arguments. When one spouse respects the other they always find a reason to end an argument because they believe that their spouse must be right as they are a good, decent, level-headed person who is usually correct. When a husband, for example, fights with his wife whom he respects and looks up to as an honest, non-argumentative and humble individual, he will find it far easier to end the argument and apologize to his wife because he will assume that *she* is justified and that the reason for the argument lies at his doorstep. 'I'm just being stubborn,' he tells himself. Without this kind of respect, marital disputes would drone on endlessly with each party believing that they are correct and insisting that the other party must capitulate.

Stated in other words, the esteem which one accords a truly special and precious spouse serves as the pretext for capitulation in the heat of an altercation since: (a) one does not wish to cause pain to a good, honest, and decent person who gives you love and care, and (b) one finds it easy to give in to someone whom one admires since it is not belittling to assume that they are the one who is correct. In fact, it is easy to accept good people as our moral superiors. I believe that we find the existence of good, decent and honest people in our midst absolutely redeeming.

They are like a breath of fresh air. Being married to a person whom we respect feels like a privilege, a privilege not easily forgotten even in the midst of battle. We therefore put an end to the marital strife in the belief that it is an honour and privilege to be married to this admirable person who stands before us. Therefore it can be seen that respect in marriage is not only important as a context to love, but also serves to provide the solution to fighting and strife.

What adultery does however is not to erode this mutual respect gradually, as do ongoing marital altercations and bickering, but to destroy it in one fell swoop. The moment a spouse hears that the person to whom they are married, the one for whom they labour and toil, has behaved with such thoughtlessness, insensitivity and recklessness, they cannot help but view that person as vain, selfish, and uncaring. They see them not as the good, honest person they thought they were married to but as a *bad* person. Worse still, they will be viewed as only half a person; weak, with no will, bereft of conviction and force of character. To our great dismay, this may indeed spell the death knell for any marriage. This is in addition to the fact that your spouse suddenly becomes a stranger – you thought you knew them but suddenly you discover that they have been leading a double life. Your security is now totally undermined and all the closeness and familiarity that have been built up over time is called into question.

Loss of Trust

The real danger of adultery comes in damaging your partner's ego and in breaking the trust which is the basis for a good relationship. Of the many casualties of every act of infidelity, loss of trust is perhaps the most significant. Why? Because if a husband yells at his wife and then apologizes, she can forgive her husband for his unacceptable behaviour in the belief that his apology is sincere. And if a wife tells her husband that she loves him, notwithstanding his character flaws, he can believe her. Through every crisis in marriage, it is trust that pulls us through because it is trust that allows us to forgive and love in return. Even after a terrible marital altercation, if a husband tells his wife, 'Please forgive me because I really do love you and I didn't mean any of the things which I said,' they can continue a normal and happy life together as long as she can still believe him. But what if she can't?

If he has a bad temper, then one facet of his personality is flawed. But there is so much left to love. She'll just try and avoid him when he shouts, or at least calm him down. And if *she* is immature, then he can still appreciate all the other wonderful things about her. But what if he or she doesn't tell the truth? What then is there to love? Everything the adulterer says is suspect. If he has a bad temper and calls his wife names, he can still apologize later, and she can accept it. But if he is dishonest, why should she accept his apology? Maybe he doesn't even mean this. It is not merely that he possesses imperfections, rather there is nothing about him to love because there is nothing about him which is authentic. Nothing is real enough to engender loyalty and devotion. To be sure, they may still be trustworthy in other areas, just as someone who cheats in business may still be faithful to his wife. But what is important in this situation is not the way things really are, but rather the perception which is created. And she thinks him to be a scoundrel. Not everyone is as forgiving of catching their spouse in an adulterous affair as the Duc de Richelieu who, upon discovering his wife with her lover said: 'Madame, you must really be more careful. Suppose it had been someone else who found you like this?'[1]

After a husband commits adultery, after he has led the duplicitous life which is necessary in an affair, after he has told two women simultaneously that he loves them, after he has shared the most intimate moments and the personal details of his life with someone who is not his wife, what is there to trust? Even if he apologizes, the wife will not be able to forget that just last week he was telling her how much he loved *her*, but at the same time running around behind her back with someone else.

The Road of Return

One of the central tenets of the Jewish faith, which also serves as a foundation and cornerstone for faith in our lives and humanity, is the fact that we can always repent and save a bad situation. We can for ever return to our previous state of innocence. Every single one of us is taught to believe, and must believe, that no single situation exists which cannot be repaired or rectified. In my opinion, the belief that we are never beat, and life is never over, and that we can always reinvent ourselves regardless of our past and previous history is the most important tenet of human living. It is so important because it means that we are worthwhile and our lives are signficant. So significant, that we can never be written off. It is not over until it is finally and truly over. We possess the ability to recreate ourselves at all times; to start life over as if we were new. At present, only death has the power to defeat us, and maybe we will even think of a way of skirting that as well in the future. But there are no other excuses. You make a mistake, pick yourself up and continue. The spiritual soul within us lends us an infinite capacity for life. And because it is pure, the dirt into which we immerse ourselves, and the stains which we put on to our soul, are merely superficial and never really stick. Thus, even after an adulterous act, we can restore our marriage to where it was before, and even make it better than before.

But here we are saying that adultery has irreversibly eroded away the trust in our relationships since we have done something that can never truly be forgotten. Does an act of adultery constitute the point of no return? Is there any way of re-instilling the trust in our marriages even after we have been unfaithful? Of course there is. Like I said, it ain't over till it's over. There is a way of always reinventing ourselves in life and starting from anew. But it requires a bit of a radical strategy, albeit temporarily.

Restoring Trust

The love and trust that once existed in marriage can indeed be recaptured fully even after an act of infidelity. Moreover, I believe that it can even be built upon to a great extent. The secret lies in waiting, being patient and going to a temporary extreme.

The celebrated medieval Jewish philosopher, Maimonides, discusses, in his treatise on human character, 'Laws of Dispositions', what a person should do if they are in possession of a very negative quality trait. First, he identifies what is a good quality trait, and what is evil. What is surprising is that he basically says that any character trait which is extreme is evil, and can only be corrected by being brought into moderation. In fact, Maimonides goes as far as saying that the very definition of good and bad is moderation and extremism. Even too much of a so-called 'good' character trait is bad. So, for example, a parent should not be too giving or too generous with their children. It will spoil and destroy them. This is not generosity. It is cruel, and it is an injustice. The rule which Maimonides lays down is that we must find the golden middle path in each and every character trait which will, in turn, bring us virtue.

But what if we are already extremists? What if we lose our temper too often and over trivial matters? The way forward which Maimonides charts is to temporarily go to the opposite extreme in order to compensate for one's imbalance, which will lead to a state of moderation, and equilibrium, later on. Thus, the cure for the person in question is this: for a limited time, say a few months, they should not allow themselves to get angry and lose their tempers over *anything*, even over those things which warrant anger. Through this strenuous exercise of extreme self-control, they will learn how to bring their emotions under their control. Once this is accomplished, the individual can then return to a happy medium whereby they stand firm and safe-guard their interests against abuse, while not shouting at any-body and everybody over matters that do not warrant anger or indignation.

The same thing applies to restoring trust in a relationship. Since the entire breach of trust was brought about through a husband or wife showing a sexual interest in another person, and acting upon it, the way to undo the damage is to go to the opposite extreme: to show no attraction or feelings for another person whatsoever. This rule extends even to movie and pop idols. If you have gone as far as actually being unfaithful to your spouse, which is undoubtedly an extreme and evil thing to do, go to the opposite extreme and show your husband or your wife that you are interested in them, and them only, that no one else excites you in the slightest.

One woman told me how she even refrains from compliment-ing the handsome male actors on the screen. Her husband reciprocates and consequently she feels like the most desirable woman on the planet. 'I am careful never to harm his ego or destroy the trust he puts in me by showing that other men, even on TV, are more attractive than him.'

When a wife discovers her husband's infidelity, she becomes paranoid and assumes that he is attracted to everyone on the planet but herself. Her self-esteem is shattered notwithstanding that this feeling has no basis in reality. What her husband must therefore do is restore her confidence and undo her misconceptions by showing no emotional or sexual attraction to any woman whatsoever, *even if this too has no basis in reality*. I am not advocating that he lie. Rather, he must behave unnaturally and stifle any automatic interest he would normally take in someone else, even on a completely cursory level. Although this might be highly artificial, and he will feel that he cannot be himself around her, nevertheless, it is necessary for a limited time until his wife's confidence in him and in herself is restored. In any event, would anyone argue that his wife's constant paranoia *is* a healthy, real, or natural state of affairs? Can he really be himself when he must accommodate his wife's hurt, pain, and suspicion? Let him give in to his wife's current demands for extraordinary affection and attention to the exclusion of everyone else on the planet. Let her feel whole and human again. Convince your wife that you're off other women. Show her that you're bored with the glamorous movie stars.

Therefore, every time a wife suggests to her husband that they go to the latest Madonna movie, I say in all seriousness that the husband's response should be that he has no interest in seeing it. Let him say, 'I don't find Madonna attractive. I love you, I don't need that.' And when his wife switches on a late-night movie, with explicit sexual scenes and nudity, he should turn over and read a book or go to sleep. And when his wife points out the latest Cindy Crawford *Vogue* cover, he should look, yawn, and turn the page.

Lest I be accused of encouraging husbands to be dishonest with their wives about their sexual interests just in order to regain their confidence and trust, I would like to point out that this is necessary therapy for the husband as well. He too must undertake the advice which Maimonides delivered. The fact is that he *did* act upon a sexual attraction to a member of the opposite sex in the most insensitive way. Thus, not just his penance but his *therapy* is to go to the opposite extreme for a certain duration and fight his attraction to others, even though this may be highly unnatural. The point here is not that he act synthetically *in order to fool his wife*. He is doing it for himself. He is going to an extreme and making himself feel nothing for other women, even the most attractive, so that later he can find a healthy equilibrium where he notices his natural attraction to other women, yet controls his thoughts, speech and action, and focuses his sexual energy on his wife. He should abstain from the constant diet of nudity and sexuality fed to him by television and the movies. He should not concentrate on the sheer see-through blouse that the girl at the check-out counter is wearing. He should not stare at the slit in the skirt of the woman standing in front of him on the bus. He must gain control of his life and direct his attention away from things which have a pernicious effect upon his marriage.

Outright sexual repression is not healthy, and can lead in the long term to neurosis. I have also argued in this book that although we may be happily married, we should still be cognizant of the natural attraction posed by all the men and women who surround us. I mentioned that the realization that, amidst being in love we find ourselves *naturally* pulled to others, is actually healthy for a marriage since it causes us to choose our spouses daily, and thus keeps our marriages alive and fresh, instead of them resting on a stale commitment pronounced years earlier. Notwithstanding this, for the husband who has already committed adultery going to an extreme and divorcing himself from any and all forms of attraction to members of the opposite sex is healthy, until he learns to appreciate the beauty and attractiveness of the opposite sex in a detached and non-lustful way.

So, by pursuing this extreme course of action the husband is not merely attempting to fool his wife, he is actually ridding himself of a dangerous disposition. It is natural to feel an attraction to strange men and women, even when we are not married to them. But it is sinful and evil to betray our marital vows by losing control of our sexual selves, or releasing our sexual energy with anyone aside from our beloved spouse.

Begin with an Effort

As a corollary, the benefits of this procedure are clear: the wife may not believe that her husband finds Kim Basinger boring and unattractive. She might also be incredulous about her husband's sudden loss of interest in television sex. However, she will definitely feel that, whether or not her husband is focusing all his attention on her and is bored by other women, *he is at least making a strong effort in that direction* and to being faithful at all times.

Not only will his wife's paranoia subside, and her faith and confidence in him be slowly restored, but she will love him more than ever before. She will see a man before her who undoubtedly stumbled, and caused more hurt to her than anything she has ever known. But she will see also a man who, amidst his blunder, loves her with all his heart, and is prepared to make Herculean efforts to remain faithful and ensure that he never hurts her again. She will fall in love with her *new* husband, her husband who struggles with a process of rebirth, and goes to a great extreme in order to undo his wife's pain, assuage her suffering, and give her confidence that he shall remain her loyal, focused and unwavering husband for ever more. And she will feel like the most wanted woman in the world.

SOURCES – CHAPTER NINETEEN

1.   *Sex and Sexuality*

CHAPTER TWENTY

HOW TO STAY IN LOVE

'I'm seriously looking for a wife and my friend Rob wanted me to take out his former girlfriend, Stacey. "She's a real screamer," he told me, "and a really nice girl." I subsequently heard from two other friends that they had taken her to bed, too. So I won't take her out. I don't want to compete with all the former men she has had, many of whom are far more handsome than me. I don't know that my ego can handle it. It just isn't nice.'

WHY IS IT that we sometimes feel so dissatisfied with our spouse? We compare their looks and their actions to all the men and women that surround us and sometimes, inevitably, they are found wanting in comparison. We then use this deficiency to justify extramarital affairs, whether real or imagined. Can we learn to be more satisfied and appreciate what we have?

The Very Definition of Love is Subjectivity

I am convinced that one of the principal causes in the breakdown of today's relationships is that we have become *objective* about the people we love. We've become objective about things that we were never meant to be objective about.

In seminars that I have conducted around the world I have asked the members of the audience to posit a one-word synonym for love. These are the most common responses: 'devotion', 'respect', 'admiration', and 'a longing' and finally 'selflessness'. These are all insightful responses, but they somehow miss out the essence of love. To me the best synonym for love is this: '*subjectivity*'. Being in love with someone means not seeing faults, or being aware of the faults but relegating them to the realm of insignificance. When you are in love with someone you no longer treat them in an objective fashion. Your love for them colours your perception of them, and *to you* they appear beautiful and glorious, irrespective of what the objective facts really are. 'The person is so important, I know they have faults, but it does not matter. To me, they are the most special person in the world.'

Conversely, falling out of love is objectifying the person you are with so that you are in a constant state of appraisal, always comparing them with the people around you. The breakdown in relationships is due to the fact that we have become objective about the people we love. We are in a constant state of revaluation as to whether or not the person we are involved with or married to is still worthwhile, or whether perhaps we made a mistake in marrying them.

The greatest example of a choice being presented that must first be approached coolly and objectively by the intellect and even the emotions, yet then committed to fully out of love, is marriage and the choice one makes with regard to one's spouse. At this point, objectivity must be relinquished in favour of an emotional and hence subjective appraisal and evaluation of their virtue and aesthetic appeal. But increasingly, this isn't happening any more.

One woman who came to complain to me about her husband said to me, 'To be honest, Rabbi, Jeffrey, who I know from work, seems as though he would have been a lot more suitable as a lifelong partner. He's funnier, more patient, loves kids, and is far more affectionate than my husband. It's a pity that I didn't meet him five years ago before I married.' It's easy to see how this kind of attitude can result directly in an adulterous affair. Even after marriage, this woman is still comparing her husband to everyone around her. Even after marrying, she still has not closed off her possibilities, in her own mind, about finding a suitable life-long partner. She is still objective about her husband. So where is the love?

The Most Beautiful Woman in the World

Contrast her attitude with the following story. When I was a student in rabbinical seminary, I was once invited to the home of an elderly couple for dinner by their grandson. During the course of the meal, I dropped a fork under the table and bent down to pick it up. When I did, I noticed that this couple, both of whom were in their late seventies, were holding hands under the table. Coming as I did from a broken home, I was impressed; tears came to my eyes.

As I was leaving, I couldn't help but mention how happy I was to have witnessed this display of romantic love between the couple, and how their feelings for one another had not diminished through time. 'You are the world's greatest romantics,' I said. 'It's amazing!' The wife blushed at my words, but the husband did not. He just looked at me with a quizzical stare, as if he did not really understand me. 'You sound surprised that we can remain in love for all these years. Why, for me it's very easy. After all, my wife is the most beautiful woman in the whole wide world,' and he kissed her as he said this.

What amazed me was that his sincerity was beyond question. I couldn't believe it. He was completely sincere and it showed. Why was I surprised? Because it was blatantly not true! Surely, however attractive his wife was, I didn't expect to wake up the next morning and find her face on the cover of *Vogue*! In fact, *objectively* speaking she looked like she was 900 years old and had so many chins that I couldn't even count them all!

And yet, amidst my own appraisal of the situation, not only did he mean every word he had uttered, but he was also accurate.

What he was saying was this: *to me*, she is the most attractive woman in the world. I love her and therefore I am subjective in my evaluation of her. I don't want anyone else. Just her.' My personal opinion of his wife didn't matter. In his world, in his realm of experience, she was the most glamorous woman alive. But how could this be? If you had asked ten men to *objectively* evaluate his wife's looks on a scale from one to ten, she might have scored barely a one. But this is the point. He wasn't objective and he didn't care about any outsider's evaluation. His love for his wife totally coloured his perception of her. That was the secret of how they stayed romantically in love for so many decades. And this is the way things ought to be. A man and a woman should indeed view their spouse as the most special, most beautiful person on the planet. A husband and wife's love for each other should alter the very way in which they perceive each other.

If this does not happen, then there is something missing, something inadequate, in their love. If you disagree and feel that this is too high a standard, then consider how you would feel about a parent who thought their child ugly or stupid, even if it were true. Would you applaud their honesty? No, you would probably be horrified.

The fact is that every parent thinks that his or her child is the cleverest and most precious in the galaxy, and every one of them is absolutely right. This does not pose a tremendous contradiction because in the eyes of each individual set of parents who acts as judge, their child is the most special and the most wonderful. They wouldn't trade him for the world. Their love for their child colours the way they perceive them.

Did it ever happen that you were patiently sitting in a doctor's waiting room, and someone's kid doesn't stop crying, sneezing on you, staring at the inside of your nostrils, and generally making you wish that you could strangle him and put everyone in the waiting room out of their misery? Then, just as you finish tying the noose to do the dirty deed, you see the child's mother, looking starry-eyed at her son, as she says looking right at you, 'Isn't he adorable? He's so sweet!' Of course, it's blatantly untrue. But the love which a mother has for her child is capable of transforming a monster into an angel, at least in her own eyes.

Now, we seem to accept that this should be true of children, but we do not correspondingly accept that the same should be true of our partners in relationships and marriage. But why not?

People would never consider 'cheating' on their own children. We wouldn't creep over to the neighbours' house bringing chocolates to their children in the middle of the night, and secretly agree to take these neighbours' children to the zoo instead of our own. Not one of us can even contemplate the parent of one child walking over to the neighbours' child when one's own children are not looking and telling them, 'You know, my children don't understand me. Mickey, it is really you that I love. Would it were that you were mine. I love you very much. You are like my real son, and when no one is looking I'll be giving you all of my own kids' toys and buy you presents. But let's keep this a secret between us. I know that the time will come when I will finally be able to flaunt this love to the entire world. Instead of us having to play computer games together late at night under your bed, I can see a time when I will finally take you to football matches notwithstanding who will be looking, and then I will leave my own children and make you my son. I only ask that you please give me a chance. I really will leave my son for you. But for now, we must continue to meet only in secret.'

The very thought of a parent choosing someone else's child over their own is ludicrous and laughable. Why will it never happen? Because a parent feels deep in their gut that their child is a part of themselves, and they simply cannot live without them. No parent who has lost a child to accident or illness can ever fully recover. The idea of being desirous of children other than our own is ludicrous. Our children are part of ourselves; they are our family; they are our very flesh and blood.

In the same way, a man or woman who truly feels that their spouse is a part of their very flesh will find it very difficult to consummate a sexual attraction with a stranger. They will feel that they are violating their own bodies. But why don't we view our spouses in the same way? Our spouse is a part of ourselves, a part that was joined together in holy matrimony under the wedding canopy. Why aren't we as subjective? Everyone of us is perfectly capable of cheating on our spouse in a way which we would never do to our children. The reason: whereas we might compare our children to other children, but still never find ourselves seriously dissatisfied with them, the same is not true of our spouse. Husbands and wives are evaluating each other constantly, with adultery the direct outcome.

A husband may look upon his ageing wife and compare her to a younger woman in much the same way he compares his 1990 Sony Walkman with the newer, more feature-laden 1994 edition. And just as he sells the old Walkman to buy the new model, he can do the same with his wife: trade her in for a newer model, either through divorce, or, an apparently far less messy solution, by having an affair.

Dating too has become quite arbitrary. The features we focus on are aesthetic appeal, youth, sense of humour, earning potential, social standing, education, common interests, and many other features that are totally ancillary to human essence. Of course, human goodness is also important to us, although not necessarily more important than those features listed above, certainly nowhere near as important as aesthetics and looks. Once, on a Friday night a young couple came to have dinner at our L'Chaim Centre who were known to me but not to our students. They were engaged to be married. She was exceptionally beautiful, but he was overweight and not very handsome (objectively speaking). I remember hearing the murmuring of the students as they asked, 'Why on earth is she marrying him?' The fact is that he was one of the kindest men I had ever met, with a real heart of gold. Yet the students naturally assumed that she would not be interested in him if he were not handsome.

Think for a moment. If you heard that a woman who was beautiful and from a prominent family, married a divorced car mechanic who was short and had a long scar on his face, wouldn't you be a bit surprised? And conversely, if you heard that a young dashing lawyer, whose father was a well-known politician, married a poor ugly girl with only a state-school education, would you not raise your eyebrows in surprise? My point here is that you wouldn't immediately consider that perhaps this girl was so special and beautiful on the inside that her husband could not help not only loving her, but even feeling as if he was the luckiest man on earth.

In his insightful book, *Why Men Are the Way They Are*, psychologist Warren Farrel invites his female readers to take the following test:

CASE 1: You are a single woman. You are about to bring home to your parents a man you are about to marry. He is tall, handsome, articulate, warm, tender; he listens carefully, understands you thoroughly, and expresses his feelings. He works as a night-watchman in a local junkyard. How do you feel your parents would react to your marrying him? Would you seriously consider marrying him? .... Yes .... No.

CASE 2: You are a single woman. Your friend would like you to meet and go out with a short friend of hers. She explains he has had plastic surgery four times, often wears makeup, and has a high, squeaky voice. Some people think he is gay – but she is fairly sure he is not, and he has taken an interest in you. He does have odd habits, like watching some movies as often as sixty times. It seems he may even have a glove fetish. Interested? .... Yes .... No. His name is Michael Jackson.

Searching for the Best

In marriage, each one of us is not interested in someone who is good enough, and suits all of our needs and desires. What we want today is *the best*. I cannot begin to relate how many times I have heard young successful people justify breaking off relationships with men and women with whom they were once very serious, not because of any real problem, but simply because, in their estimation, they did not reach their high standards. What they want is the best so they will keep looking. What we forget is that, while we can speak of the plushest house, the fanciest car or the finest cigar, because they are superficial material objects with no depth, we cannot speak of 'the best' person because every human being has infinite depth and is special in their own different way. No wonder, then, that we often go out with the wrong person since we do not seek someone that suits us, so much as someone who is judged to be 'the best' based on values that are arbitrary and superficial. Sometimes I really think that if a woman could have a CD player with speakers implanted into her hip, this would be viewed as another reason by a man to marry her. In addition to her heart and soul, she also comes along with a hi-fi system! That's how superficial things have become as we elusively pursue 'the best'.

But there is no such thing as 'the best' in marriage; there is nothing better than *good enough*. We should treat marriage like a glove that fits. The person who makes us happy and whom we miss when they are not around, and who seeks to make us happy and fulfils all our needs is the one who is usually perfectly suited to us. But people often refrain from marrying such a person, especially if they are one of the first people they date, since they feel they *must* first shop around, see what else is available, because maybe it will turn out that while this person is *good*, they are not *the best*.

The wife I married was, thank God, the very first girl I dated, and when I tell this to our students at Oxford they look very surprised. 'Look, Debbie is a great wife,' they admit, 'but could you have been sure that she was the right girl for you if you had no one to compare her to?' And armed with this philosophy, the students date and date in search of the very best possible partner for life, and in the process ensure that no one will make them happy since it is not human warmth which they seek, but accolades.

If this approach to marriage and relationships were confined to the time before marriage, it would be forgivable. The problem is that once you teach yourself to objectify people, it won't stop even after you marry. Even those who are already married fail to find satisfaction with their spouse since they still scrutinize their other acquaintances to see if they could have done better. A worse scenario is if they carry on extramarital affairs with the excuse that they find their lover more exciting and 'better' than the person to whom they are married. In short, *marriage means choosing one partner for life, and closing off all other possibilities*. The search has now been terminated. *Adultery means keeping the search alive, and continuing to choose partners long after it should have ceased.*

But apart from the 'search for the best' betraying a superficial personality, it also means that we are not in love and, I fear, have lost the capacity to love. Love means the ability to no longer be objective about a person. One simply cannot say that on the one hand they are in love with Sally, and on the other hand remain objective about Sally. Because being in love means losing your objectivity as you fall into adoration of Sally. She is so special *to you* that you see in her a completely new light compared to all the other people in the world. No one else can compete simply because you love her and not them. Love means not focusing on a human being's ancillary features, in which they can be compared and weighed against other competitors. To feel love for someone is to make that person unique and singular, and to put them into a category all by themselves where there is no competition. If you truly love your child, you don't sit around comparing him to all the other children you meet, although they may be more successful or more beautiful than your child. No one else can compare with the person you love because they are in a class by themselves. If we can compare our spouse with another, then we are playing silly games and leading a shallow life.

To love means to make someone unique; to isolate them, to say this one is mine. People don't cheat on their kids so how can they cheat on their spouses? We don't witness 'parental infidelity' because people see their children as a part of themselves from which they cannot be divorced. There can be no substitute for your own children. Why don't we look at our spouses in a similar fashion, as part of ourselves? You aren't focusing on the relationship if you are bringing other people into it. Love means the ability to lose all objectivity with regard to the object of your love. Love does not mean that you are unaware of your spouse's faults, but rather that those faults, while present, are utterly insignificant compared to the beauty of their total being and their essence. You see their wrinkles as they grow older, but that doesn't in any way change how beautiful they appear to you, and how attracted you are to them.

An objective stranger may look at your spouse and ask, 'What does he have that makes her love him so much? Surely I have met men who are so much better?' But to her that kind of comparison is ludicrous. Why not ask her why she loves her father so much? Surely there are better parents as well! She loves her husband and can see no other men who can even remotely compare. He is unique to her.

Love means being utterly subjective. This is not something negative, for it means focusing on essence. It means transcending cosmetic and superficial layers and concentrating on the deepest, most special part of a person, the part of them which cannot be assessed or appraised. This kind of deep love is not instantaneous; it can only be achieved through sharing, living and striving together. It can only come about through extraordinary commitment and sacrifice: primarily through marriage.

Premarital Sex and Marriage

One of the most significant obstacles to this penetrating love is when people engage in extensive sexual relations before marriage. Statistics show there is an exponentially increasing rate of divorce with the number of sexual partners and the amount of sexual experience one has before marriage: 'Unfortunately, it does not seem that the greater acceptance of prenuptial experiment in our own day has led to happier or more stable marriages. In the UK, the number of divorces increased sixfold between 1961 and 1990.'[1] This is borne out logically as well. If we engage in numerous relationships, and come to know many people intimately, later when we marry we will begin to compare our spouses to the people we knew so well before. How could we not? We see that they don't measure up, because no human is so multi-faceted that they could possibly embrace every human attribute that can be pooled between so many various partners.

So if you have been intimate with ten different men, and to you they begin to blur into one composite image, how could you possibly be completely satisfied later with your husband's sexual performance? Mike was special in this way, Jeff was special in this way. But how can George, whom you marry, possibly encompass every wonderful character trait under the sun, which one may come to know through being intimate with so many different people? Even more damaging is when we begin to compare their bodies and anatomical features, which they can hardly improve, with previous sexual partners. This destroys the confidence of our spouse, and they become depressed and morose. I will never forget how once, a couple came to see me to patch up their marriage after the wife's infidelity. She loved her husband, but felt that she could not now enjoy him after her affair. 'Why?' I asked. 'Is it because you feel guilty?' '*Not at all*,' she said, in her husband's presence. 'The other man's "equipment" was better, and therefore I enjoyed it more. And it's difficult to go back to my husband.'

Having many sexual partners before marriage and many intimate relationships leads us to the single most destructive force in marriage: objectivity. People cannot be compared. Our spouse, who should be the most special person in the world to us, becomes a number who can be rated on a scale compared to others we have known and met. This kind of thinking is a demoralizing and degrading process whereby human beings are dehumanized and treated as material objects which can be evaluated.

I believe the over-exposure of sexuality in film and books and magazines makes it difficult for us to be satisfied with our lives as well. Each and every one of us will be compared to a perfect ideal which has no bearing in reality. When you see Madonna and you are attracted to her on screen, you don't see her portrayed realistically. That what we see in films and magazines is simply an illusion is demonstrated by Dr Warren Farrel who quotes the Canadian National Film Board who maintain that it takes 22,000 snaps to make the perfect *Playboy* centrefold spread. In addition, he points out that movies substitute pictures of a different actress's buttocks so we won't see the imperfections in the rear of the star, and countless other electronic manipulations are carried out to enhance the man or woman being presented in the specific medium in question. So we get some idea of how every woman who looks at a centrefold feels inadequate next to the airbrushed best of thousands of photos (*Why Men Are the Way They Are*; p. 74). So it's pretty unfair to compare the person you're living with to the illusion of beauty as found in magazines and movies.

It becomes slightly more difficult when you actually were intimate with many partners before marriage. This will lead you to an even greater objectivity. It takes great discipline to focus your mind on who you are with. You must slowly allow the strong images of the past to fade by not focusing on them ever. This is the way to rectify damage caused by over-exposure to sexual images and over-indulgence in sex with too many partners. You must not allow these images, and you must dismiss them when they are conjured up in your mind. Banish them from your thoughts. Don't allow them to encroach upon the intimacy you seek with your spouse. Even if the person you are with is on the whole better than the person you were with before you will still find areas to compare. The fact is none of us is divine, and none of us can incorporate so many diverse faculties, virtues, and traits that could possibly equate with 10 or 20 people who preceded us. No person can incorporate all of those magnificent features. This is why one of the most destructive things in a relationship is the search for the 'best'. There is no such thing as the person who is the 'best' in marriage only the person who can make you happy, who assuages your loneliness and who makes you feel complete and whole, treating you with a great respect and love. What more is there? Let's stop comparing our spouses to phantoms that don't exist, or pretending we would be happier with someone else.

The larger problem which must be addressed is the consequences of today's very open sexual society: the incessant images that make their imprint on our minds, and the sexual symbols which are constantly paraded before us, luring us and creating fantasies.

The Talmud makes an interesting pronouncement about a divorced couple who remarry, saying, in effect, that when they make love there are four people in the bed. The meaning of this statement is quite straightforward. Even if they don't consciously seek to compare their current and former spouse, still it is inevitable even if it's just the simple memories of their sexual encounters. They may compare the performance of their current lovers with that of the former. Maybe in certain respects they don't feel as satisfied with their current spouse than they did with their ex. More importantly, the above considerations can seriously infringe upon the secret of a satisfying and passionate sexual life in marriage: that secret is intimacy. The problem of course is not confined to those who have been married previously, but affects all those who have had other sexual partners. There can be no greater satisfaction in love-making than to be totally and utterly absorbed in the act, and focused on the person you're with, to the exclusion of anything and everything else. Making love is an act of the greatest intensity, and has the power, unlike any other human activity, to pull us into the activity to the exclusion of any other care in the world. The isolation and sense of seclusion felt by two people who lock themselves into the bedroom is the most special human experience known to humankind. But it can be severely and adversely affected if something creeps into the bedroom with them, especially something like the thought of another person with whom the very same experiences were shared previously. When the thought of other partners creeps in, can the experience be said to be intimate?

The Ghosts of Lovers Past

What makes something special is the fact that it is distinct and unique. For example, in Jewish thought the very word holy means 'separate, distinct, and different'. The Sabbath day is holy by virtue of the fact that it is different to the other days of the week, and it is treated differently. If one is to treat it in exactly the same way in which one treats Tuesday, if one goes to work and drives the car, then it is not special. The same applies to another, more personal special day: a birthday. Only when one treats one's birthday differently to the other days of the year, and when one's friends join in with surprise presents and parties, does the day assume significance. Otherwise, it passes by without so much as a whimper and is rendered ordinary and unimportant.

The same applies to intimacy. What makes a sexual moment exciting is the fact that it is only the two of you who experience it. But when the ghosts of former lovers enter your minds, the whole experience suffers.

This is especially true due to the nature of human sexuality which is almost entirely a physical experience. Memories are strong enough when they involve a conversation, a laugh, an emotional exchange. But they are positively stifling when the experience remembered involves strong physical pleasure, excitement and fulfilment. Inevitably, one will bring those memories into the bedroom and rate one's current partner and sense of satisfaction alongside that of previous experiences leading directly to the problem of subjectivity.

The above is not only an argument against vast sexual experience and promiscuity. I lament also the very explicit nature of modern-day media, television, art and film. Which husband or wife, after watching an explicit sex scene, will not bring some of those images and personalities into their bedroom? Indeed, I would argue that it is totally unnatural, nay impossible, to be totally unaffected by such powerful images. It has always been a source of curiosity to me why it is that the same wives who become furious with their husbands for frequenting strip-joints and nude bars, could not care less that their husbands consume far more powerful images nightly on television, and with their wives' approval and often their participation.

The *Hite Report* quotes story after story of wives who feel hurt and betrayed upon discovering that their husbands frequent, or have attended a strip-joint. Here is a wife whose husband has a mistress: 'He does not satisfy me sexually because I have this constant competition with his other woman on my mind. "I'm probably not as good as she is. My body is not as nice as hers. What am I not doing that causes him to go seek out others? To try and help the situation we started trying new things: exotic lingerie, positions, locations, etc. This was fine until he then started frequenting strip-joints. Now I feel degraded and am not interested in that sort of thing any more.'

What boggles the mind after reading this statement, is this: why didn't she get upset about the probably hundreds of movies with passionate sexual scenes in them that she no doubt watched with him? Is it because the strip-joints are real, while the movie is only on film? Surely in the mind of any husband one image is just as real as another, and the disruption caused between one and the other to this setting of intimacy is equally strong.

Memories fade and they are not as powerful as time elapses. The remedy to the problem of objectifying a spouse based on intimate experiences with other partners before marriage is to never conjure up the image. Never allow it to have the same potency in your current life that it did in your past life. If you've seen too many movies with naked men and women whom you adore, first, stop watching them. The price you pay in loss of intimacy in your marriage is not worth the momentary thrill you receive from these movies. Second, even if their images pop up automatically in your brain, banish them. Forget them. Let your spouse be your sexual outlet, and don't be so unfair as to compare them with events and scenarios where they simply can't compete. After all, if you met a film star in real life, you might find him arrogant and self-centred, even though on the screen he can appear so flattering and loving. So it's pretty unfair to compare the person you are living with to the illusion of beauty as found in magazines and films. At the same time you also have to be realistic. No one person can possibly embrace and encompass all of the best positive quality traits that you have discovered in twenty former girlfriends or boyfriends.

In the process of undoing the subjectivity which can result from extensive sexual experience before marriage, I strongly advise against informing your fiancé, or your spouse, of sexual liaisons – boyfriends, girlfriends, one-night stands and so on – that took place before you met your spouse, or before you married them. You have to allow those previous images, however powerful, to fade, and the most effective way of doing this is never to discuss them. It is simply none of their business, and even if they want to know, don't indulge their curiosity. It can bring nothing but harm and unnecessary pain. It doesn't increase trust or faithfulness. Discussing your previous relationships with your newly married husband or wife is bound to hurt them, however slightly. Worse still, those memories might lead you to compare your current happiness and satisfaction with that experienced in a previous relationship. So why allow this to become a subject of conversation? It is imperative that a husband and wife begin life anew and fresh. They should not bring the ghosts of relationships past into their marriage.

While I wouldn't expect that any of the readers of this book would describe to their spouse the minute details of their previous loves, I suggest not describing or discussing them at all. It serves no beneficial purpose, and can only lead to making an unwitting comparison between those intimate acquaintances of the past and the spouse of the present.

Love in Marriage

Love means the ability to lose objectivity, whereby insignificant, ancillary, and shallow features lose their importance and we begin to descend into a world of depth where essence encompasses and overwhelms us. We become subjective and forget the glaring, overt details of a human being, instead choosing to embrace their core. A lack of love means objectifying a relationship and comparing its details; feeling cold in a relationship rather than allowing the infinite human warmth and essence to spring forth to enlighten and enliven us. A person's infinite soul, when allowed to shine forth through all of the transient coverings which surround it, becomes truly fulfilling and powerful enough to sustain everlasting human excitement and commitment.

SOURCES — CHAPTER TWENTY

1.   Lawrence Stone, *The Family, Sex and Marriage in England 1500–1800*, 1991

TEN EASY STEPS TOWARDS RESTORING PASSION IN MARRIAGE

'It is as absurd to say that a man can't love one woman all the time as it is to say that a violinist needs several violins to play the same piece of music.'
Honoré de Balzac, French novelist, nineteenth century

THIS BOOK IN its entirety has been based upon two powerful and undeniable premises:

1. That retaining passion in marriage is indeed unnatural, practically very difficult, and therefore poses a very great challenge indeed; and
2. That it is still possible and that the very same and even greater passion which exists in premarital and especially extramarital sexual relationships can be brought into marriage as well by adopting a new state of mind and focusing all of one's sexual energies on one's spouse.

In the long prelude to this book's publication, I was invited to many parts of the world to lecture to audiences of various persuasions and denominations about its contents. The religious and the atheists attended as did Jews and non-Jews. Let's face it: it's not every day that a rabbi writes a book about adultery! So they came in their droves to discover its contents. In the question and answer session which followed each lecture, I was invariably asked, primarily by the women, to summarize the practical steps we can take to restore and retain passion in our marriages.

It is to address this all-important question, so essential to a happy marriage, that I have written this epilogue: to give precise and down-to-earth advice, drawing on what we have learned from other areas of the book. Forgive me if we repeat some of the material, but remember: what we are looking for is a new state of mind, not just new techniques. And in order for people to be able to think in a completely new way, it's got to be drilled into their heads many, many times. Feel lucky that I repeat this only once!

1. *Make your spouse come alive for you as an exciting sexual object. Talk through their fantasies with them, remove all their inhibitions. As long as it is just the two of you who are involved, throw propriety to the wind. Marriage is of profound significance. It deserves courage and forthrightness. Become a totally sexual being. Sexual inhibition has no place between two married adults. By persuading your spouse to expose their full sexual nature you transform your partner from a mundane husband or wife into a seductive man or woman who will do anything for sexual intimacy and is therefore always attractive.*

Here's a real story that encapsulates the first point. A married man once told me that his marriage was full of strife due to the constant bickering between him and his wife. He said to me, 'Let me be honest with you. Our marriage has a lot of problems, and really the fighting is a result of a lack of interest in one another. We've grown bored, tired of each other, and we've grown apart. Nothing has really helped us.' He was already thinking of divorce. He was also honest enough to tell me that some of the most severe problems with his marriage resulted from his extra-marital dalliances. 'What can I do? I'm not wood, and my wife simply doesn't stimulate me any more. So I've shopped around a little bit, but never anything too serious. There are also the kids to think about.'

I told him that his attitude was a cop-out, grossly sinful and insensitive. He had given up on his wife as a woman too quickly. But how to rectify the situation immediately? I told him to sit his wife down at his first opportunity, and ask her to disclose all of her sexual fantasies, especially those which pertained to other men that he knew. 'Tell her that she should tell you about any men she has been attracted to, especially your acquaintances and friends. It's not going to be easy, and she may not want to open up to you. People feel really inhibited about these things. But it is imperative that you do this, and do it straight away. Have her take you into her confidence. Because you can be pretty sure if you have lost interest in her, she feels it and has probably lost interest in you as well. This may hurt you to hear, but by now she's bound to have developed an interest in someone else through your neglect. Go and convince her that you are really interested in her fantasies, and that it excites you to know all about them.'

After some prodding, he agreed to this. At first he didn't really want to, convinced that it was wrong and that his wife had no interest in any other men. 'She's not really into that sort of thing.' I told him that it is precisely because he thinks that way about her that he feels bored with her. Men get bored with women who are bored with sex, and vice versa.

A few days later he called back, clearly shaken. 'I feel like a knife has been stuck in my stomach.' I asked him what had happened. He said when he asked his wife, he thought it wasn't possible that she could be attracted to anyone. He was convinced that she had no real fantasies. Therefore, he wasn't afraid to discuss it. 'Finally, we were sitting in the car together. She was driving. She pulled over to the side and began to speak. Suddenly, she started telling me about men she really felt attracted to, particularly two of them whom she fantasized about considerably. "You always ignore me," she said, "but they give me a lot of attention. They seem to return the interest that I show in them."' The more she spoke, the worse he felt. Suddenly she mentioned the name of one of his best friends. 'I think he is particularly nice,' she said. 'And do you think he likes you too, or is it just one-sided?' he asked. 'It's hard to tell,' she answered. 'I've been thinking a lot about that. I don't know if he likes me, but I do catch him staring at me whenever I bend over, and especially when I'm dressed really well. Once a button in my blouse was accidentally left open and I found him peering in from the side. He's always looking at me; something which you stopped doing a long time ago.'

Having opened the floodgates of emotion she now dropped her bombshell. 'What I hate the most is the way we have sex. You climb on top of me, no kissing, no foreplay. I can see that you're not really interested in me and that you're thinking about somebody else. You have to be thinking about someone else, since my body doesn't turn you on. You never watch me when I undress. So right after you finish, roll over, and go to sleep I stay awake in tears feeling abused. I think about those other men hugging and kissing me. I'll never do anything with them, but sometimes I feel that I really do need them badly.'

The husband had heard enough. On the one hand he felt like he wanted to kill himself, it was painful and hurtful to find out that his wife liked other men and even more so that she fantasized about them. On the other hand he now loved her like never before. He was completely crazy about her, and found that just by hearing this from her she assumed an immense air of passion and mystery. Suddenly his wife was a sexually alive creature, who had fire in her soul and could even excite the passions of other married men. This man's perception of his wife changed instantly; he was reminded that night that she was a woman and that she had needs. She was attractive and sensuous, men wanted her and she was interested in them as well. To prevent the possibility of adultery, he had better do his utmost to re-seduce her and earn her affection and admiration, lest she find love and passion with the men who surrounded and admired her. Instead of spending his time seducing other women, he would now have to focus all his efforts on seducing his wife.

They stayed in Oxford another six months, during which time he told me that his marriage was better than ever before. He gave up his treacherous extramarital dalliances, and found renewed interest in his wife.

Remember: sexual inhibition leads to monotony and boredom. By contrast, sexual adventurism leads to passion and excitement. Marriage is holy and central to human living. It is a divine institution and must be preserved at all costs.

2. *See your spouse through other people's eyes. Use jealousy to your own advantage by placing your spouse in environments where their attractiveness will stand out.*

Always remember that if you aren't excited about your husband or your wife, it is not because of any intrinsic fault in them. Rather, it is because they are too familiar to you. The men and women who attract you more than your spouse are not necessarily more handsome or beautiful, and even if they are objectively, this is not the source of the attraction. It is rather their newness and the unexplored possibilities which they represent which make them appealing. And just as you are looking with envy at someone to whom you are not married, others are looking at your spouse in very much the same way.

'Celebrity Man Syndrome' is a classic example of this attitude – men who are married to beautiful models, and yet who are reported to have numerous affairs with other women whose looks, objectively speaking, could simply not be compared with their wives'. So what did they have over her, that Celebrity Man forsook the wife of his youth, the mother of his child, and the woman who had sacrificed her career for him, in favour of these others? The answer: *they were new, she was old*. He was excited about the novelty they presented, and dulled by the monotony that the accustomed relationship he had with his wife presented. Of course, he sought to justify his actions by telling her, as reported in the press, that she was no longer a 'spring chicken', 'Have you looked in the mirror lately?', etc. But all of this is balderdash. His unfaithfulness to her had nothing to do with the real facts about his wife, but rather his mental outlook toward her.

It is imperative for a husband always to notice how men react to his wife, and a wife to notice how women respond to her husband. For example, when two married couples go out socializing together, both should notice how their spouse is seen as a man and as a woman by the opposite sex. A husband is reminded at every moment that his wife is a woman, and she is reminded that the husband she has grown bored with is a desirable man, and if she doesn't want him there are plenty of others who do. A husband who has lost interest in his wife, or a wife who has lost interest in her husband, is convinced that no one else is interested in them either. It comes as a great shock to find that this is not the case. If you don't continually show your spouse affection, those affections will go to somebody else. Everyone needs love and they will do anything to find it.

Marriage thrives and prospers when a couple are reminded of their attraction to one another, and not just their mutual interests. Jealousy can destroy marriage utterly, or it can enhance it. In every interaction between the sexes there is some level of attraction between a man and a woman. The *possibility of adultery* that exists in each and every one of us affords us the opportunity of being a new sexual partner to our spouse at all times, since we are not boring and predictable. In fact, the most pious among us is fully capable of profound sexual sin. In other words, why does a wife appeal to a stranger or acquaintance, but not to her own husband? Simply stated, to the acquaintance she is new; to the husband she is old. Let him see that other men find her desirable and interesting. This is not to advocate that the modesty of a marriage, or of either spouse, should ever be compromised, which it shouldn't. Husbands and wives should not flirt with strangers and thus enrage their spouse. Rather, without purposely provoking any glances from members of the opposite sex, just always be cognizant of, and pay attention to, the fact that your spouse is indeed attractive to other men or women.

The corollaries of this attitude as far as marital fidelity is concerned are obvious. I have stated throughout this book, and am firmly committed to the belief, that every couple is fully capable of leading the most passionate sexual existence, so long as they set their minds to it. It is not about how your partner looks, but rather about what you think of them.

3. *Remember at all times that the person to whom you are married is profoundly interested in love and intimacy and has real sexual needs. Therefore, they can never be fully trusted to remain faithful, and must be shown affection and love constantly.*

Marriage is an unnatural state and must be worked on constantly. Put the same degree of time and effort into your marriage as you did while dating. When you were courting one another you were on your best behaviour because you understood that you had not yet won over this person, and they were in essence still a stranger. Well, the fact that the possibility for unfaithfulness lurks within each and every one of us teaches us that we have no security in our marriages and that our spouse is really still a stranger who must be seduced with love and hunger always. Strangers always present exciting sexual possibilities.

The book of Numbers discusses the laws of a suspected adulterous wife, the famous *sotah*. She is brought by her husband to the

Temple where she is given special waters to drink, into which are immersed the holy name of God. If she has been wrongly accused, she is restored to her youth and gains exceptional beauty and rarely gifted children. If, however, she has indeed defiled herself, then her stomach bloats and her thighs fall away, and she dies a horrible death. (Her lover suffers the same fate at the same time, notwithstanding how far away he may be geographically.) But why is this story mentioned at all? How could there have been an adulterous woman in Temple times? These people were witnessing daily miracles and could look into the holy countenance of colossal figures like Isaiah. Were these the men and women who were tempted into adulterous affairs? Could it have been possible?

But in truth by telling us this very important section of how to deal with adulterous men and women, the Bible is out to convey something positive as well. Every single person is a potential adulterer. Every single woman, even those living during the times of the Holy Temple and the prophets like Jeremiah could still be seduced by a man who was not her husband. And the reason: because we are *all* sexual. There is nothing stale or boring about us. And our sexuality is that aspect of us which is most central to our entire being. Love and affection is something that everybody needs and everybody wants. Note that in the Bible there is no word for wife. Rather, Sarah was '*the woman* of Abraham', and Rebecca was '*the woman* of Isaac'. A woman never becomes a loyal and devoted wife. At all times she remains a sexually expressive *woman* who needs passion and attention. If her husband won't give it to her, she'll fantasize about someone else. Work, therefore, to preserve your spouse's interest always.

The fact that the potential for adultery lurks in each and every one of us, far from conveying our weakness, speaks of our most special attribute. Each and every one of us is sexy, desirable, loving, attractive, new, and endowed with affectionate and sexual needs, which draws us to other humans and ensures that no one need live life alone. It is the blessing of humankind that we are not immune to the displays of affection from fellow humans, not the curse. People stick to each other so long as they are affectionate toward one another. In essence, there is nothing wrong with this at all. But what God demands, and what is best for us, is that we channel this obsession for affection into one powerful relationship which we call marriage which is special because it is for ever, and which must remain passionate if we are not to stray.

4. *When you feel most uninterested in your spouse, it is time to add as many new components as possible into your marriage. Organize that night out at a hotel; do something erotic and different. Without compromising the modesty or decency of your marriage, be adventurous and embark on a novel path.*

Now that you know that the only thing that has brought about this monotony is a lack of newness, bring as many exciting and new things into your relationship as possible. Don't be afraid of running away for a weekend on short notice. If you had an important business meeting you would do it. And if you had a mistress or a lover you would do it too. Give your spouse at least as much attention as you would give your business colleagues or your illicit lover.

Do everything possible, be at your most creative, to make your marriage exciting and new always. Give each other sensual massages, break out of your normal love-making routine; throw caution and inhibition to the winds; talk openly about sex to one another, do today what you didn't do yesterday. Be creative and imaginative. Treat your marriage like a business. When a store doesn't bring in customers, you immediately think of new ways to market your goods. Dress up your marriage in much the same way. Rearrange things constantly so that it doesn't fall into the monotony of a boring storefront whose display items are never altered. Live out your fantasies – so long as they are always about just the two of you together.

As part of this advice, don't be afraid to take radical measures to reinvigorate your marriage when things feel particularly dead. If you were to leave your husband or wife on their own on a bar stool you will quickly discover how they are preyed upon by roving members of the opposite sex. You would see that they are desirable.

This is a healthy way in which husbands and wives can play with, and thereby learn to appreciate, each other's sexuality. But remember to retain modesty at all times. Don't do anything stupid that will make your spouse hate you or accuse you of having degraded yourself. Simply allow your sexuality to speak for itself or them, for that matter.

Always retain a healthy sense of jealousy within the marriage. Don't purposely provoke your spouse or hurt them by giving too much attention to someone else. But don't ever let them believe that no one is interested in you either.

To be sure, these are radical techniques, and should only be done if felt absolutely necessary. They are not normally advisable since they have the potential of compromising modesty. After all, who belongs in a sleazy bar? And what husband or wife will truly be satisfied with a spouse who they think to be a flirt? On the other hand, I see these techniques, at times, as being absolutely necessary, and I liken them to the powerful electric charge which is put through the body of a person whose heart has stopped. The same applies to marriage and relationships. If a husband and wife have come to the point where they feel utterly uninspired with one another, they must then undertake serious action which displays each one as attractive and exciting. They must at times use even the intense shock therapy of jealousy and envy in order to shock some intensity and passion into the marriage.

I recognize that one of the principal objections that can be raised against this entire theory is this: people will say that it only works if your husband and wife really are attractive; if they are not, then even putting them in the sexiest possible situation will not get anyone else interested in them. My first reponse is this: what percentage of the people you see walking down the street, within your general age group, are you *not* attracted to in some form or another? When I asked this of about one hundred people, the consensus was that eight out of ten would catch their eye, some just for a moment, some more intensely. Eighty per cent of men and women within our general age group then pose *some* sexual attraction to us. For the remaining 20 per cent, I suggest that even they, given the right setting, are attractive and interesting. Remember, the average supermodel takes a photo session of thousands of shots in order to select just ten for a magazine spread. Dr Warren Farrel quotes the Canadian National Film Board who maintain that it takes 22,000 snaps for each *Playboy* centrefold spread, 'movies substitute pictures of a different actress's buttocks so we won't see the imperfections in the rear of the star, so we get some idea of how every woman who looks at a centrefold feels inadequate next to the airbrushed best of 6000 photos.'[1] Even men and women with the most superlative bodies need to be placed in the right setting, and their photos taken with the right lighting and from the right angle, in order to be seductive. And how do you know that the men and women that really catch your eye as you walk right down the street would also do so if you saw them immediately upon waking up in the morning, when their breath was horrendous, their hair frazzled, and their face as flat as if they had been chasing parked cars throughout the night?

5. *Use the power of fantasy to your advantage.*

First, pretend that a stranger or friend is watching you with your spouse at all times, the way you speak to them, the way you compliment them, etc. This will make you into a romantic. Sex does not live or thrive in a vacuum. We are mostly sexually attracted to those who flatter us and make us feel special and unique. The advice I give husbands and wives as to how to treat one another in everyday situations in the privacy of their own home is this: always pretend that a friend is watching you at all times. You wouldn't yell at your spouse in front of a friend, so don't do it in private either. You would probably always remember to compliment your spouse and speak to them affectionately in front of a friend. So do it at home as well, and be consistent. Remember that marriage is unnatural. Don't fret if you have a period of monotony in your life. It will get better, but only if you create a general ambience of romance and adoration, always. Remember, retaining passion in marriage, like marriage itself, is not natural and thus takes constant effort.

Second, fantasize about your spouse being in very erotic situations that are pleasurable to you. Afford them the quality of newness by mentally placing them in novel situations, especially during sex.

Every husband and wife can create the kind of setting and environment in which their spouse becomes appealing to them and those around them. So what if some people need to put more time into looking fantastic than others? The important thing is not only how we look naturally, but what the result of our efforts produces. I have argued throughout this book, and believe it to be a simple yet powerful point, that marriage is not natural and thus must be constantly worked upon. And there simply is nothing to be ashamed of in the fact that, just as one must work at marriage, one must also work on appearance, and constantly rejuvenating our attraction. These arguments of the modern age that real passion is spontaneous and automatic are ridiculous. These momentary infatuations come and go. Passion, like any other emotion, can be induced and must always be sustained. But it needs a framework, a support network. And this means a general setting of love and affection. Call your spouse at/from work. Show them you are thinking of them. If you see something beautiful, tell them it reminds you of them. Buy them little things which they love and which show them that they are always on your mind. It is everyday acts like these that engender and maintain a constant threshold of affection and romance which in turn leads to long moments of sexual passion. Make your marriage into a fairy tale by animating it constantly.

One of the best ways of doing this is to fantasize about your spouse during love-making. Be your own movie director. Every man or woman, put into the right setting, becomes attractive. Never make the terrible mistake of thinking for even one moment that your spouse is not attractive. Neither should you ever degrade your spouse by fantasizing about other people. Secondly, mentally placing your spouse into inventive situations ensures that they appear new and exciting to you as you watch them in an erotic situation.

I was once sitting in a car dealership for three hours, waiting for my car to be repaired. All of the employees had to wear a standard uniform consisting of a white top and blue trousers or skirt. The women's white tops were slightly see-through. It was amazing to observe how every male customer who walked up to the counter noticed their dress and their undergarments, the outline of which was visible through their tops. And the majority of the female employees were in their fifties and sixties, and weren't necessarily overtly attractive. But that did not stop all of the men from looking, and most of these men were young. When my car was finally finished I walked up to one of these women, who was in her late fifties, and said to her, 'Be honest with me, do you notice that men are aware of you women and what you are wearing? Let's face it. These uniforms are slightly transparent.' 'Of course we notice it,' she replied. 'You'd have to be blind not to see it. We ask them if they want to pay by cheque or credit card, and they respond not to our faces but to our busts. It happens all of the time.' When you take a woman, and put her in a uniform which her feminine bra straps show through, men are going to look in almost every case. Because all men and women are attractive, given the right setting. Passion in marriage comes about when we always seek to create this setting. Mentally superimpose any erotic item on to your spouse – so long as it's always your spouse.

Most people think that only incredibly attractive people elicit this sort of response. But this is not the case. Why did the men look at these women with the see-through tops? People look at these attributes, low cut shirts, or slits in skirts, because they are *suggestive*. It is something that excites a mental attraction. A woman seems to be conveying to you that she wants you to notice her. She comes alive as a sexual being by dressing in a provocative way that seems to call out to you saying: *notice me*.

If you are on holiday on a tropical island and you meet a woman on the beach in a bikini, you may be impressed with her figure but you probably won't be greatly stimulated just by seeing this. Now imagine that at night you see the very same woman in a hotel corridor, walking around in her underwear. No doubt this would excite you far more than the bikini. But why? She is wearing the same amount of clothing which she did in the morning when you saw her on the beach. The reason is that you are not excited by seeing her body, but rather by the signals she is sending by walking around in her intimate attire. She is saying, 'I know it is unnatural to walk around this way. I know that most women don't walk around in their undergarments. So I'm doing it to be sexy. And I know that I will be noticed and perceived as a sexual object.' By virtue of her dress, she is inviting you to look. She realizes that you will stare, and you're sure that she wants you to stare. She is sending you a personalized message: 'I want you to look at me.' And this is sexy. At the beach, however, she is just wearing the appropriate attire for swimming.

Another example that I trust women will appreciate is this: a man accidentally leaving his zipper open is not seen as sexy by women, but as clumsy, and often embarrassing. Very few women will get sexually excited at the sight. If anything, they will giggle at his humiliating omission. But when a man wears jeans with a gaping hole near his bottom, a great many female eyes will gravitate toward the bare flesh. It's just different. Here, it is exciting and sexy, rather than clumsy and stupid. Stated in other words, sexy dress is when a man or a woman wears something which convinces all of their onlookers that it was purposely put on to impress *them*. It makes you feel like the person wearing it wants you, personally. *It is personalized attire.* At the very least, they want you to notice that they are sexy and to appreciate them as such. There are countless other examples which demonstrate this point, namely, that sex is all in the mind. Use this knowledge to your advantage. Fantasize about your spouse in very erotic situations that appeal to you and make you want them more. The possibility for fantasy is endless. Don't squander it. To be sure, don't make the mistake of fantasizing about people to whom you are not married but insert your spouse into a situation your mind desires and which makes them come alive as a powerful sexual object.

6. *Bring modesty into your relationship. Don't overexpose yourselves to each other in marriage. Also, dress in a manner in which your respective masculinity and femininity are accented. Men and women are attracted to each other specifically through their differences.*

Dress modestly around the house. If your spouse wants to see your body, make them earn it. Make them slowly seduce your clothes off you to see your nakedness. Don't get bored with each other through over-exposure. Don't parade around the bedroom in the nude unless you want a passionate sexual encounter. Never allow your marriage to suffer from sexual overexplicitness. Always remain just outside of each other's grasp and never be too easy. There must remain a part of you which is always just slightly off limits and retains its mystique.

Furthermore, in everything we do, our sexuality as men and women should be accented. I wholeheartedly reject today's Western liberal mindset that says that men and women are first humans, and only after subdivide into male and female. This is not only mistaken thinking, it is deeply damaging to our sexuality and to the passion in our marriages. The feminine or masculine traits which we possess are not ancillary or incidental to our being. They are essential and fundamental. Stated in other words, there is no such thing as people, who then subdivide into men and women. The two cannot be separated. Society is not made of people. It is comprised of men and women. The society in which we live today is deeply suspicious of differences. Because so many people and things which are different have been taken advantage of and abused, society therefore seeks to obliterate differences, saying that in essence, everything is really just the same.

But different does not mean inferior or unequal, and I have the firmest conviction that whilst the sexes are equal they are also inherently different. And it is these differences that constitute their beauty and attraction. And it is these differences, therefore, which must always be sustained and respected. Men should dress and act in a way which accentuates their masculinity, and women should dress and behave in a manner that always reinforces their precious gifts of femininity. This is not to say that we should return to the female stereotypes of women at home with the children. But it is to say that women should never use men, or even their husbands, as role-models of what they should be.

7. *For husbands: during marital relations, always ensure that your wife climaxes first. And always focus only on your spouse when making love.*

This is not a sex book, and I have tried throughout to avoid direct advice about sexual technique or to be directly sexually explicit. However, I have decided to include this point about female orgasm because I feel it is absolutely vital to focus exclusively on one's spouse in bed. There can be no greater insult to one's spouse than to think about someone else while in bed with the person we love, which in Judaism constitutes a grave sin. To avoid this, we must be able to watch our spouse enjoying the experience, which further focuses us on them and gets our minds off other things. Sex at its best and most loving is a completely overwhelming and consuming experience. And its ultimate purpose is to draw a husband and wife closer together in holiness and love. While other religions maintain that sex is exclusively for procreation, and Western mores sees the purpose of sex as generating pleasure, Judaism has always proposed the purpose of sex as serving as the strongest possible glue to keep husbands and wives firmly bonded together in happiness and contentment. There is no greater abuse or impediment set in the path of this objective than to fantasize about someone else's face or body when one is making love to one's spouse.

The problem is that too many husbands just don't take the time to make their wives enjoy the experience and the ratio of male to female orgasms in marriage, according to one survey, is thirty to one, with some women claiming that they can go six months without their husbands giving them pleasure, and others saying that they have never climaxed. The losers in all this, however, are not just the wives but the husbands. Few things are as erotic for a man than to witness the woman they are with blanking out and becoming totally responsive to the intensity of the sexual experience. And few things are more sexually stimulating to a man than to watch the wife who previously seemed absorbed in a profession, or being a mother, or caring for the house, suddenly abandoning herself completely to her sexual dimension. Through this he can witness her coming alive *as a woman*, and not just the wife with whom he is overly familiar. In the act of love-making, there is nothing more powerful. In addition to this, the Bible actually mandates, and this is codified in Jewish law, that a husband is *obligated* to provide his wife with three essential items, one of which is sexual and erotic pleasure. Thus, ensuring that one's wife always enjoys love-making is pivotal for the holiness, as well as the passion, of marriage. Sex should never be a solo or selfish experience and thus both spouses must ensure that each enjoys the experience equally.

The problem is that human physiology is slightly unbalanced in that men climax quickly and easily while for women it takes greater time, concentration, and effort. This leads to a strange situation whereby husbands have had their fun while their wives have hardly begun. In addition to the fact that this leaves many women unsatisfied, it also leads to all too many husbands complaining that they don't find their wives sexy or voracious in bed, and therefore have to resort to foreign images or even the faces of other women to get excited. And too many wives who feel their husbands not concentrating on them, complain of getting turned off in bed and losing interest in the whole enterprise. The usual resort of this mutual disillusionment and dissatisfaction is that a husband climbs on his wife, has sex with her (yes, sex, this can hardly be construed as 'making love' or intimacy), rolls over and goes to sleep. A husband and wife are hardly brought closer together in situations like these. This is an extreme form of unkosher and hence, unholy sex.

The solution is for a husband to take the time and effort always to make his wife enjoy the experience and climax first. What this achieves is immediately to paint her in a sexy and seductive light. When a husband just sees his wife lying in bed, he may not feel stimulated. But if he sees her responding enthusiastically to all the sexual activities he initiates, he will see the sexy woman within her. This is truly one of the most reliable and proven methods by which to ensure that there is passion in marital sex. Even husbands who initially don't feel like getting into anything seriously sexual at night, and would prefer something quick, will change their attitude and get far more involved once they have ensured that their wives have enjoyed themselves first. *Just make the damned effort. It's worth it, even if you don't at first feel like it.* The biggest killer in marital passion is plain old laziness. All the wonderful sex manuals and technique guides still forget one thing: the only way any of these new positions will ever serve to enhance any marriage is if the couple first and foremost *agrees to even try them.* To do that you need passion. You have to be interested enough at least to overcome your laziness in bed. The woman who desires and reacts to sexual pleasure, and whose whole body responds to the power of erotic enjoyment, can excite and elicit the heretofore latent interest of her husband. In fact, there is probably no quicker way to transform a spouse from a wife into a woman than to watch her abandon herself utterly to the love which you show her. And there is nothing that will so quickly change a husband's opinion of the sexiness of his wife than to watch sexual desire overwhelm her entire being, as he sees her lose all physical control and surrender her conscious processes to the pleasure he provides. This is the very definition of passion and, I repeat, all it takes is simple effort.

Remember, make your wife into the equivalent of an adulterous woman. Focus on her body and make her sexual pleasure paramount, until she responds by abandoning every earthly concern, ascending the heights of sexual passion, pulling you along with her and in the process becoming your mistress as opposed to your everyday partner. Marriage is special and glorious. Allow this to be reflected in your marital relations.

8. *Insert a period of sexual separation and abstention into your marriage for ten to twelve days each month. Physical abstention leads to obsession with each other.*

There is nothing in life that can sustain human interest constantly or indefinitely. And sex, notwithstanding its power of pleasure, is no different. No advice in the entire world, be it a new attitude, new technique, or new daily settings, will preserve sexual passion in marriage indefinitely. For sex to really retain its presence and potency, it needs a bit of a break. Therefore, if you are Jewish, live by the laws of Jewish family purity, which mandate a forced period of separation for twelve days each month, followed by immersion into a *mikveh* as described at length earlier. And even if you are not Jewish, insert a similar time of sexual abstention into your marriage.

To be sure, ceasing all physical contact for a near two-week period is not at all easy. But its rewards are immense. And in those marriages where the cessation of physical contact is complete, the couple never know the loss of passion or the onset of monotony. In the final analysis the most effective way of making your spouse feel and appear new to you is for them *to actually be as new.* A period of sexual and physical separation leads to a time when you rediscover your spouse as a totally new sexual partner. You discover the feel of their skin anew, the smell of their bodies anew, and their sexual response anew as well. You also yearn throughout that period to be reunited with your spouse. This constant yearning transforms your spouse into a lover and your marriage into an illicit affair. You long to be together in much the same way that two forbidden lovers think always of one another and pine for the next embrace. So sexual abstention for short periods of time every month provides for a constant period of reunion, a new honeymoon if you will, every single month.

9. *Abstain from masturbation or other forms of sexual self-gratification. Work your hardest at reducing the vast number of sexual outlets, be they mental, verbal, or otherwise, that have become available to us in the modern age and focus and channel all your sexual energy toward your spouse.*

I don't give one damn about all the flood of wonderful advice that millions of sexual self-help books have given about the wonders of masturbation. I still oppose it and see its effects as almost entirely harmful. My objections are not only religious and I am not trying to return us to a time when girls and boys will once again believe that they will go blind if they masturbate. But the purpose behind masturbation is to grant a man and woman a form of sexual self-release. Who says that this is positive or proper? Aside from the fact that male masturbation is prohibited by Biblical law, it is harmful to marriage.

The purpose of sex as seen by Judaism is not merely for procreation, nor is it merely for pleasure. Rather, it is to draw a husband wife closer together, in pleasure and joy. It is for this reason that it is imperative we make our husbands and wives not just one sexual outlet among many, but the only one. This is what makes sex truly exciting. When we have been careful not to allow our sexual steam to leak out through dirty jokes, blue movies, and especially masturbation, we create an environment in which we yearn to have sex with our spouse because we feel we need it so badly. This irrepressible and irresistible craving is the very definition of passion: to want something so badly that upon getting it we go wild.

In her new and witty book on sex, Jewish comedienne Vanessa Feltz happily advocates masturbation, saying that one's spouse should never have the burden of having to serve as the exclusive outlet for one's sexual lust and desire. But this is ridiculous for two reasons. The first is that the whole purpose of sex should be to make a husband and wife draw closer together. They should not have an outlet outside of each other because this lessens their interest and dependency on one another. Secondly, when husbands and wives release their sexual lusts through masturbation, they are almost guaranteed less passion-ate encounters later on, because they have found an outlet that lessens their hunger. The simple and undeniable fact is that a man and woman who abstain from sex and masturbation for a period of 10–12 days will lust for one another and become obsessed with their upcoming night of reunion in the most passionate and powerful way because libido has to be built up if it is to be truly explosive.

10. *Limit the amount of sexual images that enter your life through television and the other media, causing you to become subjective, and find your spouse inadequate.*

Perhaps one of the strongest deadeners of passion is the incessant comparison which muddles today's marriages. These days it is so easy to compare one's spouse to others who seem so much more remarkable. Supermodels and film stars, both male and female, parade through our lives nightly, making it almost impossible for us not to feel somewhat disappointed as we turn to the right and peer at our less than perfect spouse. It may even be said that modern society leads directly to the impossible yearning on the part of all of us to be married to a Greek god or goddess as portrayed on television and in the media.

As stated earlier, the first reason this is unfair is that we are comparing our spouses to illusions that do not really exist. Every actor and actress has the benefit of make-up artists and perfect lighting to enhance their natural beauty. But more importantly, this incessant bombardment of sexual images leads to the most damning and destructive force of all in marriage: namely, *objectivity*. The very definition of love is subjectivity. Love means that our emotions colour the way we perceive people and things. Thus, every parent is convinced that their child is the most handsome, the cutest, and the brightest. But this same kind of subjectivity is essential to marriage as well.

Passion in marriage is predicated on the feeling and conviction that the person we are married to is beautiful and special, and thus worth the exertion needed to make the marriage work and stay passionate and special. People cannot be passionate about those things which don't impress them or which they perceive as being mundane. Not believing that your spouse is unusually beautiful and attractive leads to tedium in the marriage and a state whereby every effort at passionate love-making feels like an exercise in futility as well as a terrible burden.

The antidote to this destructive influence is to finally cease making comparisons between our spouses and everyone that passes by, and to limit the sexual images which bombard us as much as possible. Get the TV out of the bedroom. Wives are usually deeply hurt when they discover that their husbands have gone to a striptease joint. Yet, every night they allow that very same striptease to invade their home. Today's TV is not much better than actually stripping off, and who needs to invite unfair and unreal competition into the privacy of our very own bedrooms. Passion cannot arise when we constantly compare our spouse to phantoms, or especially when we have the effrontery to think of these phantoms during love-making with our spouse, thereby destroying the intimacy of sexual relations and reducing our spouse to a mere masturbatory tool.

So do your spouse a favour. Don't compare them to others. It's not fair to them, or you for that matter. Accept marriage for what it is: an ingenious device on the part of the Creator whereby each and every one of us would have someone around us who feels that we are the most attractive and worthwhile person on the globe. And every one of us needs to feel that way. It's what makes us impregnable and immune to all the pain of life and the hurt which is to be found in our world.

In one of its most beautiful and romantic passages, the Talmud declares, 'He who has found a wife has found goodness.' The same of course applies to a husband. And we should dedicate our every effort toward ensuring that our spouses are always appreciated for their personalities and their bodies and that indeed our marriages always are and remain, a constant source of holiness, pleasure, blessing and goodness. And let us all, once again, fall in love with husbands who are in love with their wives, and with wives who are in love with their husbands.

SOURCES

1.   Dr Warren Farrel, *Why Men Are The Way They Are*, p74, (pub?)

The Erotic Silence of the American Wife, © 1992 Dalma Heyn, published by Turtle Bay Books, a division of Random House, Inc

The Janus Report on Sexual Behaviour, © 1993, published by John Wiley & Sons, Inc

How to Get Him Back From the Other Woman, © 1992 Diane Baroni and Betty Kelly, published by St Martin's Press,

The Hite Report on Female Sexuality, © 1981 Shere Hite, published by Ballantine Books, a division of Random House, Inc

Thy Neighbour's Wife, © 1981 Gay Talese, published by Ballantine Books, a division of Random House, Inc

How to Satisfy a Woman, © 1982 Naura Hayden, published by Bibli O'Phile Publishing Co

Tempted Woman: The Passions, Perils and Agonies of Female Infidelity, © 1994 Carol Botwin, published by William Morrow & Co,

INDEX

Index

and passion 94–5, 111, 141, 155–6, 199, 201–2
  reinvigorating marriage through 299–300
  and separation 112
nudity
  and married couples 141–2
  nudist colonies 137

old age, marriage relationship in 153
one-night stands 12–13, 63, 142
  wives' attitudes to 230–1
open marriages 163, 170–1
orgasm, female 306–9

paranoia, of spouse of unfaithful partner 259–61, 269–70, 272
parents, love between children and 127–8, 276–8, 282
passion
  dulled by overexposure 141–2
  loss of in relationships 8–9, 130–45, 180
  and newness 94–5, 111, 140–1, 159
  rekindled by jealousy 158–9, 167
  restoring passion in marriage 108, 198–208, 291–314
  retaining passion in marriage 71–83
Peel, Robert, *The New Sexual Revolution* 179
physical attraction *see* attraction
polyandry 61, 62
polygamy 62–3
pornographic magazines, and sexual boredom 131–2
pornography on television 140, 151
Prager, Dennis 121
premarital sex 100
  attitudes to 27, 28
  and the Kinsey Report 21
  and objectivity 283–9
prostitutes 41

'radar syndrome' 121
rationalist thinkers, views on marriage 51–2
religion

marriage as a religious institution 50–1, 52
  see also Judaism
religious people, and extramarital sex 22–3
repression 98, 271
  and Judaism 98–9, 217
respect, loss of 261–5
romance
  preserving and restoring 203, 204–6
  and sexual boredom 136–7
Russell, Bertrand 163

Sarah, and Abraham 243–4
Schindler, Oscar 31
secrecy
  in adultery 88
  in marriage 87
separation, periods in marriage 9, 86–7, 107–18, 309–10
sex manuals 5–6
sex/sexuality
  casual sex 10, 133–5, 137–8, 147
  importance of 85–6, 96–7, 100–5, 146–53
  and intimacy 286
  overexposure to 284–5
sexual abstention
  temporary periods of 85–6, 107–10, 113–15, 309–10
  see also separation
sexual attraction *see* attraction
sexual boredom 130–45, 147, 199–201
  as cause of divorce 11, 140–1
  overcoming 72–80, 194, 292–5
  as trigger for adultery 81, 138, 190–1
sexual desire
  controlling 214–16, 269–72
  in the mind 41–2, 72–80, 81, 202
sexual experimentation in marriage 202–4
sexual fantasies
  as breach of trust 255–7
  encouraging partners to talk about 292, 293–4